W9-BKA-640

COUNTRYSIDE, GARDEN & TABLE

COUNTRYSIDE, GARDEN & TABLE

A New England Seasonal Diary

Martha Adams Rubin

Fulcrum Publishing
Golden, Colorado

Library of Congress Cataloging-in-Publication Data

Rubin, Martha Adams.
    Countryside, garden and table : a New England seasonal diary /
Martha Adams Rubin.
        p.   cm.
    Includes index.
    ISBN 1-55591-137-4
    1. Gardening—New England.   2. Country life—New England.
3. Cookery.   4. Natural history—New England.   I. Title.
SB453.2.N3R83   1993
635'.0484'0974—dc20   92-54761
                                                                      CIP

Printed in the United States of America
0 9 8 7 6 5 4 3 2 1

Fulcrum Publishing
350 Indiana Street, Suite 350
Golden, CO 80401-5093

For my grandchildren—Malika, Hannah and Willow

TABLE OF CONTENTS

ACKNOWLEDGMENTS

Thanks to my husband for always being there, and to our children and our grandchildren simply for being. Thanks to Barbara Raives, a friend who read my first chapters and encouraged me to continue, and to Risa Pollack and Pam Wright for reading the last chapters and holding my hand. Thanks to Dr. David Wolf for keeping me healthy. Thanks to Kate Norkin for her horticultural help. Thanks to Robert Baron for publishing this book, and to David Nuss for coping with its editing. And always thanks to our rugged Connecticut hills for their beauty and their permanence.

INTRODUCTION

As we reach a certain age, the temptation to look back and examine the processes that shaped our lives is difficult to ignore.

That one fears airplanes, loves chocolate, enjoys Brahms or hates the oozy clay bottom of a pond reflects not only heredity but environment. It is the mix of experience and proclivity that turns us into teachers or technicians, musicians or mechanics, farmers or factory workers, ballerinas or ball players. We are less free to choose a specific path than we may think.

The course this book will follow incorporates three basic and related affinities that surreptitiously wove themselves into my brain at an early age to rest there dormant for a time and then rise up to eclipse the more fitting activities of the urban woman. These elements are simple, and they are all related to food: cooking, gardening and their source—nature's earth. I suppose these inclinations settled on my soul long ago, and an adult lifetime in the thick of New York City never uprooted them.

Looking back, my fondest early memories are of tramping over the Texas plains with my father, looking for fossils, arrowheads and horned toads while he took geological readings. The rough and dusty prairie floor, the miracles of life that grew from its inhospitable surfaces and the mysteries of its age and evolution were wondrous secrets I shared only with him. The sometimes ominous thrills of discovery, of danger and of solitude were my own. They certainly took precedence over the quieter pleasure of the smell of bread baking in my mother's kitchen and the slow and steady growth of a tomato in our victory garden, but those sensations were significant too.

My parents and extended family represented a remnant Victorian culture even at the time I was born in the early 1930s. Decorum was of major importance, and all things sensual were looked upon with suspicion—all things, that is, except food. My grandmother, my great-aunt Jennie and my mother were all accomplished cooks and expended much effort in providing the freshest and best for the daily table. Any secret libidinal yearnings they might have had were redirected to the shameless domain of the kitchen. There they shone. I remember my aging mother once said, "I can measure my life by the wonderful meals I have eaten." And so, in such a tradition I was raised, taking for granted the fine, fresh food set before me and the efforts made to procure and produce it.

I was born in the midst of the Great Depression. We lived in a small west Texas town, better known for its dirt farms, cattle ranches and wildcatters than for its cuisine. Food was regional and simple and, necessarily, cheap. Our ordinary everyday fare is referred to as soul food today: turnip greens cooked with salt pork, black-eyed peas, fried chicken, hominy grits and corn pone. The extraordinary included domesticated versions of Mexican food—the term "Tex-Mex" was not yet used—but the most admired recipes (or "receipts," as my Mother called them) were those my great-grandmother had brought from Missouri when she and her new husband migrated to Texas after the Civil War. Whatever the preparation, we made do with local products and traditional methods—of both thinking and cooking. Food was not fast or frozen but fresh and familiar.

Such exotica as bagels, sour cream, smoked fish, Italian pasta, pizza and dishes cooked in wine sauces were to come much later into my life. In fact my hometown, widely acclaimed as "the buckle in the Bible Belt," was a dry town in a dry county. Legal beer was a 60-mile drive away, hard liquor a 150. Wine was an unknown. These evils were not available to us even in sauce form.

I would like to say that the activities involved in the acquisition and production of food back then fascinated me, but they did not. I remember driving to a nearby farm for eggs and fresh chickens, picking boysenberries at the height of the season, never buying a melon until the sound when one thumped it was just right and spending what seemed like endless hours going through the farmer's market in Weatherford looking for the best and cheapest fruits and vegetables. But my attention was directed elsewhere into a world of daydreams and fantasies. The importance of food, not only as sustenance but as love, would surface later. It was always there.

As a shy and solitary child, I dreamed of a life that I had read of in books and heard of from my father. His extravagant tales of a probably Spartan childhood on a Pennsylvania farm imbued my senses with the perfection of a harmony in nature that did not exist elsewhere. The books he urged upon me, from Gene Stratton Porter's *Girl of the Limberlost* to Mary O'Hara's *My Friend Flicka,* created a world that made my small west Texas town too confining. I longed for the vastness of a Wyoming I had seen in my mind's eye. I, too, wanted to find the rare luna moth and tame the feral horse.

These fantasies moved underground as I grew older, surrendering to a teenager's preoccupation with boys, cars and popularity. The goal for most high-school girls in our town was to solidify a nuptial arrangement by graduation time. A dismal failure at that, I went to college and graduate school, and only later realized my high-school classmates' easy ambitions. I became a teacher, married, raised four children, became a teacher again and quite forgot those simple fictions of childhood.

My family, whom this book is not about, but who creeps into it now and then, is another of those elements that have shaped my life, probably the most important element of all. Family—the core of culture, the heart of civilized life—is very strong in me. I am out of touch with much of my mother's family and have never met most of my father's. Many of my husband's Jewish relatives have been unable to accept our "mixed" marriage. We live great physical distances from most of them, in any case. But our own nuclear group, that is a different matter. It is expanding now with a son-in-law, a daughter-in-law, two granddaughters, one grandson and an almost daughter-in-law. We are a conglomerate mix of African American, Asian and Caucasian, Jewish, Catholic, Protestant, Muslim and Buddhist. Individually we represent varying ratios of mix and maintain varying degrees of religious piety. None of us is bothered by our differences. We are not always in agreement—far from it—but we are bonded as a family, a bond that connects across numerous miles and years.

I have lived in and around New York City for thirty-three years, doing many things, even finding a luna moth one summer attached to a screen door on Martha's Vineyard, but never taming anything—certainly not the children. Then, sixteen years ago, by a series of fortuitous circumstances, we bought an old farmhouse on a hillside in northwestern Connecticut. It wasn't Wyoming, but for the first time raw nature was outside our window. Well, almost raw. Acid rain was browning our maples in midsummer, chemical fertilizer was washing down from the neighbor farmer's field and killing the fish in our pond and salt from the winter snowplows was weakening our trees.

Even our own early attempts at improving our property did little to settle the balance between humans and nature. We poisoned the quack grass in our driveway and the poison ivy on our back wall. "An eye for an eye," we could have said, watching the creature that had stung us and caused us pain wither and die. Wasps were sprayed with lethal gas, the kind now outlawed in human warfare, and the wasps had nothing but their failing stingers with which to retaliate. Bushes and trees were sprayed with other deadly products to protect them from invisible or nonexistent predators. Such processes, recommended by friendly neighbors and even friendlier gardening services, were not to last long.

Two things happened that changed that forever. I started a large vegetable garden and found I had breast cancer in close succession. From then on, there simply seemed to be no logic to consciously covering food that was to be eaten with poisons.

Instead we began using compost, manure and other natural fertilizers on our land. We found organic means to exterminate severe pest infiltrations, but as our garden grew more vigorous, we rarely needed them. Our garden is strong and healthy, and our efforts are repaid with flavors we had forgotten—the flavors of our childhoods.

We have had our garden for fifteen years. It is bigger now, and there is a small orchard nearby as well as a patch of raspberries and blackberries. Blueberries grow down near the wall, and we're trying our hands at shiitake mushrooms in the woods. We have herbs growing by the kitchen door and a couple of espaliered peach trees in a protected sunny corner.

Chickens give us eggs every day in exchange for unadulterated grain, summer greens, leftover spaghetti and a large area in which to roam. Three white Embden geese, originally meant for Christmas dinner, provide protective squawks, neatly shaved grass and, in the spring, more of their own kind. A fifty-pound tom turkey has so endeared himself to us that he remains long past Thanksgiving and commands a post of authority in the barnyard. Two donkeys and a sheep mow a field and transform it into wool and fertilizer. All of this is a symbiotic system, if incomplete.

Other sources of beauty and occasional bounty are in our meadow and our woodland. One child's camp experience brought us knowledge of wild edible plants, and now we eat lamb's-quarters, milkweed buds and sometimes mushrooms from the woods. My love for mushrooms has not diminished my fear of their potential toxicity, and I carefully check all that I cannot positively identify in a mushroom field guide. The most beautiful mushrooms I've found were classified as either Destroying Angels or edible Agaricus mushrooms, I couldn't be sure which. I didn't eat them.

With all of these treasures available, we buy fewer vegetables now. We have everything we need during the late spring and the summer, and the excess we store in the autumn helps us through the winter. We do not, however, pretend to lead some sort of environmentally unblemished life. We eat in restaurants and with friends and buy popcorn at the movies, hamburgers at the drive-in on our way to the country and greasy fried onion rings at the Goshen Fair. We may do better than some, but we compromise just the same. Anyway, there is no such thing as a pure world now. We all know that. We make compromises by breathing the air.

I went to Antarctica several years ago. After we sailed across the Drake Passage, icebergs began to appear in increasing numbers floating like jewels on the water, and the world seemed fresh and genuine. Then, on our first landing, I noticed a bedraggled piece of plastic lapping against the shore.

I have written somewhere in this book that Mother Nature really has the upper hand, but sometimes those words remind me of Peter Pan crying, "Yes, I do believe in fairies," to save Tinkerbell. The only difference is that I don't believe that believing will make it so.

I am not presumptuous enough to pretend to offer a panacea for our environmental problems. I contribute to them every day. I haven't given up our automobile, electricity or central heat, but do conserve them as I am able. I avoid using products that pollute the water and the air. I make the garden and the food we eat as untainted and nutritious as possible. I wonder if it matters. Does making a small difference make any difference when concerns are monumental? I only know that I must do it—for myself and for my grandchildren.

As in most books of this ilk, I include practical suggestions for both the garden and the kitchen. You will find they can't be classified as time-saving gardening methods or recipes, although some are quite easy and take little time to do. That is due to their simplicity rather than to any trick of hurrying things along. "Saving time" is a pair of words we read or hear often. Why must we save it and for what? A metaphor for twentieth-century life might be speed: speed of travel, speed of accumulation, speed of cultural change and speed in finishing tasks. From the time we begin taking timed exams in school and are rewarded for finishing first, whether it be in a race or a thought puzzle, we are infused with thinking that faster is better.

In my gardening and cooking tasks, I often find that faster is sloppy and haphazard and that the care that produces the results I want must be slow and mindful.

In the early days of our marriage, the fast food dinner became popular. Brides exclaimed at both the novelty and the ease of devising a meal from several packaged wonders that could be mixed and cooked in seconds. Remember the casserole of potato chips and tuna fish united with canned mushroom soup? Or the ubiquitous dip of sour cream and onion soup mix? These represented the contemporary way. They were easy, different and speedy—no meat chopping, no vegetable cleaning—just a quick mix. And most of them were awful.

Food preparation, whether in the garden or in the kitchen, can be a mindful task, not to be rushed through so that one can rush to some other activity. Each thrust of the hoe, each chop of the cleaver presents its own pleasure, satisfaction and meaning.

Thich Nhat Hanh is a Vietnamese Zen master and Buddhist writer, whose small manual *The Miracle of Mindfulness* I read after our oldest son became a Zen Buddhist. Nhat Hanh's approach to consciousness or mindfulness in daily tasks, daily existence and even in washing dishes is an opportunity for examining the miracle of life. He says, "There are two ways to wash the dishes. The first is to wash the dishes in order to have clean dishes and the second is to wash the dishes in order to wash the dishes." One can be an onerous task, the other ...

> While washing the dishes one should only be washing the dishes, which means that while washing the dishes one should be completely aware of the fact that one is washing the dishes. At first glance, that might seem a little silly: why put so much stress on a simple thing? But that's precisely the point. The fact that I am standing there and washing these bowls is a wondrous reality. I'm being completely myself, following my breath, conscious of my presence, and conscious of my thoughts and actions. ... If while washing the dishes, we think only of the cup of tea that awaits us, thus hurrying to get the dishes out of the way as if they were a nuisance, then we are not "washing the dishes to wash the dishes." What's more, we are not alive during the time we are washing the dishes. In fact we are completely incapable of realizing the miracle of life while standing at the sink. If we can't wash the dishes, the chances are we won't be able to drink our tea either. While drinking the cup of tea, we will only be thinking of other things, barely aware of the cup in our hands. Thus we are sucked away into the future—and we are incapable of actually living one minute of life.

If exulting in washing dishes seems excessive, try mindfully tending a pot of rosemary placed on a sunny windowsill. Try putting in a row of bean seeds by the back door, and watch the way the seed opens to release the first two newborn leaves, then blossoms and finally bears fruit. Take a sprig of the rosemary and a handful of the beans, wash them, simmer them in a pot of water and present them to be eaten. This is a mysterious process you will have participated in, and each step an encounter with a miracle.

Although there are recipes in this book, their instruction should never interfere with the creative invention of the cook. Cooking is really about combining flavors and textures in tasty, digestible and nutritious ways, using available food materials. A slave to arbitrary measurements and inflexible ingredients cannot be a creative cook. Measurements are often meaningless, in any case. One onion, for example, can be a hundred different sizes and/or degrees of strength. Even a teaspoon of baking powder will differ in its power to make something rise depending on how old it is. Herbs and spices differ enormously. And so it goes.

The key to imaginative and palatable cooking is knowing how flavors interrelate, knowing a few tricks about the habits of certain foods and being brave enough to use available ingredients in ever-different ways to add variability to the menu and interest to the diet.

The perfect cook might never need a cookbook at all. Virginia Lee, who taught me a lot about Chinese cooking, used to roll her eyes and sigh when a student asked for the exact measurement of an ingredient. She would put whatever amount she planned to put into a dish in her hand, then measure it out into a spoon or cup, look at the student sardonically and say, "Well, one and one-fourth tablespoons, this time."

The organization of recipes in this month-by-month account of a year's cooking is not arbitrary, though it may seem so. In months of plenty, most of the ingredients come straight from the garden at the times they are at their best. For example, asparagus sprouts and flourishes in May, and so it is discussed in the May chapter; purple cabbage is best left until after a frost, when it is sweetest.

Winter is another matter. In those months I have relied to some degree, but not entirely, on foods from the garden that are storable and preserveable. After all, this is the twentieth century and few of us must subsist on our own production. The stores amassed from the garden that I do mention are indicative of the possibilities that exist for home eating innovation.

March is the only departure from the garden mode, the month our laying hens, after a two- to-three-month hiatus, begin their spring presentations. Their eggs not only contribute to many recipes but remind us that spring is only moments away.

As you read these pages, if the thought comes to your mind that what I describe represents a great deal of work, more than you may have time or desire to do, do not turn away. Try only a little. It has taken fifteen years of expanding for me to reach the level of rural complication I describe. I have even hired a hand to help with the gardening for the past four of those years, yet every moment of weeding, planting and digging is a contented one for me. There is simply not enough time to do it all alone anymore. But do what you can. I recommend it for your health and for your sense of joy. The work of gardening and the work of cooking should neither be onerous nor a drudgery to be finished quickly in order to have a cup of tea, for it is an engagement with the process of living.

So many of us, in our daily labor, do only bits of things. We attach a piece to an automobile on an assembly line, write a draft about a merger that we'll never be involved with again or sell an item we don't know or care about to a customer. It sounds quite old-fashioned, but there's something quite satisfying about planting a seed and finding it growing, nurturing it and finding it thriving, harvesting it and using it to prepare a table for family and friends.

JANUARY

While the earth remaineth, seedtime and harvest, and cold and heat, and summer and winter, and day and night shall not cease.

—Genesis 8:22

The Land

If a January diary seems an odd way to begin a book about planting, harvesting and cooking, do not be deluded by the earth's winter slumber. The genuine gardener, when not too busy maintaining his or her territory, needs time for planning, seed ordering and daydreaming about projects past and future. So January, in truth, is an excellent time to begin. And if you, the reader, plan to follow along in any of our enterprises, perhaps you'll need the less complicated winter hours as we do, to anticipate and prepare, as our ancestors did, for the lengthening days and the earth's coming gift of renewal.

January is a quiet month in the north country. The feasting of Christmas is over, and time is spent catching up on things both inside and outside, both physical and metaphysical. Children and grandchildren have dispersed back into their own domains, their own lives. We miss them, but the rare solitude of a blustery cold night and a cheery fire represent different, milder pleasures: a game of gin, a thick book, a sweater knitted for a grandchild, an hour of tinkering with a broken appliance, an evening framing pictures.

The usual January thaw has been extensive this year, and there is nothing left of the December blizzard except pools of water that can't drain off because of the frozen ground beneath them. Yesterday I found watercress, small and spindly, growing in a tiny stream near the house. There was also a crop of mache (which reseeds itself) struggling to mature in the garden. Homegrown salad rather than snow in January? It may be a miracle, but I fear it's the greenhouse effect.

Snow is referred to around these parts as "poor man's fertilizer." Its insulating abilities prevent the recurrent freeze and thaw that is damaging to root systems, and its protective cover helps prevent erosion and the leaching out of nutrients into the subsoil, too deep for many root systems to reach and make use of. Snow also ties up water so that it can fill our streams and reservoirs in the spring when it is needed. Snow's continuous winter cover over the centuries has helped to keep New England green in the summer.

This year farmers and gardeners worry about root damage to their unprotected plants and expect a summer drought. Skiers disparage machine-made snow and bemoan the brown landscape of the mountains and slopes. Some folks tell tales of the old days, of being snowed in for days or weeks, of tunneling through snowdrifts to the barn to feed the animals or, in more recent years, of living for days without telephone service or electricity. The house we live in is a mute reminder of these other times and other ways of living.

The original part of our farmhouse was built around 1800, not long after the American revolution, Shays's Rebellion and other political events of the late eighteenth century had shaped the New England ethos and character and affected the lives of the men and women buried in the little graveyard just down our road. The father of our dwelling's builder and original owner fought in the Battle of Lake Ticonderoga during the

Revolution and helped put down Shays's Rebellion a few years later. The son of the same man died a hero's death in the battle of Spotsylvania during the Civil War.

Ours is a simple house, built for functionality, with few adornments. In the older part the rooms and windows are small, the ceilings low and the walls insulated with wide chestnut planks, all early methods for keeping cold out and warmth in. The shallow hearths throw back the heat of the fire as efficiently as an open hearth can, and enclosed stairways hide themselves behind walls and doors to inhibit the naturally rising heat and prevent draughts. With our modern central heat set at sixty and a fire in the kitchen fireplace, we are snug and comfortable. With a very efficient wood stove burning, we are sometimes sweltering.

The house is now patched both with memories and with three enlarging additions, but the heart of the home is still in the earliest section, its massive center chimney opening into the well-used fireplaces that provide both physical and mental warmth and cooking fire.

When such houses as ours were built in the eighteenth and nineteenth centuries, a cellar was dug first, then a fieldstone foundation was made to line its walls and finally a single immense fieldstone chimney was constructed squarely in the center of the house-to-be. Only then was the wooden frame, which was often made of chestnut, erected around this stone heart. Our chimney has five openings: three fireplaces on the first floor in what were a parlor, a borning room and a keeping room; one in a bedroom on the second floor; and a mysterious opening with an immense, ovenlike interior and flue in the cellar—probably an oven for an old summer kitchen. There is a smaller oven to the side of the keeping room hearth. This center chimney construction serves secondarily as a primitive central heating system, for so long as the stones are continually warmed by ascending smoke, they radiate heat, though weakly, throughout the house.

Yet another ingenuity apparently helped cozy up the place in winter. We are situated on a hillside, and there is a cellar entrance and a passage to it dug out of the lower incline so that a cart or animal can be brought straight in. I've read that this was created to give easy access to farm animals during the snowy winters. As cellar dwellers, they were not only easier to get to for feeding, milking and tending, but their rising body heat helped to warm the house. The dirt floor absorbed what it could, but the barn smell must have followed the animals and given the house a special flavor along with the warmer molecules that were provided.

Other structures on our bit of land reflect techniques for meeting other needs of the era. An ancient icehouse reminds us that ice was cut and stored for summer use in a subterranean shelter. Our icehouse consists of a high-ceilinged room with a trapdoor in the floor leading to a deep, stone-sided cellar where blocks of ice were stored after being cut from a frozen pond or lake. A series of wooden vents open and close to allow warmer air to escape to the outside when necessary. Straw was piled on the ice to further insulate it so that it could survive the hottest weather. Apparently it did.

A shed and a small barn of unknown age complete our immediate farm complex. The large original barn is now only a stone foundation, a repository for the detritus of yesterday and the artifact of today: a rusty plow head, a broken bit of china or a cracked iron pot. The small existing barn houses chickens and geese. The shed has become a potting shed, and a larger barn, once a neighbor's, hides around the bend in the road and is home for our two donkeys, sheep and an occasional temporary calf. No signs of a pigsty, an outhouse, a smokehouse, a milkhouse or a springhouse endure. Our needs have changed now, but it is not tedious to live within a space that tells us an old story.

The Garden

January in New England is the traditional time of planning for spring and doing the chores one is too busy to do at other times of the year. The mildness of this particular January makes such things as fence mending, wood chopping, barn cleaning and manure spreading slightly less onerous tasks. It's one thing to work up steam skiing across a shimmering white meadow or down a glossy slope. It's quite another to paralyze one's fingers reconstructing a toppled fence section or sawing away at a dead elm tree.

The garden itself may seem a barren place this month, but it isn't in the mind of its caretaker. Frozen soil heaved up by frost or covered with snow sparkles with crisp green abundance in the fantasies of the gardener poring over January's annual gift, the seed catalog. Those Bibles of the cultivator, anticipated with prudence and scrutinized with recklessness, are often ordered from with wild abandon.

Seeds—what an evolutionary coup it was, this method of reproduction. Before seeds, living things simply divided. Poof! It was done, but it limited the complexity of an organism, and the process had to be completed on the spot. There could be no time lapse, which was often probably quite inconvenient and led to micropopulation explosions.

Seeds, hiding within themselves those tiny diagrams of the new generation, can wait for months or years until the right moment to burst forth. Even animals seem to know when to plant their seed so that it will be born at the most suitable time of year.

Seeds have evolved techniques to space themselves too. The spiraling rotors of the maple seed, the angel hair that carries milkweed seeds on the breeze and the burrs that catch on one's pant leg or jacket (the hitchhikers of the plant world) all know how to travel. Seeds surrounded by fruit use birds and their digestive systems to provide not only transportation but fertilizer. They are deposited already covered in what they need to flourish.

Domesticated seeds, however, usually need a lot more human help than their wild cousins, for as cultivators and manipulators we often want our seeds to stay put and grow bigger. For example, the earliest known wild ancestor of corn or maize was smaller than one's little finger and huskless. The seeds could fly several feet or yards when they dried and popped off of the ear. Those that escaped a hungry animal's notice stood a good chance of germinating and spreading the species farther afield. Since maize cultivation first began in Mesoamerica five or six thousand years ago, we have developed huge husked ears that would be doomed to extinction without human help. Husks protect the seeds or kernels from animals and pests and keep the kernels from falling off, but they also prevent seeds from transporting themselves to a fertile spot. We plant our maize where we choose, keeping most of it for the pot, and we have cultivated it for that purpose.

Seeds are our sustenance and our basic source of survival. They have become a metaphor for beginnings, growth and life itself. Whether they be seeds of passion, discontent, love, weeds or vegetables, seeds remain primary in our daily course.

So it is that in January I think a lot about seeds. I spread seed catalogs, last year's half-used seed packages and envelopes of seeds saved from our own garden over the kitchen table, sorting, studying and deciding whether to purchase Scarlet Nantes or Chrisna carrots or one of a dozen other varieties. I am a child in a candy store salivating at each description, culling possible purchases with regret, agonizing over decisions. I know I don't need twenty kinds of lettuce—twelve will do—but the temptation is to order more and more.

All gardeners must have their favorite seed companies, but in these days of mail-order living, each year brings forth another batch of four-color wonders as well as more modest newsprinted listings. It would take a stern soul indeed to rely on only the standard choices.

I make a rule of ordering primarily within my own geographical zone on the premise that seeds from more temperate areas will be less hardy in New England. I also try to buy only untreated seeds that have been grown organically. This process began years ago when our oldest son, a confirmed environmentalist, recommended a small seed company in Maine. Until then I had usually ordered my seeds from a couple of well-known seed megacompanies, suspicious of the Maine company's modest newsprint catalog, I purchased half from "Megaseed" and half from the Maine company. We then planted duplicates of a number of things side by side. As one might guess, the megaseeds paled against their Maine competitors. The germination rate of the Maine seeds appeared to be double that of the others, and the plants, were larger, more beautiful and more vigorous. This small experiment convinced us all. Our little organic company's seeds so far outshone the famous ones that I have never turned back. Since then, I have discovered several such companies through the miracle of mailing lists. Most of them send black-and-white newsprinted literature, to ecological and economic advantage. Color appears later, in the garden where it grows abundantly.

A related area of seed manufacture that has asserted itself in recent years is the reintroduction of heirloom seeds, the old-fashioned, open-pollinated varieties that are being lost in the whirl of commercial hybridizing.

In the beginning there were only open-pollinated seeds. Each plant flower either pollinated itself, as peas and beans do, or was cross-pollinated, the male pollen being transferred from its own flower to another by the wind or a foraging insect. Corn is cross-pollinated, so when you read instructions that advise planting it in clumps so the tassels can be blown from one stalk to another to touch each other, this is the reason why.

Hybrids, like mules, are offsprings of parents of different plant varieties or even species. They can be vigorous and very uniform plants, bred to combine positive traits of two or more disparate ancestors, but they cannot reproduce themselves with exactitude. That is the work of the scientist in the lab. Hybridizing became popular in the 1930s when seed companies became popular. Until then most folks who gardened or farmed saved seeds from their own plantings and returned them to the earth the following season. Now most gardeners order their seeds each year with rarely a thought of saving them.

I have saved seeds from time to time, with varying results. The first seeds were big, easy ones from the center of a squat, whitish Patty Pan squash. I did not know then that squash is cross-pollinated, and I was growing zucchini as well. The following year my frugally saved seeds produced long, pale-green squashes, disk-shaped dark greens and bulbous, white, nameless others, a Mendalian dream-come-true, and hardly what I expected. I don't remember there being a true Patty Pan in the lot.

Squash seeds are actually useful for planting if only one variety is planted in a garden, and self-pollinating plants give the gardener no problems. I often plant bean seeds and pea seeds saved from the year before. But if you are interested in saving seeds, you must make sure they are not hybrids or you will be disappointed.

Why bother at all when seeds are cheap and labor is dear? Sometimes you might have a variety that can't be bought again, such as seeds brought from a distant place. Also, just the idea of saving open-pollinated varieties is a happy one. Seed banks and organizations are attempting these days to protect many disappearing species. At a time when the number of plant species is diminishing worldwide, and plant pests are becoming more resistant to the chemicals we feed them, we may need these lost varieties more than we think. Despite the notion of hybrid vigor, there is an advantage to diversity in more areas than the stock market. Different plant species have different resistances to disease. If numerous varieties are planted, the chance of all succumbing to a problem is much lessened. The Inca of Peru planted forty to fifty kinds of potatoes in their fields. The Irish planted one. If they had used Incan methods, there might never have been a great potato famine.

My last seed-ordering policy is to try a few new vegetables each year. This is not a hard rule to follow, and I have never been able to find room in the garden for all I have purchased. Who could resist blue corn, golden beets, red lettuces and purple cauliflower, as well as the countless varieties of Asian vegetables that tempt the potential buyer with such descriptions as "A red-leafed amaranth grown for its leaves rather then its seed. Popular in southern Asia, Africa and the West Indies and known by many names including Calaloo."

Though plant species are diminishing across the globe as megaagricultural systems replicate fewer and fewer varieties, the home gardener seems to be gaining access to exotic plants from all over the world. Chinese and Japanese greens and cabbages are common in many seed catalogs today. Fifteen years ago when we began our vegetable garden, I could only buy them in New York's Chinatown, where I was taking cooking classes. Italian tomatoes, broccolis and peppers are easily available now, but I remember planting my first Italian tomatoes from seeds brought to me by a friend who had traveled in Italy.

Both my daughter and I puzzled over planting instructions written in Japanese on seed packages she had brought from Kyoto when she returned from studying there. The vegetables that emerged from those seeds were so exotic that I didn't know what to do with some of them. Today one seed company in Vermont, which now sells such exotics, sends a few recipes with the seeds just to help you along.

My orders this year include seeds of French, Italian, Chinese, Japanese and American extraction. Many are favorites from the past, but some are untried and experimental. Now that only two of us remain in the household as daily consumers, I plan for more preservable items: beans that can be dried, potatoes that last for months, tomatoes that can be canned. Even when the children were in permanent residence, it was impossible to consume all the lettuces before they bolted in the hot midsummer. Now we plant a little less and give away more.

New additions this year will include Baby Oak Leaf lettuce, Chinese celery, vegetable amaranth, Rubine Brussels sprouts and a mystery root called Gobo, a favorite of a Japanese friend who brought it complete with indecipherable instructions. Three new winter squashes called Chestnut, Orangetti and Delicata will be planted along with our traditional favorites, acorn and butternut. I'll plant three or four pumpkin seeds and thin them to two. We love pumpkin pie, pumpkin soup and pumpkin soufflé, but the processing of more than five or six pumpkins becomes an ineffective task. I have too often found several jars of frozen pumpkin puree many years after it was put into the freezer. It is then that I respect the compost pile as a repository always available for use.

Other garden staples include many kinds of beans, three kinds of beets and cabbage family products such as Brussels sprouts, broccolis, cauli-flowers, red and savoy cabbages and Chinese cabbages. We try carrots of varying lengths, from the round baby Paris markets to the deep growing Nantes longs. Celery and celeriac; many rows of sweet corn; cucumbers small and large; leeks, onions, garlic and shallots; a few melons; sugar snap and regular peas; red, yellow, brown, green, hot and sweet peppers;

parsnips, summer squash; and tomatoes ... They are in the mind's eye and on the catalog page, the memories of their tastes and textures heralds of the spring that seems so far away.

Our vegetable garden is a medium-large one. It measures seventy by seventy feet, which is only an eighth of an acre, but it is sufficient for all our vegetable needs for half the year. The garden has had several expansions since we first plowed a patch in the field in 1977. It started at less than half its current size. I don't think I would recommend starting a garden on such an ample scale, especially in untested soil, but I ardently recommend starting some sort of garden, be it a small patch or a window box.

Suggestions for a Moderate Garden

Lettuce, four kinds, one short row each to be repeated in midsummer
Carrots, two kinds, short and long, one longer row each
Sugar snap peas, as many as you have room for
Summer squash, one mound of six to eight seeds
Winter squash, one mound of six to eight seeds
Large tomatoes, three plants
Cooking tomatoes, three plants
Green beans, one long row
Peppers, two kinds, four plants of each
Eggplants, one kind, four plants

The Kitchen

January to the gardener ... The fresh sweet tastes and smells of the summer are only memories, but there is still the larder, and it is packed with the fruits of last summer residing under various guises. Stored homegrown foods fall into four categories: frozen, canned, dried and those that keep on their own. The latter are the ones we use more quickly, before they deteriorate, and the larder gets emptier each week as we cook leeks, onions, carrots, beets, cabbages, winter squash, celeriac and potatoes. We have enough onions and potatoes to last until spring—and they do—but other unprocessed resources have less staying power. Potatoes and winter squash are piled in baskets and wooden barrels and kept in a cool corner. Onions are hung from a beam in braided lengths along with drying thyme, sage, basil, oregano, savory and other herbs. Carrots, leeks, cabbages and celeriac are refrigerated, and dried beans and tomatoes fill jars on the pantry shelf. Other jars hold tomato sauce and pickles made of zucchini, cucumbers and green beans, as well as chutneys and jams and whatever else we can invent to take care of a harvest excess. The freezer holds the rest—corn, peas, strawberries, cherries, rhubarb— enough to allow us to keep our pact to continue to live at least partially off our land.

Aside from vegetables, our freezer is also packed with the butchered parts of a veal, two lambs and several chickens we or neighbors have raised organically. The dairy farm next to us sells off its male calves in the fall, and one raised in the comfort of our barn amidst sheep and donkeys provides enough veal for a year. It also eases our guilt at eating commercial veal that we read has been mistreated, abused and filled with questionable chemicals. It is not surprising that a calf that has led a short but happy life living off of fresh milk before going off to the butcher tastes better than the commercial variety.

We buy two organically grown lambs, already packaged and frozen, from a neighbor and kill our own chickens when we need them. I confess that I do not do these deeds myself. I am, well, chicken-hearted. But I can defeather and clean with no qualms. I attribute this ability to a childhood of watching while someone else wrung chickens' necks and cleaned them. I remember sitting on the back porch waiting for the moment when head and body parted and the poor headless creature ran around in circles until it dropped at last, to be gathered up and prepared for the oven. This is plainly the etymology for the adage "running around like a chicken with its head chopped off," one of many examples of an agrarian heritage that persists in our language. It may also be an example of a child's insouciance in the face of violence. I believe I viewed the killing of chickens in the same way I viewed the violent cartoons at the movies every Saturday afternoon— with a sense of unreality and distance. I wept only once, when a little hen I had made a pet of met her end, but our connectedness made that a different matter.

Raising chickens is so easy, dressing them is so little bother and their flavor is so much better than anything store-bought that I am surprised so few country people do it anymore. Commercial chicken is admittedly cheap, but the flavor of a natural, free-range fowl is another matter altogether.

Our initial venture into poultry slaughter began one spring when ten of the sixteen baby chicks born to our coop turned out to be males. We had two roosters already, a father and son struggling in true Oedipal fashion for the favors of the hens and the rule of the roost. A total of twelve roosters, as the young reached maturity, was too many. Their range, no matter how free, was not big enough for the lot. The daily battles would have interested a cockfight enthusiast, and the coop became a hotbed of dissension and discontent. Half the group took to nesting in a nearby pine grove. The rest often emerged from their perches in the morning, limping noticeably and displaying battered cockscombs and missing tail feathers.

It was decided that we must relieve these fellows of their warlike and territorial ways and relegate them to the stew pot. This we did one Saturday morning with the help of two friends and one of our sons, who had observed the art of slaughter at a bucolic summer camp in the Adirondacks some years ago. Our son caught each bird and held it upside down for a minute, apparently a calming device, which proved effective. One neighbor then placed the head on a tree stump block and with one swift blow beheaded the creature. Each bird was immediately plunged into a large pot of boiled water to loosen the feathers and make picking easier. The feathers can then be removed in two or three minutes' time. Leaving the bird in the hot water too long tends to make the skin come off with the feathers and should be avoided. After defeathering, a T-shaped incision is made above and down through the anus. From this hole one can reach in and pull out all the entrails in seconds. Liver, heart and gizzard may be saved, but care must be taken to remove the gall bladder without breaking it, for it can add a note of bitterness to anything it oozes upon. Removal of undigested grain from the craw completes the cleaning and the fowl is then ready for either oven or freezer. The roosters had had a free and well-fed life. I did not mourn.

After many years I can remember why, as a child, I preferred the dark meat. In a fowl that has lived on earthworms, toads, grass, excess garden greens and grain, the dark meat is distinctly different. It is browner in color and has a hint of gaminess that creates a hearty flavor, a flavor that needs no sauce to disguise its blandness, a flavor our New England forefathers presumed to be timeless. Little did they know that in three hundred years, chickens would never see earth or grass and would live on commercial mash, antibiotics and hormones.

Today our freezer contains carefully packaged fauna that have ranged freely and eaten wholesomely. Our winter larder can sustain us.

Recipes that invite one's culinary interest in January are often of the hearty, stomach-filling sort, the kind that can cook for hours on the back of the stove or in a pot on a hook in a cooking fireplace.

Our farmhouse has one such fireplace in the kitchen, the room once called the keeping room. In the nineteenth century all cooking was done here, usually with cast-iron paraphernalia for boiling, roasting, broiling and baking. A large, open hearth is the foundation for this fireplace, much higher and wider than those in the other rooms. The back and sides are built of massive pieces of fieldstone, but it is faced on the front with brick, undoubtedly a more difficult item to come by than stone, the abundance of which leads old-timers to remark that only in Connecticut does stone grow. The hearth area contains a movable iron crane for hanging pothooks and houses a beehive-shaped brick oven once used daily to bake bread.

When we first moved in, I was entranced by the notion of heating the room with the same heat we used to cook our food. We found some old iron kettles with hook handles at auctions and even in a few farm-supply stores. We experimented with different recipes and different woods, with smoking, braising and boiling. I even found an old reflecting oven that could be placed in front of the fire to bake bread or roast a bit of meat. It takes forever! A Dutch oven placed in the coals and covered with ashes does a quicker job of it. We have never used our built-in brick oven because the original iron door is missing. Someday I would like to replace it and give that a try. Apparently brick-oven baking is done by making a big fire in the oven, letting it burn down and then baking the bread with the retained heat.

As one might imagine, cooking over an open fire is less controlled than that on a modern stove, but it has its place, which is not the same as using charcoal briquets on the outdoor grill. Food cooked over wood retains a distinctive, subtle wood flavor quite different from that created by briquets, even when it is concealed in a covered pot. Several years ago, when our regular oven proved too small to hold the two geese we needed for a large family Christmas dinner, we roasted a second Christmas goose in the reflecting oven in front of the fire. It was slow, and we had to finish it off in the stove, but the velvety hint of apple wood is memorable yet.

Here are some recipes using winter garden vegetables that are suited to fireplace cooking. They may also grace the back of your sleek electric range with only mild detriment.

Broiled Veal Chops with Dried Fennel
He may have been reinventing the wheel, but this was the creation of one of our sons when he was a child. We often grilled meat in the fireplace using a portable double gridiron with a handle, which clamped the meat

on both sides and held it fast. One turned the whole mechanism rather than just the food. We were inserting thick veal chops, preparing them for the fire, when Jim noticed some fennel fronds hanging to dry. "Why not cover the meat with the fennel?" he asked, and being a resourceful child, he proceeded to make a layer of fennel fronds on the gridiron. He placed the chops on this, covered them with more fennel, closed the contraption and placed it over the fire. The meat arrived at the table juicier, less charred and hinting at that delicate licorice flavor of the fennel, a scrumptious surprise. Would that more of us had the sagacity of the unencumbered mind.

Since then we have tried the same method with dried basil plants or sage branches, both with satisfying results.

INGREDIENTS:
>   *Veal chops, about 3/4 inch thick*
>   *Olive oil, good quality*
>   *Salt*
>   *Pepper*
>   *Lots of dried fennel, basil or sage branches*

PROCEDURE:
1. Make a wood fire and let it burn down to a bed of red coals.
2. Coat the chops with a good olive oil, then salt and pepper.
3. Cover the grill with the dried herb branches. Place the chops on the top. Add more herbs to cover. This is easier with an enclosed two-sided gridiron, as it holds the whole lot firmly and can be turned easily.
4. Cook the meat over the coals until just done through. This will depend on the heat of the fire and the thickness and temperature of the chops. It could be 10 minutes or 20.
5. Remove the chops from the heat. Most of the herbs will have burned away. Scrape off any unappetizing bits and serve either as is or with a light mustard sauce.

Chicken and Dumplings

This is a recipe that symbolizes a cultural maxim of times past. It is the notion of saving, making use of seemingly useless items and making do. In these days store-bought chicken is normally not more than ten weeks old and is as tender as the chemicals and hormones it was raised on. But what of the tough old bird, whose flesh will not lightly succumb to a knife and fork, but whose flavor is unsurpassed by its younger relatives? It was to one such fellow, a rowdy old rooster, that we wielded the axe and created a dish of old-fashioned luxury. When it was butchered, the fowl's meat was the color of beef, thick-skinned, tough and fatty. It would have been a disaster broiled or roasted, but stewed in an iron pot over an apple wood fire, it made a sumptuous feast.

INGREDIENTS FOR STEW:
1 6-pound stewing fowl, cut into serving pieces
Cooking oil
2 medium onions, sliced
6 to 8 medium carrots, cut into 2-inch lengths
5 or 6 celery stalks, cut into 2-inch lengths
2 celeriac bulbs, cut into half-moon slices
Bay leaves
Thyme to taste
Salt to taste
Pepper to taste

PROCEDURE FOR STEW:
1. Simmer the neck, back and giblets in salted water. Reserve. Pour the oil into a large skillet and add the chicken pieces. Brown them briefly and transfer to a large, iron fireplace pot. Brown the onions and add them to the casserole. Add the salt, pepper and herbs and cover with water. Hang the pot above a medium-high fire, burning a flavorful wood if possible. You may have to adjust the distance of the pot from the fire. When the water has come to a boil, move the pot to a spot where it will simmer gently. Cook until the chicken begins to feel tender to the touch of a fork.
2. Add all the vegetables to the casserole. Stir to mix with the chicken pieces and add more liquid, if necessary, to cover. Simmer for another hour, skimming grease from the top occasionally. If the water evaporates, add strained broth made with giblets and other chicken parts.
3. When the chicken feels tender to the fork and the vegetables feel tender but firm, remove enough pieces so there is an even layer of liquid on the top of the dish. Set these pieces in a dish on the hearth to stay warm.
4. Shape the dumpling dough into balls about the size of a small ice-cream scoop. Float them on top of the simmering broth. Put the lid on the casserole and cook for 12 to 15 more minutes. Test the dumplings, which should triple in size, to make sure they are done in the center.
5. Serve in wide soup bowls, adding chicken and vegetables first, then broth and finally dumplings on top.

INGREDIENTS FOR DUMPLINGS:
2 cups unbleached flour
4 tablespoons baking powder
2 eggs
1/2 to 3/4 cup milk
1/2 teaspoon salt
1/2 cup fresh parsley, minced, or a bit of thyme or rosemary (optional)

PROCEDURE FOR DUMPLINGS:
1. Sift the flour, baking powder and salt into a mixing bowl. Make sure it is well mixed.
2. Beat 2 eggs into a 2-cup measuring cup. Fill to 1-1/2 cup level with milk. Add this and the herbs to the dry ingredients, mixing but not beating. Work quickly. Don't overmix. The dough should be stiff enough to form into balls but should not be dry. If it seems too dry, add more milk. Let it sit for 10 minutes before cooking.
3. Add the dumplings to the casserole. Cook with the lid on for 12 to 15 minutes. Serve from the pot into large, flat soup plates.

Vegetables Roasted in Hot Coals

Years ago we spent summers in a little town on Long Island just across from an uninhabited part of Fire Island. We often took a ferry or sailed across to the vast beach there and had picnic suppers, five families together with our fourteen collective children. A fire was built with driftwood, cooked upon and sung around as the evening grew darker. Along with the customary hamburgers and hotdogs, we often took a burlap bag of fresh corn which we soaked in the roiling brine at the edge of the sea. Twenty years ago we were not suspicious of the ocean's purity. We then roasted the marinated ears, husk and all, in the embers. Sometimes we took Idaho potatoes, which we wrapped in foil before baking the same way. I now cook yams, beets, onions and parsnips by the same method in our own fireplace.

INGREDIENTS:
Potatoes, beets, onions, yams, sweet potatoes, parsnips or unhusked corn
Salt
Pepper
Sweet butter

PROCEDURE:
1. Wash the vegetables. Peel the hard layers from the onions. Peel the parsnips. Wrap the vegetables in foil and place them among the embers. Cook until tender.
2. Serve with salt, pepper and sweet butter.

Dutch Oven Dessert

Anything can be cooked in a Dutch oven that can be cooked in a regular oven, so long as it can fit in the space. My Dutch oven is made of heavy cast iron. It has a close-fitting lid with a lip around the edge to facilitate the positioning and maintaining of hot coals on the top. It is big enough to hold a medium-sized roast, half a ham or one large, round loaf of bread. I place it on a bed of coals, put more coals on the lid and replace them as they burn out. I've never tried to cook anything delicate, such as a soufflé, in a Dutch oven, but I'm sure that it can be done.

This New England dish uses only ingredients that would have been available two hundred years ago in the northern woodlands. In the original recipe, the spices—the only imported ingredients—were called for in minuscule amounts. I wonder if their rarity and expense was the reason.

INGREDIENTS:
1 butternut squash, peeled and cut into 1-inch slices (about 2 pounds will do for the amount of seasoning listed below; if squash is larger, add more seasoning)
Equal amount of sliced apple (about 4 apples)
1/3 cup honey
1/4 cup butter
1/2 to 1 teaspoon cinnamon
1/2 teaspoon nutmeg
1/2 cup chopped walnuts or pecans

PROCEDURE:
1. After slicing the squash and apples into relatively uniform pieces, place them in a buttered Dutch oven.
2. Drizzle them with honey and dot with butter. Sprinkle with cinnamon, nutmeg and chopped nuts.
3. Place the Dutch oven in the fireplace on a bed of coals. Pile more coals on the oven cover. Replace them if they cool.
4. Bake for about 45 minutes. The dish is ready to eat when the fruits are soft but not too mushy.

FEBRUARY

I always wanted my own land but it was a secret. Everyone has a garden inside of them. But you have to find your garden. Some people never do. Life doesn't offer it to them.

—Gailard Seaman, gardener, The Bronx

The Land

February, the bitter month, distinguished by little save cold and brevity, is an impatient time for the gardener. Actions must be mental rather than physical, and gardens grow only on paper and in the imagination.

We sit at the kitchen table, the fire at our backs, bird feeders out our window, frozen ground beyond, now covered with an inch of snow, now bare and desolate, grass hay golden and sparkling with frost. Helping the wild birds in their winter search for food is a distinctive winter pleasure, though one hears it makes them lazy, less able at foraging for themselves. We are careful never to let a feeder run scant of food in case they have lost their hunting nature. They come in groups of their own kind, chickadees, purple finches, evening grosbeaks, juncos, contending for spots there. A pair of blue jays appear, and all others scatter. Two red squirrels who seem to live within our walls set to work under the feeders collecting all fallen remnants. A wild cat who frequents the area waits quietly for the precise moment to pounce. I chase her and, inadvertently, the birds away. A pair of cardinals make their daily appearance. A downy woodpecker zooms in. I watch and dream, and think feebly of springtime and the garden to come.

Our land was never a horticulturalist's dream. A previous owner, who had purchased the house and forty acres in the mid-1930s, chuckled when she told me once that "Old Allyn certainly knew which forty acres were totally useless when he sold them off during the depression." Old Allyn and his forbears had farmed this hill and its surrounding valleys for almost two hundred years at that time. His son, grandsons and great-grandson are today our closest neighbors. Their dairy farm is one of a handful of "Farms of Distinction" in Connecticut and their fields have been worked by the same kin group for almost 250 years. It would have been most foolish of Old Allyn to sell valuable farmland to a writer and his family, as these first nonfamily-related owners of our house were. It was fortuitous that the expanse is as pleasing to the eye as it is untillable to the hand.

The land is a north-facing, saw-toothed wedge cut out of our neighbor's domain. The house and outbuildings were erected north of an east-west road that cuts across a hill rising upward to the south and down into a valley on the north. Ice-age glaciers have strewn it with automobile-size boulders, moss-encrusted outcroppings and almost buried stones of unimaginable size that clutter an area that begins as a watershed and ends in a wetland a hundred feet below. Streams and rills gush or trickle, depending on the season. The largest stream, once used along its route for a forge, a gristmill and a sawmill, meanders through another neighbor's high pasture before reaching our boundaries through a culvert under a highway. There it skirts a pasture that contains our donkeys and sheep and tumbles down a hillside, creating three waterfalls, two only thirty feet apart and another perhaps three hundred yards downstream. The upper two falls plunge between cliffs of sedimentary rock carved and chipped along their layers, in some places making crude and precipitous steps fit for a long-legged giant with unusually small feet, in other places obscured by boulders as high as a house but looking as if they had been dropped unpredictably and scattered as mere pebbles. One such stone has fallen at a slant to form a small, rather damp and dark cavelet, the sort that might spell discomfort to the adult but magic to a child.

Beneath the second upper cascade stand the rocky remains of a mill, which one I can't be sure. There is a pool large and deep enough for swimming if a person has the courage to withstand the icy waters flowing through. The rapid movement of the water prevents the stream from ever completely freezing, but it also never seems to warm to a degree I can tolerate. Small, delicate, thin children who come to visit splash with relish in water temperatures I find cold enough to stop one's heart from beating.

The lower fall is the one I most often visit. It is the tallest and deepest in the woods. Several large flat rocks jut out in front of it on the embankment, making spacious resting places. This waterfall generates an aura of solitude that comforts and renews.

My favorite time for contemplating nature by the waterfall is now, in the silence of winter. First of all, there are no gnats, a scourge we shall investigate as summer approaches. Second, even in a snow-poor winter, a frosty fairyland builds itself here until spring decimates it. Geodes of ice rise up and around the rocks and falling water to form a pattern of complex design. Whorls and globs of iridescent white, silver and gray only partially hide the roaring water underneath, each globule building one upon another, forming mounds of connections. Icy stalactites both strong and fragile reach out for the rushing water below, glittering like momentary jewels. If one is well bundled and doesn't mind the creeping cold that quietly sitting produces, here is the place to meditate, to forget the compromises of our own creations and try to fuse with a perfect natural setting.

The remainder of our steep and rocky hillside, once a pasture behind the house, faces north and is afflicted with long winter shadows that keep snow from melting and ground from thawing until late in the spring. Even so, it becomes verdant in summer where goldenrod, wild raspberry, barberry, chokecherry, Joe pie weed, milkweed and a hundred other wild things reclaim the pasture in the places where we don't mow or graze animals.

A path we have cut leads to a pond near the bottom of the hill that we dug fifteen years ago. We haven't stocked it with trout since our first batch succumbed to watershed pesticides that drained down from a farmer's field above, but the pond has surviving salamanders, frogs and a turtle. Once it sheltered a water snake and another year a pair of teal ducks and their baby. I believe muskrats live in the banks for I see the remainders of the reeds they dig up to eat.

When it first emerged from the bulldozer's sculptings, the pond was a raw, torpid mass with no detectable life. I often sat beside it or swam in it, wondering if it would always look like a scar on the landscape, but I needn't have fretted. The astonishing thing is the speed with which it was found and settled by water plants and animals—dragonflies and cattails, frogs and reeds, salamanders and algae. Today the pond has its own ecosystem with all sorts of flora and fauna, known and unknown to us. Snow tracks tell us that deer, coyotes, rabbits and wild turkeys frequent its frozen surface. Springtime brings us the chorus of peepers that live on its edges. Summer is a circus of interactions: dragonflies copulating in the air, water bugs walking on the water's surface and the turtle doing his disappearing act.

Beyond the pond there is a marshy area that levels into a hay field tended and reaped by our neighbor and, beyond that, woodland that widens and narrows until it is ours no more.

It is within these unlikely parameters that we have forged a large vegetable garden, a kitchen herb garden, several perennial flower beds, a poultry house and yard, a sheep and donkey pasture and a small orchard. We've gone about it in a deliberate if innocent way, making mistakes and rectifying them, having successes and celebrating them and all the while learning. If ever there was a misrepresentation, it is that of the happy, slightly simpleminded farmer, thoughtlessly tilling the fields, for living near the land generates an almost uninterrupted series of surprises and decisions based on those surprises. Unexpected events from flood to drought, snow to windstorm, insect infestation to bumper crop, raccoon attack to unexpected chicken hatchlings make each day a fresh experience, each season a unique one. The seemingly laconic attitude of the cultivator is bred of a lifetime of changes. Nothing can surprise a farmer—a snowstorm on the tenth of May, a rainless April, a frigid July or a balmy February. As weather forecasters howl and newspapers headline such anomalies, the farmer shrugs and goes on with his or her labor.

The Garden

A garden can be anything from a few pots of herbs or nasturtiums on a windowsill to an expanse the likes of Kew Gardens. So many of us feel the need to plant something and watch it grow that one sees evidence of it everywhere. Could it be our heritage? We began as nomadic gatherers and hunters several millions of years ago. Our ancestors wandered from place to place, finding whatever they could on which to survive, probably first gnawing on raw wild grains (as shown by fossil teeth abrasions) or scavenging the lion's leftovers, only later learning to form tools with which to hunt. But even as we harbor this image of the ancestor as hunter-cavedweller, we know that we began basically as eaters of plants. So important was plant life in our diet that about ten thousand years ago, people began to settle down in order to really get at this business of making plants grow. They learned, as my husband and I have learned as we commute back and forth from city to country, that keeping a garden in good health is difficult if one is not around to tend it most of the time.

The first permanent town or village undoubtedly followed the concept of ordering—to some degree anyway—the procurement of vegetable nourishment. Food cultivation and production gradually replaced simple gathering. People found it necessary to stay put and probably work harder. Building dwellings, preparing and caring for fields of plants and maintaining accumulating possessions must have required more energy than roaming, gathering and hunting. Why did they do it? There are a number of theories, often based on the needs of an exploding population and competition for food and territory. Whatever the original cause or causes, this simple but basic change in survival technique has quite changed our world.

Because in present-day hunting and gathering societies the vegetable gatherers are traditionally women, one may also theorize that it was a woman or group of women who first conceived the notion of planting. How eccentric she must have appeared to her nomadic comrades, and how uncompromising and strong she must have been to withstand the ridicule of those who, like most of us, reject the new and innovative. It is to this mythical figure I look for geoponic guidance, this woman who planted the first seed, for she has sent her message forth clearly throughout the world. We see her descendants wielding mammoth tractors in Iowa and mindfully pruning the roots of a bonsai. We see one of them in the aged woman on the top floor of a brownstone behind us in Brooklyn meticulously cultivating the potted plants in her window, and we see another in the kindergartener who glows at the sight of a bean sprouting in a jelly glass. They are all of the same human seed.

How widely that human seed has spread itself. Evidence is everywhere. There was the tiny patch of cabbage we saw in the center of Shanghai, stuck into a corner where the pavement was broken. Despite the city's coal fumes and human traffic, these Chinese cabbages were tall, full and healthy, clearly tended with love and intelligence.

On the Caribbean island of Martinique there was an eccentric stranger who drew me off the street into her meager courtyard to view her hibiscus collection, perfectly tended and perfectly pruned, perfectly beautiful and the heart of an elderly woman's existence.

Perhaps my favorite testimony to the prevalence of the human need to grow things was a bower in a village on the coast of Yugoslavia. My husband and I and our four children were driving down the coast toward Dubrovnik. I had read of a charming inn in the village of Trsteno, so we stopped there and inquired about rooms for the night. That none were available was a disappointment, for the inn was small, whitewashed, clean and perched on a hill over the Adriatic Sea, whose waters sparkled like jewels. As we returned to our car, a middle-aged man wearing a sleeveless undershirt, short pants, dark high socks and dark leather oxfords approached us and, searching for a common language, communicated that he and his wife would have room for us in their home.

Private bed-and-breakfasts are common in eastern Europe, but we had not stayed at one before. We drove back to the highway that cut through the village and left the car there. The upper part of the town could only be reached on foot because it was terraced ever higher, a clutter of stone steps, walkways and houses built cheek by jowl with one another, dipping down the steep and stony hillside toward the sea. Our mentor's house was like the others, modest in size and architecture but clean and charming. I remember linen sheets edged with real lace that smelled of the sun under which they had been dried. I remember best the small cement patio where we ate dinner and breakfast. It sheltered three tables under a homemade trellis that created a bower of unrivaled practical splendor, for edging the area was a continuous row of large tin cans in which were planted every vining vegetable one could imagine: squashes, melons, cucumbers, tomatoes, beans and peas. They all rose and came together over our heads to form an edible canopy. A ripening melon was entwined with a string bag to prevent it from crashing to the floor as its stem loosened from the vine. Cucumbers hid in the greenness of their leaves. Squashes added gold and tomatoes red. Here was beauty bonded to the need for food, and a tribute to both.

All of the above are gardens. They don't compare in size and style to the elegant structures of Soochow or the expanses of our own Brooklyn Botanic Garden, but they are meaningful gardens nevertheless, for they each reflect an individual's connection with the earth. They are planned, attended and a significant part of their owner's lives.

No unequivocal rules can ever apply to planning a garden, for each garden, each site, each climate has its own peculiarities that make it distinct and intractable. The hardpan earth of west Texas is no match for the fertile loams of the Northeast, but the Texas season is longer, milder and sunnier. Rain is a major problem for the southwestern gardener because watering is often restricted during a drought. In New England frost and fungus are greater sources of worry and woe.

Garden planning, whether done haphazardly at the moment of planting or fussed over on a winter's evening, is an exercise in juggling variable—at least the expected ones. To begin with, one doesn't want everything in the garden to ripen at once, nor does one want more than can be consumed, frozen or given away. These can be problems for the unseasoned gardener that most seed catalogs do not prepare you for.

I remember the year we planted our first big vegetable garden in the field. I had ordered, among other things, one small package of perhaps twenty or twenty-five zucchini seeds. Inexperienced as I was, I planted the whole package, and was faced six weeks later with dozens of zucchinis. I couldn't pick them fast enough. They became giant clubs capable of bludgeoning a strongman with success. Nor could we eat them fast enough. They became zucchini bread, zucchini soup, zucchini pickles and, finally and most happily, zucchini compost. We learned. Now I plant one mound of zucchini—five or six seeds—and after a few years we have learned to like it again.

Seed packages and catalogs don't provide much help on such things as the zucchini problem, but they do impart useful information that one should not ignore. Most catalogs list the number of days of growth required from planting to harvest. This is important to note, and though the numbers are not writ in stone, being dependent upon rain, sun and temperature, they give you an approximate time of arrival for each mature vegetable.

Another important factor is the cold or frost resistance of an individual plant. Some vegetables may be planted much earlier than others because they germinate in a much colder soil, and the seedlings will withstand and even enjoy cool days and frosty nights. Some plants grow well only in a cool climate and tend to bolt when temperatures rise. Others thrive on the heat that makes other plants—and people—wilt. Knowing this information and the plants' maturation rates can help in planning serial sowings. For example, rapidly maturing lettuces and Bok choi may be planted in April to mature from mid-May into July. Their emptied patches may then be replanted with quick-to-mature fall plants such as Chinese cabbage, more Bok choi or even additional lettuce, if it is shaded to keep it cool enough to germinate. This is an especially useful method for the gardener with limited space, and if cleverly executed can keep a family in ripe vegetables from May through November.

Correct spacing of seedlings is another factor rarely made explicit on a seed package. We are usually admonished to "spread seed thinly," but how thin is thinly? Lettuces can be planted just inches apart and thinned out and eaten when they are young to leave the remaining plants to grow to maturity. Cabbages must be planted about two feet apart from the very beginning, an instruction I ignored for several years, resulting in runty specimens.

I've already mentioned yield in terms of zucchini production, and it is indeed the most difficult factor to anticipate for a number of reasons. Weather variables as well as soil variation can influence yields greatly, and not always on the side of overabundance. One summer I planted twenty Romanesca broccolis, a special Italian broccoli with pale green heads that form elegant pyramids or cones. It leafed well and each plant grew to gigantic size, but by the end of November when the ground froze, we had still not seen a head form. I've raised this variety successfully before, so I was mystified at its recalcitrance in maturing. It may have been the hot summer, but I couldn't have expected it, so two rows of the garden were useless.

Each year I make a plan of the garden showing where each plant variety and species is to be placed. These I keep from year to year so I can remember never to put a variety in the same spot two years in a row. Each type of plant uses soil nutrients differently, so this rotation equalizes the use of the soil. It also discourages insect pests, such as the corn borer, that winter over beneath the plants they have enjoyed most during the previous season. This rotation method has been successful, for I have had no serious pest infestations. The soil fertility is stable and high. No one plant type has robbed an area year after year until it has depleted the soil of specific nutrients. No pest has become entrenched in an area because its favorite food was continually to be found there.

The ultimate size of a particular plant is another factor that seed packages may or may not help with, but all you need to do is think about it. A lettuce plant takes up the space of a lettuce, while cucumbers and squash tendrils can cover an area you never dreamed would be filled with green. Peas and pole beans grow high, shading other plants, and must be trellised. Staked tomatoes and corn do the same, so they might work better at the north end of a garden, unless you live south of the equator. Plants of any sort need space around them for root growth and nutrient absorption, and instructions on seed envelopes usually indicate this. However, in the richly fertilized, raised beds of intensive gardeners, plants may be crowded together and still produce well.

My own garden combines two raised bed areas, a regular flat area for large specimens and areas of perennial plants. As the garden has expanded, the asparagus patch, a perennial bed put in five years ago, is now smack-dab in the middle, though it was originally at the edge. Raspberries have been moved out of the fenced garden area into the field because they were spreading chaotically. Perennial strawberries, rhubarb, pyrethrum (a pink daisy whose petals poison insect pests) and—God forbid—horseradish remain. Don't ever put horseradish anywhere that it could possibly crowd out anything. It is a delicious root, wonderful when picked after the first hard frost, freshly grated and mixed with cheddar cheese or sour cream, but it spreads and sends down roots too deep to ever dig away completely. Even the smallest piece of root will rejuvenate and grow into a mammoth, long-leafed specimen proclaiming its survivability waving insolently in the wind. I recommend horseradish farming to anyone who might enjoy the rural routine but doesn't know much about agriculture. It is a plant that will never be defeated, however indifferently it is treated.

Our raised beds measure about five feet by sixty feet. I fertilize each in fall and early winter with donkey manure, stopping in February to let the highly nutritious stuff age and rot before planting time. Here I plant intensively, with foot-wide seeded areas rather than rows and eight-inch spaces in between. I can reach almost everything without walking on this heavily fertilized, heavily used earth. Into this area go the small things: lettuces, spinach, Oriental greens, carrots, beets, parsnips, some herbs, garlic, shallots, Bok choi and cilantro. In many cases these are also plants that can go in early and be replaced in midsummer by fall-maturing plants. Since the rows here are short, they are ideal for things that one doesn't need a lot of, such as a specific variety of lettuce or an experimental item of questionable reputation. It is here I shall plant my Japanese friend's gift of Gobo root, of which I know nothing at all.

The rest of the garden is rotated except, of course, for the perennials. We've been known to stick in extras wherever there is a spot, especially at the end of planting time when there are leftover seeds or seedlings. No plan will probably ever picture our garden exactly the way it is.

The Kitchen

What shall I learn of beans or beans of me?

—Henry David Thoreau, *Walden*

Do we ever know the humble Leguminosae? Being less ambitious than Thoreau, we produce only six or eight rows of bush beans and three or four mounds of pole or runner beans each year. This doesn't match his two and a half acres, but our production does come in handy, not only in summer but also in the middle of winter. Beans are good keepers. They are easily dried and can be stored in jars on the pantry shelf for months, possibly even years, without the need for sterilization, smoking, salting or freezing to prevent their deterioration.

This benefit has given beans a high place among peoples who live without the modern facilities of refrigeration and canning. Perhaps this is why beans are traditionally thought of as peasant food. Another benefit is the bean plant's ability to enrich the garden soil with nitrogen-fixing bacteria that live in nodules on their roots. A third benefit is their nutritional value. High in protein, beans also contain vitamin B1, folic acid, iron, calcium, phosphorus, a cholesterol-reducing insoluble fiber and starch. A free-and-easy captor of nitrogen fertilizer and a high protein resource for people to whom meat is a luxury is beneficial indeed.

Archaeologists have found evidence of bean culture nearly everywhere they have found evidence of human culture. Legumes were particularly important to the pre-Columbian cultures of Mesoamerica, their place of origin. The expanding populations of the Olmecs, Mayans, Teotihuacans, Toltecs and later Aztecs had no domesticable animal save the turkey and the dog. The dog they bred into a grain-eating Chihuahua, which was considered a necessary but inferior food. The turkey was consumed by the upper classes. But for the vast majority of peoples, other sources of protein had to be found. We know today, by using scientific technologies, that the combination of maize, beans and squash is a perfect nutritional blend, each providing the specific amino acids that maximize the protein absorption qualities of the whole. By trial or luck, the early Meso-Americans must have discovered this, for the mixture became a staple of the diet there and still sustains many individuals of the Latin American world.

The bean-grain combination is not unique to Mesoamerica. Rice and tofu in Asia, pasta and fagioli in Italy and lentils and rice in India could all have derived from the need for protein.

Beans might not be found on the menu at five-star restaurants, but there are many hearty and elegant dishes widely loved by peasant and prince alike that are based on the lowly legume. French cassoulet, lamb with flageolets, Spanish black bean soup, even chili con carne (and frijoles, of course) take the bean a step or two above the ordinary. The soybean, on the other hand, seems to have become part of practically everything we eat. Although its use in burgers has eluded me, I eat the soybean in its many Asian forms almost daily, be it soy sauce, tofu or soybean sprouts. In the Chinese markets in New York, there are even more soybean metamorphoses, each of which seems to have little in common with another except its base.

Black beans, red beans, green beans, yellow wax beans, white beans, navy beans, pinto beans, kidneys, cranberries, Jacob's cattle, tongues of fire, soldiers, China yellows, mungs, lentils, limas, split peas, fava—the list is long and varied. Beans are a worldwide staple and with good cause. They keep and they nourish.

My own romance with the bean began long before I knew of French or Asian bean exotica. As a child brought up on vegetables "properly" cooked until they were a limp and mushy mass, beans were one of my favorite edible forms.

Alta Vista, my first school, was a two-block stretch from my house. Its "high view" was imperceptible on that Texas tableland, and it was a quick, flat run from house to school. We all did it four times a day, not only morning and afternoon but at noontime as well, when we went home for lunch. There was no such thing as a school lunchroom then, and in any case, for most people in a small west Texas town, lunch was dinner and dinner was supper. Fathers came home from work for noonday dinner, and children came home from school.

Our mother, clinging to the more sophisticated model of the larger city she had come from, belittled this system. My father did not come home for lunch/dinner, and I ate in solitude, often picking at leftovers from the night before. But sometimes I was given navy beans cooked with a bit of salt pork and served in a soup plate with a generous dollop of catsup on top. I looked forward to those bean meals, and I haven't forgotten them. I remember sitting alone at my place at the dining-room table lining up beans around the rim of my plate, while other folks bustled about in the nearby kitchen, where I was not allowed to eat. I suppose it was pretty lonely in that quiet and formal room, but the beans were comfortable companions.

Although beans are eaten fresh in the shell, without the shell and dried, this month I shall concentrate on the beans we picked and dried last summer. There are several quarts of blacks, kidneys, pintos, cranberries, soldiers and flageolets on the pantry shelf all needing a recipe.

New England Baked Beans

Baked beans in New England are like chili in Texas or fried chicken in Georgia. Practically every family has an ancestral recipe, and every ancestral recipe is thought to be the only decent version of the dish. I remember a PTA meeting in Brooklyn many years ago where the women almost came to blows over fried chicken. We were planning a fund-raising supper, and each member was asked to bring a fried chicken. "Ah, yes," came the response, "but what recipe?" As it turned out, each woman felt hers to be the only one possibly worthy of use. The meeting went on vehemently for too many hours. The outcome? I don't remember.

Whatever recipe you use for beans, remember that the flavors—sweet, pungent, salty and herbal—should be in balance. Taste-testing is the best way to elevate this. Baked beans are another dish suitable for fireplace cooking. They can be hung from a cooking crane for the first part of the preparation, then placed in a Dutch oven among coals and with more coals on the lid of the pot. Slow, low heat gives good results.

This recipe is not an heirloom, but my husband doesn't groan as he often does when I attempt something his mother used to make.

INGREDIENTS:

*1 pound dried beans (cranberry, Jacob's cattle, great northern or any
    medium-sized bean), soaked overnight in cold water*
1/4 pound smoked end bacon with rind
2 large onions, chopped
2 cloves garlic, chopped
2 tablespoons molasses
3 tablespoons prepared mustard
2 tablespoons chopped fresh gingerroot
Bay leaf, thyme and winter savory to taste
Salt

PROCEDURE:

1. Drain the soaked beans. Place them in a saucepan and cover with about 2 quarts of fresh water. Add the salt. Bring it to a boil. Then simmer until the beans are almost, but not quite, tender enough to eat.
2. Slice the bacon into 1/2-inch cubes. Place it in a frying pan and sauté it until some fat has been rendered. Add the onions and garlic and sauté until they are softened but not browned.
3. Drain the beans, saving the cooking liquid. Put the beans, bacon, onions, garlic and all other ingredients into a bean pot, casserole or kettle with a lid. Mix everything together. Add enough of the cooking liquid to just cover the beans. Taste and adjust the flavors if necessary. Cover with a lid.
4. Place in a 325° oven, in a fireplace or even in a pit in the ground that has been prepared with a roaring fire gone to coals. Cook for about 2 hours or until the beans are soft but not mushy. Check the liquid level occasionally and if it gets too low, add more cooking liquid.
5. Beans can be made well ahead and reheated when needed. They are one of those better-the-next-day sort of dishes. If they seem too bland after all this preparation, add a little vinegar or even catsup to give them extra tartness. If they seem too tart, add more molasses.

Colorful Mixed Bean Salad

This Indian bean dish is a useful year-round recipe. It may incorporate whatever beans are available at the time, fresh shelled, dried or both. With a blend of colors, it can make a splendid presentation. The beans I've chosen here are arbitrary. They may be any group that are roughly the same size and offer a nice contrast in colors.

Remember that none of these recipes is inelastic. They are really only jumping-off places for new food ideas and experiments.

INGREDIENTS:

> 1/2 cup dried kidney beans, soaked and drained
> 1/2 cup dried cranberry beans, soaked and drained
> 1/2 cup dried great northern beans, soaked and drained
> 1 cup dried flageolets, soaked and drained
> 1 cup string beans or wax beans, cut in 1-inch lengths (or whatever is available when you make the dish; 5 kinds makes for an attractive combination, but it could be 2 or 6)
> 1 piece gingerroot, minced
> 1 fresh hot chili, minced
> 4 to 5 tablespoons fresh cilantro or mint, chopped
> Thyme to taste
> Lemon verbena to taste
> 3 to 4 tablespoons fresh parsley, chopped
> 1/3 to 1/2 cup good olive oil
> 2 tablespoons white wine vinegar
> 1/2 teaspoon sea salt
> 1/4 teaspoon freshly ground pepper
> 1-1/2 tablespoons vegetable oil
> 1 teaspoon mustard seeds
> 1/4 teaspoon caraway seeds
> 1 fennel bulb, sliced very thin

PROCEDURE:

1. Simmer the dried beans in slightly salted water until they are just tender, 1 to 2 hours. Drain them and allow them to cool. If you are using beans of both dark and light colors, you may wish to cook them separately so their colors won't bleed into each other.
2. Simmer the fresh beans until they are cooked but still crisp and brightly colored. Drain them and allow them to cool.
3. While the beans are cooking, combine the gingerroot, chili, herbs, olive oil, vinegar, salt and pepper in a bowl.
4. Heat the vegetable oil and add mustard seeds and caraway seeds, and fry until the mustard seed sputters. Pour this into the other seasoning mixture and stir thoroughly.
5. Add the cooked beans and fennel and gently stir until the dressing is well mixed.

Fagioli of Tuscany

On a recent September vacation we visited an Italian family in Orvieto. As is the custom there, cannellini beans were served in some disguise at lunch and supper every day. They were wonderful. Not long after our return to New York, my friend Barbara Raives published a food book with Pino Luongo about his native Tuscany, which described the Tuscan love of the bean. His bean-cooking method is simple and delicious, and reminiscent of those wonderful beans of Orvieto.

INGREDIENTS:
> *Cannellini, chick-peas or lentils, soaked overnight*
> *Olive oil*
> *Salt*
> *Pepper*
> *Balsamic vinegar*
> *Scallions, parsley, fennel, celery, garlic (or whatever you want to mix in)*

PROCEDURE:
Cook the beans until tender. Drain them, and add the olive oil, salt and pepper. You may eat them warm, or add vinegar and green things and serve cold as a salad. Add as much or as little as you please. You can't ruin them.

Bean and Squash Stew with Polenta

This is the perfect protein triad together in one dish. Italian polenta and Mesoamerican spices make a happy cross-cultural marriage here.

INGREDIENTS FOR STEW:
> *1-1/2 cups dried beans, Jacob's cattle, pinto, kidney or any other large beans, soaked and drained*
> *Corn oil*
> *1 onion, chopped*
> *2 or 3 garlic cloves, chopped*
> *3 cups winter squash, cut into cubes*
> *Tomatoes, stewed or canned with juice*
> *1 to 2 dried chilies*
> *1 to 2 teaspoons cumin*
> *1 or 2 teaspoons oregano*
> *Dash of chili powder*
> *Cinnamon stick and cloves, tied in a cheesecloth bag*
> *Fresh parsley or cilantro*

PROCEDURE FOR STEW:
1. Cook the beans in salted water until they are tender but not mushy.
2. Heat the oil in a large skillet or wok. Add the onions and garlic. Sauté. Add the squash, herbs, spices and some stewed tomatoes. Simmer until

the squash is cooked through but not too soft. Add more tomato if the mixture gets too dry.

3. Combine the beans with the squash mixture and continue to cook until the squash and beans are of the right consistency. Continue adding tomatoes if the mixture is dry. It is better if a little, but not too, soupy.

4. When the stew is done, remove the bag of spices and dried chilies (or at least warn people about them). Serve over polenta with a sprinkling of fresh parsley or cilantro, if available.

INGREDIENTS FOR POLENTA:
Good stone-ground cornmeal
Water
Salt
Pepper

PROCEDURE FOR POLENTA:
1. Boil 3 to 4 cups of water. Reduce the heat a bit and add the cornmeal, sprinkling it a little at a time over the water and stirring constantly. Keep adding cornmeal until you have a fairly mushy consistency. You'll probably need 1 to 2 cups.

2. Keep stirring. Add the salt and pepper. Continue to stir until the cornmeal is soft to taste, and the consistency is fairly solid but not dry. You may want to add a little water if it gets too stiff. If it lumps, a wire whisk will clear up the problem easily.

Bean Pasties

INGREDIENTS:
2 cups dried beans
2 or 3 bay leaves
Salt
Olive oil
2 onions, chopped
2 or 3 stalks celery, chopped
2 or 3 carrots, chopped
    (Be sure that all the vegetables are chopped into pieces smaller than the beans you are using.)
Fresh garlic (optional), chopped
Fresh thyme to taste
Fresh parsley to taste
Pepper to taste
Grated or sliced cheese (cheddar, mozzarella, Brie)
8 to 10 baked 4-inch pastry shells (see Pastry Crust in the November chapter)

PROCEDURE:

1. Soak the dried beans overnight or for 5 to 6 hours, changing water occasionally. Fresh beans need no soaking.
2. Make the pastry dough and chill it in the refrigerator.
3. Drain the soaked beans. Cook them in salted water with bay leaves until they are soft but still hold their shape. The time necessary to do this depends upon how long the beans have been soaked and how large they are. Plan for 1 hour of cooking time. Younger beans cook much more quickly. Preheat the oven to 500˚.
4. Sauté the onions, celery, carrots and garlic in the olive oil, stirring to prevent burning. When the carrots are cooked but a bit crisp, add the beans (reserving some of the cooking liquid), chopped thyme, parsley, salt and pepper. Cook slowly, stirring and adding bean liquid a little at a time to thicken into a sauce.
5. While the bean mixture is slowly simmering roll out the dough, fill the tart pans and bake them at 500˚ until the shells begin to puff and brown. Heap the bean mixture into the baked shells. (If you remove the pastries from the tart pans, it is easier to serve them later.) Top with grated cheese. Place the pasties in the oven and heat until the cheese has melted. Serve hot.

MARCH

*It was the best place to be, thought Wilbur, this warm
delicious cellar, with the garrulous geese, the changing
seasons, the heat of the sun, the passage of swallows, the
nearness of rats, the sameness of sheep, the love of spiders,
the smell of manure, and the glory of everything.*

—E. B. White
Charlotte's Web

The Land

March, the month of lions and lambs, bluster and rain, also gives us
our first peephole view of spring. Winter snows melt and the ground
begins to thaw. Days are longer and the sun is higher. It is now that we
must step up the pace. Away with those cozy hours by the fire dreaming
of spring, for it is almost upon us and there is work to be done.

After the tentative pruning we did in February, I have now called in a fruit-tree expert to diagnose our small orchard of apples, pears, plums, cherries and peaches. He comes with fine business cards printed on bonded paper that present not only the usual name, address and phone number but also an espalier design, indicating his sophistication, I suppose, and his ability to prune anything into the tortured shapes of double cordons and palmette verrier. We are planning to train a row of these two-dimensional beauties to grow along the road, replacing a row of overgrown and nearly dead arbor vitae that were already old when we moved here.

Espalier is not merely beautiful but also practical, for its invention in Europe in the fourteenth century was as a space-saving scheme, as well as a means of growing less hardy trees in a cold climate. By creating a flattened-out tree, espalier maximizes use of a space, increases cubic-foot fruit production and, if placed against a wall that faces south, steps up growth and fruit ripening, for the wall retains heat absorbed during the day, keeping the fruits warmer during the night and hastening their maturity.

We espaliered two dwarf peach trees in a sheltered spot near our kitchen door five years ago, an amateur venture into this area of arboriculture. We unwittingly used peaches, a difficult species to espalier into the form we had chosen, for they put out long branches that grew rampantly. We trimmed and snipped reluctantly because we were afraid to cut too much, troubled about unnecessary mutilation and aware that nothing could be put back once gone. We fussed foolishly, but these little trees have survived our ignorance and even seem to have become inured to their altered state. They bear bushels of succulent peaches, seem immune to pest attack and provide a feast for the eyes of anyone who comes to the house.

The arborist, unimpressed by our endeavors, suggests that we also reshape the regular dwarf trees we have planted over the last fifteen years, the middle-aged standards planted before we arrived and three remaining ancient apples. These are the last remains of an orchard planted around the back of the house perhaps a hundred years ago.

Apple trees were not dwarfed here then, and these old standards probably were originally pruned to the shape of an open umbrella, a design that made picking from the upper limbs less difficult. As they age, the widening lateral branches become too heavy and unbalanced for the hollowing trunks, and at unexpected moments they crash to the earth with resounding vibrations.

A seasoned apple tree is a wonderful thing to behold, for it is quite unlike most other deciduous trees of this area. The trunks are rarely straight but rather twisted and gnarled, pushing this way and that in many directions. The trunks of ours are often hollow, providing houses for squirrels or chipmunks. In some the outer structure is only a shell, so thin that it seems a miracle it can sustain life. In a nearby field there are old apple trees lying on the ground, still producing blossoms and green leaves.

Apple branches circle, droop and push to the sky in a thousand ways, each tree finding its own pattern, making its own statement of individuality. They seem to be saying, "Here I am, a tree unique, not your basic pine, that looks like any other. I am an ancient apple, bent with the winds and the fruits I have provided for a hundred years. I may have little time left, but I will go down in thunder."

Another tree, and a dominant one in this verdant land, plays a role in March activities that symbolize both American history and New England to many people, especially as they eat their morning pancakes. It is the sugar maple, and March is mapling season in the woodlands of the east. The mapling process was taught to early European settlers by their Amerindian neighbors, and maple sap was once the only sweetener available in outlying colonial communities. It is still bound up in the nostalgia of log-cabin life.

Maple sap rises in its glory as the days warm and the nights continue their chill hold on winter. Coursing through trunk and branch to feed the buds that are forming hidden leaves, it spills its nectar from any opening. For about four weeks, usually from early March to early April, maplers collect this sap through hollow metal taps or spigots driven into holes that have been drilled into a tree trunk. On these taps hang the collecting buckets, which fill more rapidly than one might imagine and must be emptied each day. Sap looks and tastes like slightly sweetened water and must be boiled down to about one-fortieth of its original volume to produce the sticky amber liquid that flavors American lives and palates. I remember it as a favorite childhood treat. It came in a tin can that replicated a log cabin and hinted at a romantic and patriotic time. Paul Revere must have eaten maple syrup, and Betsy Ross too. It would be un-American not to love the sweet, nutty flavor. It is the soul of ethnocentricity, purely our own.

Processing maple sap these days follows a method as old and as simple as that of the pre-colonial Indians. One simply boils it, preferably in shallow trays for maximum evaporation, until it becomes sweet, thick, sticky and of ocher to sienna hue. Simple though this process is, it takes a long time and creates a great deal of sugary steam that can form crystals on a person's eyebrows and hair and, if done naively in the confines of one's kitchen, also on one's walls, furniture and whatever else is around. Serious sugarers build sugar sheds that are roofed but fairly open and away from the house. More modest operations are outdoor affairs. In both systems, flat pans of a design suited to efficient evaporation sit above roaring wood fires that keep the sap bubbling until the magic moment when it is ready. A taste will tell you, but a few minutes too long and you'll have a charred and smoky mass that has nothing to do with maple syrup.

The latter happened to us one year, the only year we have attempted sugaring on our own. We had borrowed a cooking tray and a homemade "furnace" concocted out of an old oil drum that had been turned on its side and cut out on the top so the evaporating pan could lie flat above the fire. It was also open at one end, so that we could stoke it with gathered branches and logs too old or resinous to make good indoor firewood. The whole contraption was balanced on two iron sawhorses.

We began our cooking-down operation in the driveway on a Friday afternoon, but we soon realized that syruping is not something you can easily stop to call it quits for the night. Pails keep filling with sap as fires turn forty gallons of sap into one gallon of finished syrup. We took turns stoking, gathering and attending, enjoying the freshness of the night, the adventure we had undertaken and the painless way we were clearing up wood knocked down in winter storms.

We had been taking turns watching that proverbial pot all night long, when in the gray of early morning it began to rain. We covered our pan with a heavy metal lid that had probably been provided for such occasions, ran for cover and returned not long after to find that thin liquid we had left was now a mass of blackened lumps. Of course the lid had kept in the heat, increasing the temperature of our sap to a point that less easy evaporation couldn't compensate for. A sad sight, and discouraging to our beginner's efforts, but we scrubbed and scraped the pan back to its original condition and forged on to complete about three gallons of true maple syrup, the essence of well over a hundred gallons of sap.

Our syrup turned out a rich tea color and had a muskier flavor than the usual syrup we buy at a local store. I'm told that sap from later in the season, which this was, is darker and more "mapley." It is often sold to be added to the sugarcane syrup that makes up commercial "maple-flavored" syrup, which is only about 3 percent real maple, yet still tastes somewhat like maple and is much less expensive than the real thing. This darker maple syrup is often labeled "B" or "C" on the can, as opposed to "A" or "Fancy" for a lighter amber-colored stuff. Such grading stems from the early days when maple sugarers were competing with southern cane-sugar growers for the sweetener market. The darker variety was considered less suitable as an anonymous adjunct to coffee or a general sweetening agent for cakes and pies, and was therefore inferior. Maple sugarers dreamed of producing a white, flavorless maple sugar that might be mistaken for the blander cane variety. Even today, buyers insist on "A" syrup because "A" must be better than "B," whereas in truth each is simply different. A mild "Fancy" or "A" grade might be preferred on pancakes or waffles. A little "B" or "C" can go a long way in adding a maple flavor to homemade ice cream or maple cake. I prefer the darker grades because they are stronger flavored and less sweet, perhaps because that is what we produced on our own as mapling novices one showery March night.

The Garden

In the north country, with its short growing season and erratic weather fluctuations, many annual plants require too long a time to mature before autumn frost—that is, unless they are started indoors in flats or pots, under grow lights or in greenhouses or cold frames. If one wants slow-ripening, frost-susceptible vegetables in one's garden, they must be either purchased as seedlings at a nursery in late spring or started from scratch by planting seed indoors six to ten weeks ahead of the last frost date, depending on the individual species, its rate of germination and initial growth. Buying someone else's handiwork is admittedly easier, but growing is cheaper and not as difficult as I may make it seem. It also provides the pleasure of seeing a small, hard, dead-looking orb burst forth through the earth to reach for the sun. If such is your inclination, now is the time to begin the potting and prodding of these pesky seeds into life.

Many of the vegetables that must be started indoors are those warm weather-loving staples of summer eating: melons, tomatoes, peppers and eggplants. Others, though less susceptible to frost, require so much time to mature that a head start inside is a great advantage. Still other plants may be started indoors later in the season as succession crops, to be transplanted outside in places vacated by early lettuces, peas, beets and Bok choi.

Although most of these species are readily available in nurseries and markets all around our area, I began several years ago to start my own. The reasons are simple. Commercial seedlings are limited in variety, have been less dependable than my own plants and are rarely available in mid-summer when I need seedlings for second crops. I do buy a number of commercial seedlings, usually annual flowers, because I have limited windowsill and grow-light space, but I prefer to raise food from seeds I trust.

I dream of a greenhouse full of sunshine and bobbing seedlings and exotic plants grown from seeds from other parts of the world. I faithfully collect them wherever I go: poinciana in Guatemala, mimosa in France, lotus in India, as well as many unnamed things that I can't resist smuggling away, but alas, they languish in envelopes and dresser drawers for want of a place to grow. For a plant lover there can never be enough sunny windows.

Celeriac and celery are the first seeds I pot up for a future in the garden. Slow to germinate and slow to mature (110 days after germination, say my catalogs, and that is a minimum time), each seed must ultimately be planted eight to ten inches from its nearest neighbor. The easiest way to do this is to plant two or three seeds about an eighth of an inch deep in a small pot and, when they have germinated, remove all but the strongest specimen. If you can't stand such wastefulness, you may sow the seeds in a flat about a half-inch apart, and when they have germinated and developed at least six branched leaves and a somewhat sturdy stem, carefully transplant them into individual pots. Because I plant relatively few seedlings—only twelve to twenty of each variety—I usually start them directly in pots, since each transplanting is a shock to a seedling's system. Celery and celeriac need a temperature of seventy to seventy-five degrees to sprout, but may be kept in a somewhat cooler climate after sprouting. They are constantly thirsty, so they must be watered often. They are delicate infants that grow into robust and delicious adults, that are well worth the bother.

This year two sorts of tomatoes, Italian plum and a large beefsteak called Nepal to indicate its adaptability to cool fall weather, will also be started in small individual pots. Multicolored varieties of peppers will go into small flats and be thinned to about three inches apart. I hope they will grow into fruits with hues of purple, yellow, red, brown and green.

The eggplants I sow are never available in the nurseries of our area. I discovered them in New York's Chinatown and found them again in my Maine seed catalog. Called Oriental Express, they are banana-sized and banana-shaped, fast-maturing and have a more delicate flavor than large eggplants. They can also be sliced into rounds, an attractive shape for a ratatouille or a salad.

Melons are difficult in our climate, but each year I try a variety purported to do well in northern areas. They often have such encouraging names as Alaska, Far North or Earligold. They ripen earlier and exhibit melonlike characteristics such as juiciness and succulence, but I have never tasted a northern-grown melon that had the clear sweetness and vivid essence of its southern cousin ripened on the vine in the heat of a Texas sun. The flavors of a Pecos cantaloupe or a Weatherford watermelon eaten ice cold with a sprinkling of salt are still distinct in my memory.

This year I am trying an orange-fleshed French Charentais melon, which is smaller than the usual cantaloupe, and which I hope will absorb an abundance of the sun's heat and be sweet. My second choice is called Nutmeg or Rocky Ford, said to grow well in Vermont and northern climates. Its flesh is light green. The two might look quite respectable together sliced in a salad if they ever grow.

Other seeds that I'll start indoors are peppers, annual herbs and those of the cabbage family: broccolis, Brussels sprouts, Chinese cabbage, flowering kale and red and savoy cabbages. Cabbages are hardy in cool weather and may be put outdoors early, but they must be planted so far apart that I find it easier to start them in pots and transfer them to the garden when they have developed a couple of "true" leaves.

True leaves are usually the second pair of leaves to appear on a sprouting stem. The seed leaves or cotyledons are smaller and of a different, sometimes simpler shape. In fact, all cabbage-family cotyledons look alike. True leaves are more or less typical of the plant's later leaves.

Most newborn seedlings are unimaginably delicate, flimsy wisps of life that need correct soil, regulated temperatures, a consistent amount of water, an oxygen supply at their roots and enough light to prevent them from becoming leggy and weak. These can be difficult requirements to fill. Our house is chilly when we aren't there and often when we are there, at least by the windows. Windowsills supply limited light and water evaporates either too quickly or not at all, rotting roots in the process. I've tried various schemes, short of buying a greenhouse, with greater or lesser success. My greatest accomplishment has been Kate, a lovely young woman who takes seeds that my windowsills can't accommodate, tends them with spiritual calm and returns at the end of May with thriving samples of the horticulturalist's art.

The following are some simple planting techniques that have often brought me success despite adverse circumstances. Most of these I learned as a volunteer potter in the Brooklyn Botanic Garden many years ago.

Our first consideration in the greenhouse there was the soil we used. We made our own potting mix, gathering it from large wooden vats under the potting table. It consisted of one-third peat moss, one-third sand and one-third finely sifted, clean garden soil. Of course the soil had been sterilized, a task I never remember to do in the fall in Connecticut; and in March the earth and the compost pile are too hard-frozen to consider. Today I buy potting soil in plastic bags and hope to remember to save some good soil and sterilize it next year.

I have recently read that a Canadian researcher has been successful using two parts sawdust, one part garden soil plus 1 percent organic fertilizer (fish emulsion, manure or liquid seaweed) for potting, but again, one must use sterile soil. The trouble with packaged potting soils and packaged fertilizers is that there are no state or federal standards regulating what is actually in them. One buys, so to speak, a "pig in a poke." The Farm Resource Center in Putnam, Connecticut, recently conducted a study that found contaminants such as heavy metals in some commercial bagged soils, a discouraging bit of news that just might spur me on to save some sterile soil in the fall.

Although one doesn't sterilize the earth of the garden—nor should one even think of it—apparently the indoor seedling is prone to damping-off, a condition in which fungi may attack, weaken and even kill young seeds before or soon after they germinate. Sterile potting soil is the advertised preventative for such a potential problem because it should contain no fungi. It will also contain no weed seeds, those rugged fellows that can be confused with the seeds one has planted, and is the right consistency for a fragile seedling to be born into. Plants will therefore receive the correct amount of oxygen and will not have to struggle to break through a compacted earth.

Once proper soil is at hand, calculations must be made as to when to start a seedling and when to plant it outside. Often seeds are started too early and outgrow their pots before they can be transplanted into their permanent homes. Six weeks is usually long enough for most vegetables to live indoors, celery and celeriac and their long germination rates notwithstanding. The cabbages can be planted toward the end of March and transplanted about the middle of May. Frost-sensitive plants—the tomatoes, peppers, eggplants and melons—will be put out on Memorial

Day weekend, the customary planting day in Connecticut. That means they should be started indoors during the second week of April. Whatever the vegetable variety, it is helpful to check the seed package for maturity times and plant accordingly.

Sowing can be done initially in almost anything that has good drainage. Flats, small plastic pots, clay pots, peat pots, old milk cartons cut off four inches above the bottom and punctured for drainage, cleverly folded newspapers, even paper cups with holes in the bottom are all useful. Please don't use Styrofoam: it's destroying the ozone layer. I dislike plastic in most of its forms, but I often use hard plastic pots because they retain moisture longer than the others, they are reusable and I have inadvertently collected them by buying small plants over the years. Whatever the container, it should be at least three inches deep and have adequate drainage. Seedlings can actually drown if earth is so saturated with water that no oxygen can find its way in.

Water must not only drain out but also find its way in through the drainage hole. Never pour water directly on a newly planted seed or a tender seedling. You can dislodge a seed or crush a seedling with the strong flow.

With containers and soil at the ready, seed planting can begin. Fill each container to within about a half-inch from the top, then put in seeds and lightly sprinkle earth over them. Press the whole thing down ever so gently, and that's all. Seed packages often give the reader instructions on the depth the seed should be planted. A general rule is to plant two times the diameter of the seed. Since many seeds are very, very small, this seems like almost nothing at all. It is. In fact, some seeds do better if simply scattered on the surface of the the the soil. That's what happens in the wild. Just remember that "less is more" when seed depth is concerned.

Planting seedlings bring my roasting pans, cookie sheets, trays and serving platters into play. I pack the planted pots onto them and pour about an inch of water into the pan. Through that wonderful resource of osmosis, the water works its way up to the resting seed without disturbing its placement. I continue to water until the earth at the top feels faintly damp—never saturated. Then, if we are leaving the country for the next few days, I cover the whole pan and pots with a "sticky" plastic wrap, thus creating a minigreenhouse and ensuring that seeds will never dry out. This solution is no panacea. The whole lot can stay too wet and rot the seedlings. The plastic wrap can slip off, as happened this year to the celery, and all will dry out. The best way is to be around. There is no set rule to watering any plant. It depends on room temperatures, the amount of sun, soil conditions and, of course, the type of plant. You just have to look and feel and figure.

Until a seed germinates, it is happier in a relatively warm place, and darkness is fine. I've tried putting seedling trays covered with plastic on top of the furnace in our cellar. This works well if the seedlings are rescued the moment they germinate; otherwise they will become leggy, white ghosts searching for a ray of light. After germination, the brightest window or a grow light placed a few inches above the plants is an urgent need. Only mushrooms do well in darkness. Spindly, weak tomatoes and melons can't be redeemed later on, so give them as much light as possible.

Assuming that all has gone as it should and the seedlings are large enough to be transplanted, the final step in this process is wrenching a young delicate plant from its stable environment; shaking it to its roots; placing it in a new locus with different temperatures, brutal winds, melting sun and drenching rain; and expecting it to flourish. Usually it does, but a few obliging procedures may ensure success. If you have a flat of six or twelve seedlings, chances are their roots have become fairly well interwoven with each other. Although it is tempting to pull them apart, a healthier method is to amputate. Water the flat well, and then take a sharp knife and cut between each seedling, just as if you were cutting servings of cornbread. It may seem ruthless, but it is better to cut through some roots than to jerk them around, which may separate them from the soil and expose them to dry air, giving them quite a jolt. Pots are easier to deal with than flats, for if you're lucky, you won't have to handle the plant directly. Make sure the plant is nicely damp, dig your hole in the ground, tap the pot lightly and the earth and seedling should fall into your waiting hand in one lump. Try to place your hand so that you don't crush the plant as it arrives. Then gently put it in the ground, press it into place and water. Now it's ready to meet the world and its hazards: a rabbit waiting to ingest those succulent young petals; a gopher coming from beneath to pull it into the earth; a cutworm—the logger of the lepidoptera world—sawing through the stems of young plants. Aphids suck plant blood. Slugs make lace of leaves. Flea beetles perforate them. Birds peck them. And yet most of our plants survive these many perils, not the least being our own handling, and give back to us the gift of life.

The Kitchen

After a slow winter, actually having to buy eggs when our whole extended family was visiting in December, the hens, anticipating spring, have begun to lay again. Six or seven eggs arrive each day, and without our children here we are hard-pressed to use their daily presentations.

Even our geese have begun to lay. They are about nine months old now, massive, white Embdens bought last June when they were day-old, straight-run hatchlings, "straight-run" meaning that you don't know whether you're getting males or females. I found the first large white egg a week ago. In fact, by catching sight of a female nesting, I have realized that the larger two geese I assumed were males are indeed the females, and the smaller, whiter "female" is their consort, the gander. He is just beginning to exhibit his avian machismo by hissing at whoever comes near, chicken or human. If geese are similar to their chicken relatives, it is probably just as well that this trio is polygynous. Male rivalry isn't something we need in the barnyard.

The females, however, seem to be content in their harem role, nesting and laying bigger and bigger specimens. I've found several thick-shelled white, eggs, each grander than its predecessor. There may have been more, for the geese lay in odd and assorted places both in and out of the barn. The last example was certainly large enough to accommodate a baby brontosaurus. It weighed in at just over eight ounces, six ounces more than the average large chicken egg, certainly a tasty feast for a roving raccoon or a skulking skunk.

Since the scientific world's discovery of cholesterol, we eat fewer eggs, but with our own discovery of the difference a really fresh egg from a well-fed hen can make, we are loath to give up the pleasure of it altogether. Also, we enjoy the squawking mass of feathers we allow to wander around our yard to feed on earth worms, grass and weeds, except in spring when they nip emerging plants in the bud. We hope they prefer weeds to flowers. Fortunately our vegetable garden is fenced and so far from their territory that they have never ventured there. But an occasional toad and any insect they can get their beaks around frequently become victims of their insatiable appetites.

These natural foods, combined with the unadulterated grain we buy for them, produce eggs that both look and taste unlike their grocery store counterparts. Their flavor is fresh and light. Their yolks sit high and sprightly, almost an orb when you break them into a bowl. The whites can be beaten into soufflés of boundless rising capacity which I discovered, to my embarrassment, when I baked a soufflé in a small convection oven and found it glued to the top when I arrived to retrieve it.

Eggs seem so simple and basic—the largest cell, as we learned in high school—but as a cook I find them an endless mystery. The diet of the hen, the age of the egg and its temperature are all variables that can make or break an egg-based recipe. The power of the egg to emulsify, expand, congeal, bind, thicken, coat and clarify creates endless possibilities in the kitchen. It can also be responsible for potential disasters; the hollandaise sauce that separates, the custard that doesn't thicken, the souffle that doesn't rise, the leaden cake, the saboyan that overheats and suddenly turns into a thick golden glue or the fried egg that comes out like a piece of leather. As M.F.K. Fisher has told us, even a boiling an egg is fraught with dangers. It may be watery, hard, nearly indigestible, sulfuric or green-yolked, and if it is too fresh it will not peel properly, if at all. Despite these problems, cooking would not be the same without the egg, and some of our most luscious dishes would be lost to us.

Whether boiling an egg for breakfast or creating a soufflé for a serious dinner party, one's results are dependent on the original condition of the egg itself. A New York cab driver who had an uncle with an egg farm in New Jersey once told me that the average age of a grocery-store egg is about six weeks. Since then, I've been even more certain that my preference for my own—or rather my hens' own—product is not imagined. The freshness of the egg and the hen's diet and general health affect the flavor and adaptability of the egg in any dish.

Once you've started with a fresh, healthy egg, it would be nice to think that nothing can go wrong. Wrong. But here are a few hints that may prevent future disasters, or at least minimize them.

For most uses, eggs at room temperature work better than ice-cold ones.

Fresh eggs are the very best when fried or scrambled, but an egg less than two days old will never peel properly when hard-boiled. The thin skin between the shell and the egg won't separate and peeling becomes a fight that usually ends with gouges and splits all through the egg white. If an egg is store-bought this will never be a problem.

Patience is a virtue when cooking custards and sauces that are largely yolk. They need constant stirring and a low, steady heat, preferably over a double boiler. Surges of heat, such as when you turn up the burner in frustration that nothing is thickening, may result in the aforementioned glue.

The longer you cook an egg, the harder it is to digest. We probably tend to overcook eggs because many of them aren't so good to begin with, and the cooking actually removes flavor that can be harsh. A fresh, well-nourished egg is delicious practically raw. (Commercial eggs, however, are produced under conditions that, at times, have led to the development of salmonella bacteria. These bacteria, which can only be killed by thoroughly heating the egg, can cause sickness. If there has been news of salmonella bacteria in the commercial egg stock, it is not a good idea to eat raw or undercooked commercial eggs.)

Here are some examples of eggs thickening, expanding and emulsifying to create a variety of dishes.

Floating Island (Oeufs à la Neige)

This is a dessert I remember from my childhood. It is especially good after a hearty dinner, and it is best when made from eggs freshly gathered from under a generous hen and never, ever refrigerated.

INGREDIENTS:

8 eggs, separated
2/3 cup sugar
2 cups scalded milk
Pinch of salt
Flavoring (one of the following): vanilla extract, coffee liqueur, melted semisweet chocolate, Amaretto, rum or something of your own choosing (a few teaspoons to a few tablespoons will do, depending on the strength of the flavoring)
4 tablespoons sugar

PROCEDURE:

1. Beat the egg yolks and 2/3 cup of sugar until a ribbon forms on the surface of the mixture when you lift up the beater. Slowly add the scalded milk while continuing to beat. Transfer it to a heavy saucepan or double boiler and cook slowly, still stirring the mixture constantly, preferably with a wooden spoon. When the bubbles disappear the mixture is about to thicken. It is finished when it coats your spoon. If the custard should curdle, take it off the heat, let it cool a bit and then vigorously beat in a raw yolk. This should bind it all back together again

2. Add a pinch of salt and whatever flavoring you wish. The mixture will be dense but still runny. When it is done, allow it to cool, strain if necessary and set aside in a serving bowl large enough to hold the meringue on top.

3. Set the water to boil in a large skillet or pan.

4. Beat the egg whites until they are stiff and glossy, adding 4 tablespoons of sugar a little at a time as you beat. Add a bit of flavoring to the finished meringue and beat that in.

5. Turn the water down. Shape gobs the of meringue into large balls and poach them in simmering water. Turn them so they will be cooked on both sides. Each side will take 2 or 3 minutes, depending on the size of the balls. Drain them on a clean towel and pile on the waiting custard. Serve cold.

Angel Food Cake

Angel food cake was always birthday cake in our home. I imagine it was the same in my mother's home too, for traditions died hard with her, especially food traditions. Mother always made the cake by hand, using a wire whisk to beat the egg whites to the exact stage of "stiff but not dry" that was necessary for a cake that would rise perfectly and melt in your mouth.

Angel food cake doesn't seem to be fashionable these days, for I rarely see it in bakeries, restaurants or recipe books. But I understand why. Most examples I have had outside my home are pale and tough imitations of the cake that stands out so favorably in my memory. Angel food cake should not have the flavor of library paste and the texture of a used sponge. It should be light, airy, delicate and delectable—angel's food.

I learned to make this recipe at my mother's side, one of the few things she actually taught me how to cook. She was a very exacting cook in all things, but this cake symbolized her carefulness in each aspect of her art. She owned an electric mixer, but for angel food only the whisk, which beat in more air and made a lighter meringue, would do. Cake flour and sugar had to be sifted nine times, never less. The folding had to be precise. Dry ingredients had to be sifted over the egg mass in very small amounts and then folded in with a quick, circular motion. A special high-sided pan, used for nothing else, was filled, put in a *steady* oven and, when removed, turned upside down on the pan's "feet." Her cakes were always perfect. I cannot say the same for my own, but at least some of them have been quite wonderful. It's all in the motion.

INGREDIENTS:

1-1/2 cups egg whites (11 to 13 eggs), room temperature
1 teaspoon cream of tartar
1/2 teaspoon salt

1-3/4 cups sugar (superfine if possible)
1-1/4 cups cake flour
1/2 teaspoon ground mace or 1 teaspoon vanilla
1/2 teaspoon almond extract

PROCEDURE:

1. Preheat the oven to 325°.
2. Sift the sugar, mace and flour together 9 times. (Do not shirk!)
3. Separate the eggs. Make sure no yolk gets into the whites, or they will not become stiff when beaten. If a yolk breaks in the process, and a bit combines with the white, use an eggshell to fish it out. Yolk will magically adhere to eggshell, whereas it will prove elusive to a fork or spoon.
4. Beat the egg whites until frothy. I use a copper bowl and a large wire whisk. When the whites are frothy, add the cream of tartar (not necessary if the bowl is copper) and continue to beat until the mixture is stiff but not dry. It will have a glossy surface and will stand up straight on the whisk when lifted out of the bowl.
5. Add the almond extract and fold it into the mixture.
6. Sift the dry ingredients, a small amount at a time, over the top of the egg whites. Fold them in as quickly as possible, using a circular motion, cutting into the middle of the mixture and turning the bowl as you work.
7. Put the finished mixture into a high-sided tube pan, making sure there are no large air holes. Do *not* grease the pan. The cake's rising depends in part upon its adhering to the pan sides.
8. Bake at 325° for 1 hour. Test with a toothpick for doneness; if it comes out of the cake clean, the cake is done.
9. Allow the cake to cool in the pan. If you have an angel food cake pan with legs, turn it upside down to cool.
10. Serve the cake with a custard sauce, fruit sauce or icing. The custard of the Floating Islands recipe is good with angel food cake and uses up a lot of those leftover egg yolks. A fresh raspberry sauce is superb—just raspberries mashed with a bit of sugar and a dash of some liqueur like Amaretto or Grand Marnier. Hot fudge sauce also works well. A butter-cream icing can be spread on and decorated to make a high and handsome birthday cake. I have used pale green icing and garnished it with candy shamrocks for our daughter born on St. Patrick's Day. We have had shredded coconut nests of jelly-bean Easter eggs for our sometime Easter child. The rosettes, curlicues and jolly messages created with our cake-decorating set have been no match for the professional's artistry, but the secret hours of family preparation for a birthday child's moment in the sun have compensated grandly for the less-than-perfect rose.

Mayonnaise

After you have used twelve egg whites, what do you do with the yolks? You can put them in the compost or down the drain, for they are the cholesterol-carriers of the egg. Or you might want to make sauce or custard that requires fresh, tasty yolks. You might even put them in the freezer, a few to each package, for future use. Don't feed them to the chickens I'm told by my neighbor's daughter, for it will turn them into cannibals. They will love their own handiwork so much that they will break their own newly laid eggs to have another helping. I've never tested this theory.

Béarnaise, mayonnaise and hollandaise are three sauces of egg yolk derivation. Mayonnaise is perhaps less often made at home since the commercial product is ubiquitous and cheap, yet homemade mayonnaise is so different that there's little need to compare the two products.

Whatever the recipe, the basic process in making mayonnaise is the absorption of oil by particles of yolk. I've made mayonnaise with a blender, a wire whisk and a fork, all with good results. The only potential problem is adding too much oil for the egg to handle which causes the whole mass to separate. The answer is to start over with a new yolk, re-adding the oily mixture. It works every time.

The advantage of the homemade product is the superiority of the ingredients and the choices of additions that can turn a common mayonnaise into an elegant sauce. The basic recipe is simple.

INGREDIENTS:

> *3 egg yolks, room temperature*
> *2 cups good quality olive oil or corn oil*
> *Dry or Dijon mustard to taste*
> *Pinch of salt*
> *2 tablespoons lemon juice or white wine vinegar*

PROCEDURE:

1. Place the egg yolks in a bowl and beat thoroughly.
2. Add the salt. Add the oil a few drops at a time while you continue to beat vigorously. A wire whisk is an excellent tool for this and is easier to clean than a blender or food processor. However, a food processor does the job in seconds.
3. When the oil has been added and the mixture is smooth and thick, pour in the lemon juice or wine vinegar and mix thoroughly.

Once the basic recipe is made, all sorts of flavorful additions are possible:

- *A few tablespoons fresh tarragon*
- *2 or 3 cloves of crushed garlic to make an aioli*
- *1 to 2 spoons of curry*
- *Chopped capers*
- *Freshly grated horseradish*
- *1 handful of chopped sorrel*

Chocolate Soufflé

Soufflés are a family favorite around the Rubin house, and contrary to common opinion, are no more difficult to make than most anything else. Like so much else in life, the secret to a good soufflé is relationship, in this case the relationship between the yolk base and the beaten egg whites.

The custard base must be the solid citizen, containing the specific flavor of the soufflé, be it cheese or chocolate. The meringue must be the visionary, capable of taking the custard and soaring with it to heights of lightness and elegance. If the custard is too thick and heavy, it will hold the meringue back and not allow it to rise. If it is too thin or watery, it will not bind with the meringue and will end up a gluey mess at the bottom of the soufflé dish. If the meringue is not beaten until it is stiff and sturdy, it won't be able to lift the custard as it is meant to. But if the relationship is fitting, greatness can be achieved. It is a beautiful interdependence and when nearly perfect can make a dish fit for all.

Soufflés may be either sweet or savory. Bases may be made with egg yolks, milk or cream, flour and any number of additions such as ham, fish, cheese or Grand Marnier. A recipe traditionally calls for one more egg white than yolk and often a thickener to semisolidify the base. A French chef once told me that the eggs of a soufflé should never be too fresh, but on querying him I found he meant two or three days old—never less— but probably not more either.

This chocolate soufflé replaced angel food cake in the hearts of our teenage children. I served it topped with whipped cream and sometimes chocolate sauce as well, and the children nevertheless survived to adulthood.

INGREDIENTS:
> 4 egg yolks
> 1/3 cup sugar
> Pinch of salt
> 5 squares semisweet chocolate
> 2 to 3 tablespoons rum, Amaretto or another liqueur
> 2 tablespoons heavy cream
> 5 egg whites

PROCEDURE:

1. Preheat the oven to 375˚. Line a soufflé dish with butter. Coat the butter with a little sugar. Set aside.

2. Beat the egg yolks and sugar until the mixture forms a ribbon when lifted from the bowl.

3. Melt the chocolate and liqueur. Be careful not to burn it. Add the heavy cream. Stir.

4. Combine the chocolate mixture with the egg yolk mixture. It should be thick enough to hold some shape when a bit is held on a spoon. (Chocolate itself is heavy and dense, so it doesn't need an added thickening agent like flour or cornstarch.)

5. Beat the egg whites until they are very stiff and glossy. A good test is to lift the beater and turn it upside down. If the meringue on the beater stands straight up, it is ready.

6. Fold the meringue mixture into the custard mixture with a circular motion, moving from the center of the bowl to the outside. Turn the bowl as you work. Do this quickly and stop as soon as the two mixtures seem thoroughly blended. This is a step that must not be overdone.

7. Turn the mixture into a soufflé dish and bake it for 25 to 30 minutes. The most delicious soufflés have form on the outside and are runny in the middle. Serve immediately.

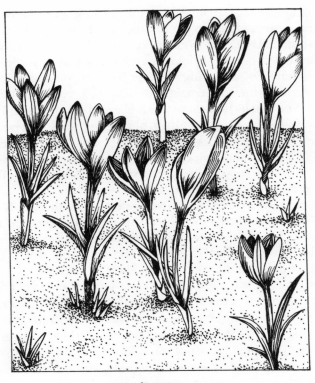

APRIL

Cold in the earth—and fifteen wild Decembers
From those brown hills have melted into spring.

—Emily Brontë
"Remembrance"

The Land

April came in this year on the tail of a thunder and lightning storm. The weather prediction for April 1 was for snow, but it must have been an April Fools' joke. April always fools us here in our corner of New England. The calendar tells us it is spring, but too often the winds blow, snow falls and rain pours. Some years it is only toward the end of the month that we see much of the world's annual rebirth without getting down on our knees and peering carefully at the earth for signs of life.

Grumbling and eager to take those discovering walks in the woods to sight the first robin, to unearth the first asparagus, to sow the earliest pea seeds and to smell the first flowers, I exclaim to friends, "This is the latest spring I can remember." They agree, and we talk for a while about the freezing temperatures, changing weather patterns, prospects for drought and whatever else the future might hold. I look back through my old journals and find that in 1982 there was a blizzard on April 5. In 1983, eight inches of snow fell on April 16 and 19, heavy, wet snow that pulled down trees, melted quickly and flooded rivers and ponds. Three inches of snow fell on April 23, 1986, and an inch or two on April 28, 1987. Snow in April … well, these are the New England hills: snow and snowdrops, floods and forsythia, all in a close continuum.

This doesn't mean, of course, that spring is not alive, only that it's a little sluggish. The birds tell us spring is near. A rose-breasted grosbeak, our usual pair of cardinals, a herd of gold and purple finches, chickadees, juncos and a hundred other birds at our feeders or pecking at the snow-flecked or sodden ground are singing their springtime melodies. The willows are wafting chartreuse branches across the yard. The maples present an ephemeral vermilion haze against the sky. The furry buds of the pussy willows quickly change to delicate flowers, and, as the days of April progress, skunk cabbage pushes up its fat, ridged leaves in every marshy place. The three leaves of the trillium and the soft curves of the bloodroot can be found all over the woods, and violets are sprouting everywhere. We must have a corner on the world's wild violet population.

On the domestic scene, snowdrops and crocuses color the yard, and sorrel, sage, thyme, mint and chervil make tentative motions upward. The dark green leaves of rhubarb unfold from their round crimson wraps with pleats on their giant surfaces, produced by the careful packaging inside their rosy cocoons. Toward month's end we find our first asparagus, a single, pale stalk pushing its way through the earth. Everywhere seemingly dormant life shows little touches of revival, from a slowly swelling bud or emergent bulb to a transparent capsule enclosing a black speck that will become a tadpole and then a frog.

It's around the pond that spring activity seems most stepped up nowadays, and observing life in the water is a mild endeavor geared to a sunny, bug-free April afternoon. My quiet and watchful groundside demeanor appears lethargic in contrast with the fearsome energy exhibited underwater.

The pond is full of salamanders now. There are hundreds, possibly thousands. They lie in a dead man's float, or twine themselves around each other in interesting sexual positions, and scurry away if they detect danger in a movement in or above their territory.

More new pond life is represented by the frog's eggs laid in clusters of jellied balls around the underwater stems of reeds and cattails. They sparkle in the filtered light, carrying their microcosms of life. If one can venture close enough to see the tiny black specks in the center of each transparent egg, one sees change from week to week. First mere grains, they soon are swimming about in their transparent cells, whipping minute tails behind them like impatient children eager to get out into the world. Judging from the numbers of eggs we see and the numbers of frogs we have about, their survival rate is not great. But that is the frog's evolutionary gambit—sire many and hope for a few to carry on.

Peepers and bullfrogs, more often heard than seen, join in a chorus repeating the same musical score each year. Whirligigs entertain us as they chase each other in circles. Water striders arrogantly exhibit their miraculous ability to walk on water. Fat, year-old pollywogs prepare for their final metamorphosis. Birds swoop and sing and all is mellow with the world, at least for these moments.

A less mellow spring activity, at least for us, is a human one, sanctioned by law and anticipated by folks from all over the countryside. Fishing season begins the third Saturday in the month, which means, to us, poaching season. Our lovely stream attracts anglers from across the road and across the state. They leave their lunch bags, cigarette packages and beer cans behind as reminders that no one's home is necessarily one's castle, and no one's property is immune to invasion if it offers amusement and free fish.

We've put up unfriendly "No Trespassing" signs, which we then must avoid looking at, for they spoil the uncontaminated beauty of the woods and water. We've asked our neighbors to call and inquire if they might use the stream. Some of them do, and we almost always say yes. We wonder whether this small paradise, which we legally own, can really be the possession of one person or family, or if it is only a gift from nature. Are we just its protectors? And if so, how far must protectors go? Must we build a great wall?

Walls—those odd inventions—give us clues about the earliest notions of ownership. They came late in the scheme of things, originating, as far as we know, between nine and ten thousand years ago to protect the accumulating possessions of the first sedentary communities in the Near

East. The oldest examples of this innovation have been found there, but the notion quickly spread or was reinvented all over the world. What began as deterrents to potential robbers of modest crop stores became obstacles to the invaders of mighty nation states. Yet even with Shih Huang Ti's masterpiece, the Chinese could not keep out the Mongols. Perhaps his Great Wall, so high and impregnable, only tantalized the foe to ever-increasing ingenuity. "If they are protecting that land to the south, it must be fine, worth owning, better than ours. Let's have at it."

Walls attempt to keep things out, keep things in, hide things and secure things. Wall technologies are always changing: stronger, higher, tighter, more clever. Walls of stone have been replaced by walls of electrical shock. New methods of encroachment require more substantial means of deterrence.

New England's first significant walls were built by the English for containing animals and defining boundaries. Their Amerindian antecedents had no use for either. They domesticated no animals and had a different notion of boundaries and landownership. To them land was like air and ocean, not a commodity, but a spirit of life, free for all to use if they used it well.

To our colonial ancestors, land was definitely owned, and one way of demonstrating that was to wall it off. The most available wall material was just what was being cleared from the forest floor to make fields for hay and grain. It was that ubiquitous glacial stone, gray and cumbersome, scattered over the land to impede the plow and deter the roots of plants. What better dual task than that of gathering up this granite detritus and transforming it into boundaries, walls and building foundations? Our small patch of land alone bears testimony to many hundreds of hours spent lifting and piling thousands of stones in long rows, defining a lane, a house, a barn or a shed that no longer exists, meandering through a woodland that was once a pasture or a field of corn.

New England may be one of the few places left in the world that is not currently being deforested and that has, in fact, for the last hundred years been returning to woodland. There is little or no primeval forest here. It is almost all secondary growth, replacing the vast, dense timberlands of chestnut, elm, oak and maple that were stripped bare in the eighteenth century by settlers moving inland in an early thrust of expansion activity who had to cut trees continually just to get an ox and wagon through. In a hundred years this rocky land was naked. Its fertility had deteriorated from erosion and overuse, and the West was opening up, to be the newest sacrifice to the axe and the plow. Families who had been fighting the granite boulders of the East heard of western territories with six feet of topsoil and land that was free if you homesteaded it, and they left for Kansas, Iowa, Nebraska, Oregon and California.

Cornwall's population, which had doubled between 1790 and 1860, began to decline, and by 1900 it was back to its 1790 level. Many farms reverted to forest and a new cycle began. Today it is difficult to imagine these green hills of pine, ash, oak, hickory and sugar maple in any other way, but the walls tell the story. There is an old house foundation in our woods, its center chimney tumbled into a mass of debris, with a hefty maple growing from its living room floor. The access road to this farm is speckled with mature trees, but the ruts of the path can be detected at one place or another, and the wall beside the path still remains, confirming that "good fences make good neighbors."

These walls and foundations were built in a manner called drywall construction. No mortar was used, but the stones were aligned so that they balanced, one on top of another—a three-dimensional jigsaw puzzle—until a reasonable height was achieved. Today a young man in our community has found a successful profession as an expert in the building or rebuilding of these historical structures, but in the eighteenth century every family was a farming family, and every farmer built stone walls.

As one looks about the countryside, it is apparent that every farmer did not have the same interest in achieving a wall as intricately balanced and well fit together as Machu Picchu. Some walls are hardly more than jumbled piles of easily toppled stones, sometimes referred to as rubble walls, their stones primarily those rounded into the smooth boulders softened by time, water and wind. Others are coherent structures built of flatter, rougher, more angular stones, fitted together precisely and weighted toward the center, with the heaviest and largest stones saved for the top off the formation. A friend who lives nearby has a wall so wide, flat and sturdy that it is said the builder drove his team of horses and wagon along its top in yearly exhibits celebrating his craft—and probably his driving skill.

Our own walls are woefully inferior, high here, low there, down altogether in another place with rusted lines of barbed wire topping the original boundary markers, reminding us that parts of our woods were used as pastures until only a few years ago, and that the stone walls were as poor at keeping cattle in as they are now for keeping poachers out.

The Garden

Despite the lack of cooperation from the weather, we have found a number of days this month in which to begin real gardening activity. Even in wind and thirty-degree temperatures, there is a sense of excitement, anticipation and pleasure in those first moments of actually digging in the earth. The leaves that eluded us last fall are raked and added to the stack that will be used as mulch. Garden soil is prepared. Early vegetables are planted, and the compost pile is renovated by turning, aerating and adding manure and a mysterious organic mixture of hibernating microorganisms that will munch and break down our winter debris with great speed.

Compost is the backbone of our garden. It is a magical mixture of leaves, weeds, bones, seafood exoskeletons, moldy or overgrown vegetables, potato peelings, orange rinds, eggshells, tea leaves, coffee grounds, carrot tops, stale bread, prunings, thinnings, spent plants, bolted lettuce heads and even chicken feathers. All are merged to become a primal essence, decomposing into a smaller, denser mass that contains enough minerals and microorganisms to nurture a plant through a healthy and hardy life.

As I have watched my neighbors carefully tie their fallen leaves into large plastic bags, cart them off to our overfilled dump (which has now been closed, perhaps forcing the issue) and then, some time later, go off to the shopping mall to spend a lot of money on fertilizer, I have used compost with a missionary zeal. I've been trying to convert people to it for over twenty years.

Almost that long ago, I kept a discreet little pile of orange peelings and browned lettuce leaves in the backyard in Brooklyn, nothing dubious like lamb chop bones or pizza crusts, just plain, unvarnished vegetable matter. But a neighbor became quite undone about it. She would wait at her window, and if she saw anyone come into the yard with anything in hand, she would berate them soundly. She was certain we—and she—would be overrun with rats. We weren't, but she continued to threaten so we gave up. Now I occasionally haul a batch of fish bones or potato peels that are too succulent to waste to the country, much to my husband's amusement. In Cornwall there is no one close by to complain.

Composting has been a part of farming for so long that I wonder if the alchemists of yore conceived the notion of changing iron or stone into gold from observing the metamorphosis of kitchen and garden waste into rich and succulent planting loam. If the alchemists had succeeded in their own quest, their product could never have been as basically useful, for the value of compost to the gardener is inestimable, and it is free.

Whether it is called compost or humus, it is the elemental medium with which organic gardeners pursue their occupation. It is used as both fertilizer and mulch. It has the nutrients all plants need to grow strong and the living organisms necessary to maintain living, healthy earth—the essence of organic matter.

Organic matter is the key to building a soil that will provide a healthy atmosphere for plants, no matter what the chemical fertilizer companies say. It is this decay that returns to the soil the nutrients that it gave up to living matter and that it needs to continue to produce life. Once composted, this mixture of manure, kitchen scraps, weeds and grass clippings becomes the feeding ground for fungi, beetles, earthworms, insect larvae and all sorts of microscopic life that busily eat and digest the debris and each other, until a large, disorganized pile becomes a chocolate-colored "mousse" to be consumed by the plants of the spring garden.

Our country compost pile consists of three chicken-wire bins situated next to the vegetable garden: one for recent acquisitions, one "cooking" and one of finished humus. Into these we throw all organic garden rejects and kitchen debris except for fats and treats for the chickens such as leftover pasta, which I believe they see as a plate of worms. This waste is layered with manure dispensed by the donkeys, which works as a catalyst to brew a steamy stew as microorganisms feast and develop, turning last week's garbage into brown gold. We water it in dry weather and turn it to increase its oxygen content, but compost will develop even if you don't do these things. It will simply transform more slowly, and weed seeds will not be eradicated by the heat of a rapidly cooking brew, but the compost will still reach an appropriate state of decomposition after a few months. It cannot be defeated.

The most monumental compost heap I've ever seen was at the summer camp one of our children went to in the Adirondacks. The camp had vast vegetable gardens that supplied the campers with fresh, organic food. With manure from horses, chickens, goats and geese; vegetable matter; and kitchen waste, the camp had constructed the "Great Pyramid" of composts, an elongated trapezoidal shape, that loomed and steamed and never smelled of anything except barnyard, which is where it was situated. The slightly outward-sloping sides and the trench down the middle of the top caught maximum rain, and the large quantity of manure kept things cooking. I don't know how they aerated it. The vegetable gardens—recipients of this munificence—were covered with a black, friable loam the likes of which I have never seen, and the vegetables responded by producing in abundance despite their geographical situation in the high northern mountains. Shades of Findhorn.

Our compost pile is certainly small potatoes compared to that, and it must be supplemented. We plant rye grass as a cover crop or green manure in the fall and turn it under now to begin decomposing. We bring over extra nitrogen-rich donkey manure in the wagon behind the tractor, spread it around and rototill it into the ground along with wood ashes to provide potassium, phosphorus in the form of bonemeal and lime (except where the potatoes are to be planted), which aids nutrient absorption. Then I shovel finished compost into each row as I plant it to give each seed or seedling extra help in the beginning. Unless the gods turn against me, this system will continue to work as well as it has thus far.

The story goes that James Underwood Crockett, the famous television gardener, was asked what it took to grow a bountiful vegetable garden. He was said to have answered, "Six hours of sun and good soil. The rest is details." And indeed, it does come down to that. Unless I'm deceived, there's nothing we can do about the sun, but the soil is a different matter. It is ours to nurture and replenish or to overuse and kill, and what we give to it, it will return in beauty and abundance.

Along with soil preparation, we begin planting the earliest food crops in April. Peas are the customary first planting, and some folks talk about planting peas on St. Patrick's Day. Well, on St. Patrick's Day on our hill, the ground has always been frozen or near-frozen, and too wet and compacted for planting. We usually plant peas the first or second week of April. This year they went in the first week but only germinated in the last. Before planting peas in the damp, cold soil, I soak them briefly in an inoculant that protects them from fungal diseases and improves their growth. I also never plant any seeds right after a heavy rain, for they can be drowned for lack of oxygen or overwhelmed by the weight of the dense, sodden earth. This year I have put most of the pea crop along an outside fence. It won't be high enough to hold them, but when they are approaching the top, I will take dozens of three- or four-foot-long branches from the brush pile and stick them into the chicken wire that encloses the fenced area. This extends the height to which the pea vines can grow, and it can easily be done in a new part of the fence each year.

No matter how many peas we grow, there are never enough. This year I've put in sugar snaps, snow peas and old-fashioned Lincoln shelling peas. They will be ripe—I hope—the last week of June and continue until the midsummer heat slays them. Sugar snaps eaten raw, right off the vine, alone are worthy of the planting effort. Our grandchildren seem to think they are candy, for they love their crisp sweetness and are always ready for a trip to the garden to pick them.

Other April plantings include numerous lettuces and Oriental greens, all cool weather lovers that mature quickly and leave room in midsummer for a fast-growing, fall-ripening crop to take their place. I plant greens in succession, a few every week or two until the middle of May, so we won't be overwhelmed with them all of the same age and quickly going to seed. This year we have planted arugula, romaine, bibb and Batavia lettuce, along with the peas the first week in April. Two weeks later, oak leaf, baby oak leaf, lollo rossa and Bogota lettuces went in. Each planting contains only a two-and-a-half-foot row of each lettuce type so that our salads can always include a colorful and tasty variety.

A French and Italian way to use such early salad greens is to combine seeds and plant them as a mixture called mesclum or mesclun. As this natural blending of textures and flavors grows to perhaps four or five inches, the very young and tender leaves are snipped off of the top to be eaten, allowing the plant to continue to produce. Packets of mesclum can be found now and again in catalogs or seed stores, but it is easy to enough to concoct your own version. I recommend it especially for the small garden or even a window box. Here are a few possible combinations.

- Chervil, baby romaine, arugula, lolla rossa, escarole and ruby-leafed lettuce.
- Red oak leaf, regular oak leaf, basil, chervil, sorrel and bibb lettuce.
- Mache, chervil, nasturtium leaves and blossoms, radicchio, Boston lettuce and early spinach.

Joi Choi Bok choi, Mei Qing Bok choi, Siberian kale, Nagoda Chinese cabbage, Tyee spinach and Taisai greens round out our early leafy production, giving us cooking and salad greens. We also put in an area of salsify, parsnips and carrots, slow growers that need a long season to mature.

All of these, save the peas, go into one of the long raised beds at either end of the garden. These beds, four feet wide and sixty feet long, are about twelve inches higher than the garden floor and what one calls intensively planted. Into this area go short, eight-inch wide rows that run the width of the bed, or squares either two feet or five feet across. Whatever the shape, I leave very little space between plantings. I plant lettuce between carrots, parsnips, beets and kale so that the greens are used up in time to make room for the expanding, longer-lived vegetables. Of varieties we won't use much, I plant only half a row at a time so we will get a continuing supply of freshly mature greens or roots. Most greens mature in forty to fifty days if weather conditions are right. Immature lettuce, of course, is edible and succulent, so since lettuce must always be thinned no matter how sparsely you think you've seeded it, it's useful to let seedlings grow to about three or four inches in height, thin them and use them for an early, delicately flavored and textured salad. In the same way, immature Oriental greens are delicious in a clear Chinese soup.

On April 30, more arugula, Chiogga and Mobile beets, fennel, carrots and radishes are planted. Carrots are slow to germinate, but radishes germinate, grow and go to seed quickly. I often plant a few radishes in with carrots to help define the parameters of the carrot bed because they germinate in only five or six days. They are mature and can be eaten when the carrots are only just emerging from the ground, so the two never crowd each other. Radishes, which love cool temperatures, get woody and bitter in hot weather, so one must plant early and enjoy soon.

I try to do all these plantings on a dry, windless day, for wind can blow seeds about and torrents of rain can wash them away. I have found Bok choi growing among the squash, lettuces tucked among the tomatoes and a parsnip, quite robust, growing out of the grass in the pasture some distance from the garden. All are demonstrations of the mysterious adventures even seeds can have when left alone.

Along with soil preparation and seed planting, attention must now be paid to the perennial beds: the strawberries, asparagus and rhubarb within the garden and the patches of blackberries, raspberries and blueberries in the field. In the fall we mulch the strawberries with salt hay or pine needles, and all the other perennials (as well as leftover leeks and parsnips) with dry leaves six to eight inches deep. Now is the time to pull back these winter shrouds and allow the sun to warm up the earth above the plants' roots. As we move the mulch aside, we carefully cultivate around the dormant plants adding the usual compost, bonemeal, wood ash from the fireplace and sometimes lime. The coming asparagus hide among the dead stubs of last year's stalks, waiting for the earth to warm. When the temperature is right they bound forth, growing inches each day.

The strawberries look sad and bedraggled now, but they will soon start sending out runners from each mother plant, and in a few weeks each attached newcomer will be covered with white blossoms. Now is a good time to thin out any areas in the patch that are crowded, for they will be too jammed together to produce well as they expand farther. Raspberries, blackberries and blueberries are now pruned of canes and stems that have suffered from winter-kill. There are many this year, another casualty of the lack of snow cover during the coldest months. As I read of global warming, I ponder future winters, scant of snow and subject to frequent thawing and refreezing. Will they prohibit our raising these fruits that taste of the New England earth? If so, they will be missed.

The Kitchen

In nonindustrialized societies, this first month of spring or its climatic equivalent is often known as "hungry season," a period when winter stores are low and new crops have not matured enough to be eaten, a period when early sprouting wild plants are sought to tide people over. Times of drought or flood can prove catastrophic, and famine and death can ensue. Watching one's resources dwindle as floodwaters rise or rains refuse to fall is an ordeal few modern Americans have weathered. Our problems tend to be those associated with the liabilities of overabundance, such as obesity, high cholesterol, high blood pressure, diabetes and the like, but ours are not the problems of much of the world. An anthropology professor with whom I studied once remarked facetiously that there is no such thing as a fat peasant, but I believe it may be true. In Mexico, Guatemala, Tanzania, Rwanda, Kenya, India, Nepal and rural China, I have looked in vain for a corpulent worker of the soil. In urban New York, only chic Madison Avenue women appear to be as thin and reedy as the populations who work and subsist on ever-smaller pieces of land sustaining ever-growing populations.

To urban populations the return of spring and its shoots of edible green mean little indeed, but imagine what they must signify to a peasant or what they must have signified to an ancestor of our own. After a winter of living on increasingly rancid grains, the delight of eating the first wild lettuce or herb must have been, or must be, ecstatic. Even today in the United States, in such rural areas as Appalachia, ramps—an early wild leek—are enthusiastically eaten in spring as a delicious and curative purge of the winter's toxins. They are reputed to have a strong garlic flavor and after-flavor. Apparently you can smell a ramp eater from quite a distance.

I've never been able to find ramps in our woods or meadows, although they are native to the Northeast, but there are other early wild and domestic plants that can satisfy the human need for green stuff after a long winter. Wild violets and their leaves are high in vitamin C and delicious either cooked or raw in a salad. Fiddlehead fern shoots are tender and succulent as they emerge, requiring only brief cooking to bring out their earthy flavor. Young nettles, before they have developed violent stingers on their stems, have leaves that make a soup reminiscent of spinach soup, but milder and more delicate.

Dandelions—that scourge of the suburban lawn—have a pungent flavor and are becoming more popular and expensive in New York vegetable markets. Dandelion greens are best picked when they are young. They are high in iron, calcium, potassium and vitamin A, and they make a wonderful salad combined with the milder violet greens or buttery tender bluebell greens, another spring plant that makes a brief appearance and then vanishes until the next year.

These and the later-blooming oxalis, purslane and lamb's-quarters can combine to make an early and labor-free mesclum wild in the spring fields. These greens, topped with an uncomplicated vinaigrette made from the best of vinegar and oil, have a taste as rare as their ingredients are common. The key, of course, is the youth of each participating leaf.

In the domestic domain, our earliest fresh crop is overwintered parsnips. Layered in fall with a heavy leaf mulch, they survive the frozen ground and begin to send up fresh leaf shoots soon after it defrosts. When picked they are sweeter and fresher-tasting than they were in the previous season, since the cold increases their sugar content. Egyptian onions and leeks also overwinter to produce delicious green tops as well as hot, spicy roots. Mache comes early from reseeding itself in the fall. Sorrel, chervil, sage, thyme, lemon thyme, lovage, chives, lemon balm, tarragon, marjoram, oregano, winter savory and mint return to their places around the kitchen door and provide fresh new tastes in soups, salads and omelets. Chervil makes the earliest appearance—another natural reseeder—its anise flavor more delicate and pungent than that of its cousin, the later-emerging, longer-lasting tarragon. Chervil is a favorite that I would be averse to living without. Perhaps it is the time of year that it comes forth or perhaps it is its lacy, delicate look. Perhaps it is the flavor, unavailable at greengrocers and not to be compared with its commercially dried and bottled form.

Whatever the reason, I look for it impatiently, carefully snip a few outer leaves as soon as the plant is strong enough to lose them and enjoy a salad, soup or omelet that is the very quintessence of spring.

By now our winter stores have dwindled to a dozen jars of tomatoes, one or two jars each of pickled cucumbers, pears, green beans and carrots and a quart or two of dried beans. There are a few onions strung up on the wall. The potatoes at the bottom of the bin are sprouting, and most will be used for planting next month. The last molding winter squash has been added to the compost. Of course we don't have to live on this meager fare, so even thinking about it is pretentious, but I can't help thinking about it anyway. We do all this because we believe it is better—better-tasting food, better nutrition—but we can always find a grocery store at a moment's notice. Our survival doesn't depend on our subsistence labor, which, of course, would have to be a great deal more arduous if we had to live solely on our own production. This partial way of life is a form we have chosen, not a necessity. We experience no "hungry time." We are not at work but at play in our joyful, abundant garden.

More than a hundred years ago, thousands of people left their farms and their land, thus ensuring the success of the revolution fostered by the first mass-production industries. I can't imagine preferring an assembly-line job (I had one once) to digging about in the earth, but I never factor in the intensity of the labor that real farming in the nineteenth century required, the farmer's accountability to his family and his land and the relative security that a paying job must have provided.

I have a good friend who was born in a village near Canton, China, in 1937, her life beginning just at the escalation of that long and complex war. She came to the United States in 1961 and is afraid to go back to China, afraid that she will be unable to get out again and afraid that her childhood will be revisited upon her. Her memories embody cold and fear and hunger, but when urged to remember she speaks of it diffidently, of moments when she would gaze at the part of her hand where the thumb meets the palm and visualize a chicken leg, and dream of its taste and its ability to fill her aching stomach.

I have another friend, a Korean woman, who lived through her country's civil war. Her husband was conscripted into the army. She was left with a newborn son and a little money, but food was scarce. She remembers trying to digest grass when there was nothing else to eat, and she remembers her baby son crying for milk when her breasts had dried up and had no more to give him.

Both of these women survived but many did not during those times in Asia, and many have not in other cruel times throughout history. As we measure out the ice cream and worry about our waistlines, we must remember that for some those times still exist.

Combining the remains in the larder with the new wild and domesticated plants that spring up to face the whimsical April weather can be an inventive task. Dried beans, last fall's potatoes and yesterday's eggs all taste fresher and better with a few recently sprouted herbs or greens. Soup with new onion greens and parsnips is better now than it is in the fall. Wild greens make a salad distinct from those made of lettuces grown in Florida and packed in cold storage for weeks.

This is a time to cook creatively, put together what is available and discover a new group of flavors.

Sautéed Parsnips

INGREDIENTS:
Fresh, sweet overwintered parsnips
Sweet butter
Salt
Pepper

PROCEDURE:
1. Pare and slice the parsnips. Parboil them in water for a few minutes until they begin to soften. Drain them.
2. Sauté them in a little sweet butter. Top with salt and pepper and perhaps a fresh sprig of herb, if available. Serve immediately.

Pureed Parsnips

INGREDIENTS:
2 pounds fresh parsnips (about 6 large parsnips)
4 tablespoons heavy cream
2 tablespoons sweet butter
Salt
White pepper

PROCEDURE:
1. Pare the parsnips and slice them into 1/2- to 1-inch rounds. Place them in a large saucepan and barely cover them with lightly salted water. Bring them to a boil, reduce the heat and simmer for 20 to 30 minutes until they

are soft and about 75 percent of the water is evaporated. If there is still too much water, pour some out.

2. Put the parsnips and remaining water into a blender, food mill or food processor and puree until smooth. Add the cream, butter and pepper.

3. Put the puree in a double boiler, cover and simmer on very low heat for about 1 hour, or until you are ready to serve. This last step softens the often sharp flavor of parsnips and cooks away the air bubbles that a food processor churns into the mixture, giving it that processor "fluff" texture.

Fiddlehead Ferns with Hollandaise Sauce

INGREDIENTS:

1 pound fiddlehead ferns
Water
Salt
1/4 pound sweet butter, cut into slices
3 egg yolks
3 tablespoons lemon juice

PROCEDURE:

1. Wash the fiddlehead ferns carefully and remove the rough, brown hairs from the stems. Their stems should not yet be unfurled.

2. Combine the butter, egg yolks and lemon juice in a double boiler and let it warm to room temperature.

3. Set a pot of water to boil. Add the salt. When it boils add the ferns. Let them boil for 2 to 3 minutes until they are bright green and tender. Remove them from the heat, but keep them warm.

4. Heat some water in a double boiler. Stir the sauce over the water until it thickens and coheres. Serve over the ferns.

Shad with Sorrel Sauce

The first leaves to take a chance on the early spring weather and show themselves in the herb garden by the back door are the long strident sorrel leaves. Returning year after year, their light, lemony flavor is a welcome contrast to winter's fare. They are useful all summer long, but their flavor early in the spring is an edible emblem of the coming season.

I use sorrel in a number of sauces and soups, but I avoid recipes that require long cooking, for its beautiful green turns a muddy gray if it is cooked too long.

INGREDIENTS:

>   *2 to 2-1/2 cups fresh sorrel, picked over and thinly sliced*
>   *2 to 3 tablespoons chopped shallots*
>   *1/2 to 3/4 cup white wine*
>   *1 cup heavy cream*
>   *Salt*
>   *Pepper*
>   *2 to 3 tablespoons butter*
>   *1-1/2 to 2 pounds shad, fileted*
>   *Skin and bones from fileted shad*
>   *Shad roe (if you feel expansive)*

PROCEDURE:

1. Prepare the fish filets for cooking. Extract any bones that might still be in them. Wash the roe, if you are using it, and carefully remove any extra filaments around the sac. Do not break the sac.

2. Put the fish skin, bones, wine and a third of the shallots in a saucepan with a little water and poach for a few minutes until the flavors have meshed. Add the heavy cream and heat through.

3. Melt the butter in another saucepan. Add the rest of the shallots and sauté them. Add the sorrel and stir until it has wilted, being careful not to let it discolor. Strain the fish and wine mixture into the sorrel mixture. Set aside.

4. Sauté the fish filets and roe in the rest of the butter. Place them in a serving dish and cover with the sauce. Serve immediately.

Leek and Potato Soup

Here is a way to incorporate sorrel or another spring herb and turn a simple soup into a dish that tastes of a new season. It can also make use of any overwintered leeks that have sprung to life as well as some of the last withered potatoes in the barrel.

This most basic of soups is a staple in our household. It may be a hot and hearty, cold weather soup or a cool summer one, and it has even other metamorphoses. The most memorable leek and potato soup I've had was in Provence many summers ago. We had a wonderful Belgian cook named Suzanne who made a delicious cream soup. Our son, Jim, then four years old, loved it so and she loved him so that she made it almost every day, changing its flavor with different seasonings.

Her basic model began with leeks and potatoes sautéed in sweet butter, then cooked in water with an addition of some sort of canned milk at the end. I have never made such good cream soup.

Perhaps it is because I use fresh cream or milk. Perhaps it is because I don't have Suzanne's touch. Or perhaps it is the climate in those southern French mountains that makes everything taste so fresh and correct. Here is my version of cream soup, inferior though it may be. As you will see, it's not really a recipe. It is a theme with a hundred variations.

INGREDIENTS:

3 or 4 leeks
4 to 6 Idaho-type potatoes,
3 to 4 tablespoons very fresh, sweet butter
Water or chicken broth
Light cream, heavy cream or milk
Salt
White pepper
One of the following: fresh sorrel, fine curry powder, basil, mushrooms,
    scallions, watercress or something of your choice

PROCEDURE:

1. Carefully wash the leeks and slice the white parts into thin circles.
2. Peel and slice the potatoes
3. Melt the butter in a soup pot and add the leeks and potatoes. Stir to coat the pieces with butter and sauté them for a few minutes, being careful not to brown or burn them.
4. Add the salt, pepper and curry powder if you wish to at this point.
5. Add the broth or water to cover the other ingredients. Simmer for about 30 minutes, adding more liquid if necessary.
6. When the potatoes are very soft and start to fall apart, remove them from the heat and put the mixture through a food mill. I prefer a food mill to a food processor for this step because it doesn't mix in air that results in a too fluffy puree. If the mixture is too thick, now is the time to add more liquid, but remember that you'll be adding cream at the end which will further thin the soup.
7. Return the soup to the pot and add any chopped greens you might wish to use. Heat it slowly to boiling, then add the cream and turn off the heat. Stir and serve.

Bread

Breads are a universal staple that can consist of a variety of grains kept and preserved from harvest to harvest. As such they are a perfect complement to food in the "hungry season."

When I was a child the only bread available locally was a form of "Wonder Bread" called Mrs. Baird's Bread. I loved its cotton candy texture and bland flavor, but I only tasted it at other people's houses, for my family clung to the notion of the nutritious. We made our own bread, apparently from an ancient family recipe. It doesn't resemble the whole-grain breads of the 1980s, but in the 1930s whole-grain flours were not available in our town, and this bread was surely more nutritious than the other alternative.

There was a debate between my grandmother and my great-aunt Jenny over whether milk or water should be used as the liquid ingredient. Milk makes a crumblier bread, which tends to fall apart when used as a sandwich. Water makes a lighter bread that sticks together but hasn't quite the flavor of the milk version. Choose for yourself. The recipe makes three loaves.

INGREDIENTS:
> *1/2 cup warm water*
> *1 teaspoon sugar*
> *1 cake or package of yeast*
> *1 cup milk or water*
> *2 cups unbleached flour*
> *8 cups unbleached flour*
> *1/2 cup sugar*
> *1 heaping teaspoon salt*
> *1/2 cup shortening*
> *2 cups milk or water*

PROCEDURE:
1. Mix the warm water, sugar and yeast in a small bowl. Let it stand for 10 minutes. This tests the freshness of the yeast. If the mixture begins to bubble, it is usable.
2. Mix 1 cup milk, 2 cups flour and the yeast mixture in a large bowl. It will be very gooey. Cover and let it stand in a warm place until it doubles in size (about 1 hour).
3. In the meantime, mix the other dry ingredients in a very large bowl. Cut the shortening into the dry mixture. When the flour and yeast mixture has risen, add it and the remaining milk or water to the dry mixture, mixing well. Knead the dough until the whole mass hangs together. Cover it with a damp towel, put it in a warm, draftless place and let it rise to double its original size.
4. Knead the dough well and let it rise again. (As you can see, this is a long process, but the extra kneading makes a smoother, tastier bread. I've skipped this last kneading and found that the bread isn't as good.)
5. Knead the dough again and divide it into three loaves. Put the loaves into lightly greased pans. Cover and let them rise again.

6. Bake the loaves at 375˚ for 1 hour or until they are nicely browned. Cool them on racks. Eating a piece while it is still warm is supposedly very bad for the digestion, but it is delicious nevertheless, especially slathered with sweet butter that melts into the warm bread.

Hot Water Corn Bread

Dried corn or maize was a staple in the New World long before Columbus landed. Today it still serves as the daily bread of Latin America and a secondary staple in the southern and southwestern United States. I have seen pine tree–shaped mounds of corn drying on the mountainsides of Nepal and strings of it in the doorways of earthen dwellings in western China. It traveled to Asia fairly late in history but has settled in well. And even though it is merely fodder for cattle in the Midwest and Northeast, most of us look with interest at an ear of fresh sweet corn in August.

Because of my limited garden space I have never attempted to raise anything but sweet corn. Last fall I dried and tried unsuccessfully to grind some of it. Rather than pulverizing into a meal, it simply made a gummy mess. I later realized that the high sugar content causes this. Subsequently, I have found a local natural food store that grinds corn into meal while you wait. It is better than any cornmeal I've tried and improves the following "hungry season" food enormously.

I've never known anyone to make this but members of my mother's family. There was never really a recipe. It was all done by feel. If it is done correctly, when each patty is cooked the inside will be soft and light and the outside crisp and thin, something like a corn chip surrounding a corn mush.

INGREDIENTS:
White cornmeal
Boiling water
Pinch of salt
Bacon grease

PROCEDURE:
1. Sift the cornmeal and salt into a bowl. Pour boiling water over it until you have the right mix, not too runny and not too dense. Let it rest for about 10 minutes.
2. Heat a little bacon grease in an iron skillet. Form the cornmeal into patties and sauté them over a low heat until the outsides are crisp and brown. Serve hot with butter.

Spoon Bread

I have made some changes here in the family recipe. There are proportionately more eggs which makes a lighter batter. I have also omitted the bowl of melted butter that was served with it to be ladled over each person's helping.

INGREDIENTS:

2 cups sweet milk
1 cup cornmeal
1/4 pound sweet butter
1 teaspoon salt
4 egg yolks
6 egg whites

PROCEDURE:

1. Preheat the oven to 375˚.
2. Scald the milk. Beat in the cornmeal, using a whisk or beater to ensure that the mixture will not be lumpy. Cook it, beating continuously, until the mixture has thickened. Remove it from the heat.
3. Cut the butter into several pieces and add them to the cornmeal mix. Stir until the butter is melted. Add the salt. Set aside to cool.
4. Separate the eggs. Add the egg yolks, one at a time, to the cornmeal mixture. Beat after each addition.
5. Beat the egg whites until they are stiff and glossy but not dry.
6. Fold the egg whites into the cornmeal batter. Do not overmix. Turn the mixture into a straight-sided casserole or soufflé dish. Bake for 45 minutes. Serve immediately.

MAY

sweet spring is your
time is my time is our
time for springtime is lovetime
and viva sweet love

—e. e. cummings

The Land

A less refined version of cummings' poem sticks in my memory, a stanza probably sung by some callow teenager in west Texas, circa 1950: "Hooray, hooray, the middle of May. Outdoor necking begins today."

For those of you who are under thirty, possibly even under forty, it might be difficult to comprehend the notion of "necking" and especially "outdoor necking," but truly, there was a time and place when many young couples spent long and hopefully uninterrupted hours in parked cars, in the dark of night, on lonely, seldom-used back roads, usually dirt roads that led to outlying farms, ranches or oil rigs. This time was usually spent necking, an activity that might be defined today as intense physical contact between necks and anything above them, or sometimes between waists and anything above those. I've never, however, heard the word "waisting," but "courting" or "courting up a storm" was a Texas expression for something more than merely necking. "Going all the way" was something else again, and a girl (but never a boy) could lose her reputation overnight if such was reported by a proud but indiscreet date. I remember a high-school football hero called Ding Dong Bell (not an alias), who was reported to have driven down the main street of town with a beautiful young girl, a new girl in our ninth-grade class, with her bra waving from his car radio aerial. This, and the widely spread tale of his experience with her, made him an even greater hero. Public response to the girl was a different matter. Her immediate rejection by her female peers led her to drop out of school and out of sight.

Of course necking, courting and even going all the way were not dictated by the spring season, but the coming of warmer weather did make these hours of fervent activity more comfortable, especially if the place of choice was an unheated pickup truck. Weather or no, the advent of spring seemed to set people's juices flowing out there on the plains.

The warming of the earth excites the sexual instincts of geese and chickens and all manner of wildlife. Perhaps the acknowledgment of a similar human instinct for spring fertility has simply gone underground. The springtime rites of the ancients were overtly ribald, celebrating fertility and birth by practicing conception. These rituals, now translated into Maypoles, spring proms, commencement exercises and military extravaganzas, phallic in their symbolism, are not so different from our rooster's Maytime struts, crows and humpings. But the question is, with all the revelry and celebration, how did the spring farm work ever get done?

May is a season of much being, much coming, much changing and much to do. Simply caring for the infant garden could take all of one's time, but there are countless other things to observe and to participate in. Wherever one turns, spring is living up to its name by bounding forth.

It is a time of feverish endeavor, and not simply human endeavor. Plants have heard the alarm clock of spring and seen the dawn. Even the laggards are springing up everywhere at their silent pace. Daffodils, tulips, lilacs, primulas and fruit-tree blossoms surround the house. In the woods, trillium, jack-in-the-pulpit, marshmallows, Adder's tongues, bluebells, bluettes and columbines wave their sprightly heads in recognition of their genesis. The world looks good. The world smells good. The plants seem to be saying, "It's O.K. Life has come."

In the animal world, activity is even more fervent, though often unseen. Robins are everywhere; spring warblers, tanagers, catbirds and orioles are in the field. A phoebe is nesting above our front door as her ancestors have done for many years. Mourning doves can be heard at dawn. In fact, the clock radio is unnecessary these days, for daybreak brings a chorus of birds in ever-different harmonies greeting the coming sun.

This year for the first time we have two bluebirds, real "somewhere over the rainbow" bluebirds, nesting in the field. They are the first real bluebirds I have ever seen. They have claimed occupancy in a certified bluebird house we purchased and erected following instructions that I felt skeptical about, but lo and behold, it has worked. The homemaking couple bring twigs and pine needles to their new residence, cautiously skirting and circling it until they hope they've fooled you as to their ultimate destination. Only then do they zoom into the hole in the manmade box.

Bluebirds almost became extinct a number of years ago at the height of DDT usage. Many birds that ate seeds containing DDT residues could not develop eggs with properly hard shells to protect the embryo inside; therefore, they could not reproduce themselves. For less prolific birds, like the bluebird, this created a critical situation, and the species was very nearly lost.

Of course, throughout the course of evolution, species are being lost all the time, but until the rise of humankind, extinctions were caused by nature's own forces: extreme weather changes, extraterrestrial mishaps such as meteor collisions with or near the earth and events that we can only guess at. Since humans have proliferated on the earth, the causes for most extinctions have become apparent. Whether we have exterminated plants and animals for food, for territory or for cash, we have been the prime destroyers.

In the case of bluebirds, there may be a happy ending, for they are coming back. We are not the only house in the neighborhood that has a bluebird family in residence.

If wild birds are in a frenzy of nesting and mating, their domestic relations are close behind in terms of springtime passion. One female goose has built a large and tidy nest of the wood shavings on the floor of the goose pen in the barn. She now sits brooding on the accumulating eggs while the male, always protective, spends his days stalking about, beating his wings, stretching his lengthy neck and hissing ominously at anything that comes near. He attacks anything that doesn't get out of his way, which includes the older, less agile hens, whose backs he has pecked until there are few feathers left. Poor things. We are now keeping the geese and the chickens separated.

Our two remaining roosters have reached an uneasy settlement of their respective ranks. The barred rock has become the ruler of the roost, a position he vied for before his adversaries were put into the freezer some months ago. Like so many people who have struggled for their position, he is a cruel master. He is licentious and utterly without delicacy. His exploits are forced upon his harem in an ever more ferocious fashion. The other male, in the meantime, can't get near the hens without a cockfight.

Until we separated our two avian species, this milder male had become friends with the brooding goose, often sitting quietly by her as she nested when her consort was away feeding. On one occasion, I found him humping her enthusiastically. She submitted to the event with calm insouciance, although the difference in their sizes made it only an academic experience for either of them. She, in turn, tolerated him as she did no one else, neither hissing nor flapping about in his presence. Now that he has been separated from this love, he looks dissolute and distracted. It's the end of an affair that was never meant to be. She is content with her eggs and has probably forgotten him already. The tragedy of unrequited love ...

The beginning of the growing season invariably brings to mind projects and problems we have put off or failed to solve. One affliction we have is a very large expanse of country lawn—consisting of grass, dandelions, plantain, clover and a hundred other wild interlopers. It undulates around the house down to an old stone ha-ha wall and spills over onto the north hill pasture, narrows as it descends to the pond where it ends in a slightly unkempt circle around the water's periphery, then loses itself in the woods to reemerge as pasture by the old barn. This mammoth greensward preceded us in Cornwall, and although I've made attempts to reduce its girth, they have been inadequate. A flower bed here, a clump of bushes there, the large vegetable garden, the chicken yard, even a tennis court—and we still have several acres of green that must be tended or allowed to turn from meadow to weed, then to thicket and finally to new forest.

Agreeable as it is to look at, sit on, run through and smell when newly mown, lawn isn't so interesting to tend, even when it is unmanicured country stuff thought of mainly as goose fodder. We have never contributed to the ten billion gallons of lawn pesticides and fertilizers that are sold in the United States each year and despoil groundwater all over the country. Our turf is what it is, though mowed.

It has seemed so wasteful of energy and time, this continual mowing, that several years ago I purchased two very young goats, which we fenced into a three-quarter-acre patch on the hill to act as mowers. They set to work denuding their area of all vegetation: bushes, trees, vines and, finally, grass when there was nothing better to ingest. They were friendly and intelligent. Our visiting grandchildren were attracted to them, so daily visits to give them treats became part of our routine. We had quite a summer together until we dispersed in the fall, and the goats grew big enough to jump over the fence our caretaker had constructed. So agile were they that they could sail over the four-foot fence like Pegasus over Mount Olympus. Then they would eat our flowers, or visit the neighbors and eat their flowers, all the while eluding capture. We resorted to keeping them in the barn, where they thrashed around in such misery that one fall day, when we were in New York, the caretaker sold them—a relief, to be sure.

The next year the grass was growing again, and I considered another solution to the mowing problem. This time I bought two lambs (one later died). After all, the fence was there and lambs can't jump very high. They aren't as friendly as the goats, nor as alert, but they eat grass down to its roots and appear to be turning this otherwise useless weed into wool and perhaps, in the future, some form of progeny.

With sheep in residence, our next concern became their safety, mainly because of the proximity of coyotes in the woods east of us. We see coyote tracks in the snow in wintertime and hear their howls echoing through the valley, lonely and expressive of potential violence. There is an urgency in those faraway moans, and the urgency is undoubtedly for food. A nearby farmer's calf was attacked in its own barnyard last fall, and while cross-country skiing a year ago, we found a freshly cleaned skeleton of a deer stag surrounded by hundreds of coyote tracks. To add to the danger of predators, two local people have recently reported sighting a cougar, and many have seen black bear, though their talent for damage is directed more toward bees than sheep.

As I was fretting about this difficulty, a neighbor called to ask if I would be interested in adopting two donkeys rescued from Death Valley in a drive to save them from the ire of ranchers. My problem was suddenly solved. A coyote deterrent often used by sheepherders in Texas is the practice of grazing a donkey in the fields with the sheep. Donkeys can "kick the bejesus" out of the most forward coyote, and a female donkey will bond with sheep, protecting them as she can.

Donkeys, used throughout the Middle East as pack animals and human transport, are considered the perfect animal by a friend of mine who has lived there. They are strong, can carry enormous loads relative to their body weight, require minimal attention and get by on less food and water than most domestic animals. Not only that, they are intelligent and responsive, and regardless of their reputation for being more obstinate than a master would wish, they take kindly to their circumstances. In Cairo one sees donkeys everywhere, loaded with everything from firewood to people, picking their way between buses and office buildings, never ruffled or stressed. If they can deal with Cairo traffic with such ease our bucolic Cornwall hill must be a study in relaxation. They have proven to be a fine solution to the protection problem. They are friendly and tame, have bonded with the sheep and keep the pasture smooth and low. The only problem is that we can't figure out how to lead them through the woods from one pasture to another, so in one place our grass still grows.

The Garden

This spring has been one of ample rain, and while it has scotched the rumors of drought in the Northeast, its frequency has generated a colder and wetter atmosphere than usual. The plants have responded by being a bit slower to spring forth in customary May fashion. Gardeners are talking about seeds rotting in the ground, and though our germination rates have been sparser than usual, we haven't suffered as badly as some. We are lucky with our sloping hillside location. The same conditions that cause soil erosion also prevent water from settling and the seeds from rotting. Raised beds do the same job on flat land, yet another reason to consider starting them in one's garden.

Our own raised beds have been thoroughly planted now with short rows of twenty to thirty different greens and roots. As I did in April, each week I put in more: lettuces in succession two weeks apart, beets and carrots to mature early and late, Oriental greens of various sorts, parsnips and salsify, coriander, fennel and dill.

As I plant each seed type, I label the row or mound, writing the species name and the day it was planted on a sturdy wooden labeling stick with permanent ink. At the end of the day, I enter the same information in my journal, showing the location of the plant on a garden map. In a large garden this identification is essential, for it is impossible to remember each seed's exact location or which row of beans was the black ones and which the cranberries. Even in a small space, it is surprising how easy it is to forget the locations of each variety. I also identify the seed company and the name of the variety, such as Chiogga beet as opposed to Sweetheart beet. This allows me to note which is most prolific, which tastes sweeter or more pungent, which matures fastest and which germinates poorly. This is all useful information when you are planning the next garden.

By mid-May we put out the broccoli, cabbages, Brussels sprouts, leeks, celery and celeriac we started from seedlings in March. We plant onion and shallot sets and onion seeds. We retrieve and plant last fall's wizened, wrinkled potatoes that are impatiently sending up white eyes for sun and sustenance. When I plant potatoes, I dig a trench eight to ten inches deep, fill it with about two inches of compost, put in the potatoes about fourteen inches apart, cover them over and then, as the plants grow, fill in the trench with compost, garden soil and mulch. This is an upside-down version of hilling up. I think it produces more potatoes that are less likely to pop out into the sun, which turns them green and renders them bitter and poisonous. This method works well on our hillside slope. However, on land with poor drainage, hilling up (building up a hill of earth around the growing plant) has its advantages.

All of this month's planting is simply a prelude to the task that customarily takes place on Memorial Day. Not until then can we feel safe from frost. Of course we have had frost in June, but only rarely and mildly. On Memorial Day or thereabouts, the planting of squash, beans, tomatoes, peppers, eggplants, cucumbers, melons and corn round out the garden.

If the weather is wet or chilly, which it often is, I nurture newly transplanted seedlings by housing them in homemade cloches made of plastic soda or milk bottles with the bottoms cut out and the screw top removed to give the plants air and keep them from suffocating on a warm day. These cloches give the plant extra warmth, keep heavy winds from breaking spindly stems and deter the malicious cutworm from chewing through a seedling at the ground level and killing it.

We now have more lettuce than we can eat, so we thrust it upon anyone who comes by and take to it everyone we visit. Of the many rows of curly, flat, loose-leafed, headed, red and green salad makings, a friend who happened by said, "Ah, and remember when we were all so thrilled when Boston lettuce came on the market and we could buy something besides iceberg?"

When I gather lettuce now, I pull each young plant up by the roots, giving space to its rapidly expanding neighbors. An alternate method, if you have too little lettuce, is to snip only the side leaves, allowing the rest of the plant to continue growing. Tender, young, buttery lettuce is something never found at a greengrocers and rarely found in a restaurant. I suspect it doesn't travel well under commercial circumstances. It wilts quickly, so we usually pick it just before we plan to use it and rinse it in the ice-cold water that comes through our tap from the well. If it has wilted, a thorough soaking in the same water will revive it. When I am taking a bunch back to the city, I put it in plastic bags along with a few ice cubes. Unless there is a serious traffic problem, it arrives undaunted or only slightly wilted.

For our last major May gardening enterprise, we now turn to the orchard and the other fruit trees scattered about the place. As our arborist advised, we have planted six tiny pear whips (year-old, unbranched saplings) of six different varieties, which we found at a fruit-tree nursery that specializes in many old types of apples, pears and plums.

We hope to flatten these whips into the elegant shape of the palmette verrier, a shape not unlike that of Poseidon's trident, although it will eventually be a quadrident, with its center prong branching into two. This is accomplished by allowing only two branches to grow from the young tree trunk. All other emergent stem must be ruthlessly plucked away, leaving two beautifully horizontal boughs that will grow out to the right and left of the central trunk just opposite each other. They will be trained along a guiding wire and eventually will be turned upward to form the trident shape, assuming that another central branch grows in place of the severed one. A final step will form two more parallel branches from that branch about a foot above the first. If we live long enough, we might even force a third branching, which will create a sexident.

All of these will, we pray, be covered with different varieties of pears: two early, two mid-fall and two late-ripening. It is said that the late varieties will keep almost all winter if picked at the proper time, wrapped well and kept at the correct temperature. These are a lot of "ifs" to think about, especially considering the many "ifs" in bringing them to maturity in the first place.

In line with this, a major project we have initiated this season is organically spraying the existing fruit trees in the field. For the first time we have set up a program that, if we are lucky and if the gods allow, will keep the worst pests away and permit us to eat the fruits of our labor. In the past our pear trees have yielded decent harvests of often mildewed pears, juicy and delicious nonetheless. Plums and cherries put in five and six years ago have yielded little fruit, although this spring they were covered with blossoms. The apples, which include the older trees that preceded us on the hill, have been uniformly riddled with insect larvae, scab and probably much, much more. A dealer in chemical sprays once told me there are ninety-two apple pests in this area alone. Of course he was selling toxic sprays, which I refused, thinking I could easily buy chemical apples at any fruit market at much less cost and effort than I expend on these capricious trees of ours. However, letting nature take its course has not been a success, at least with the apple trees, and now we are regularly applying such nominal organic poisons as we can find.

Our difficulty with them is probably the same difficulty that has caused apple growers to embrace the cause of chemical pesticides. Chemical pesticides are invented to stick and that is why residues can be found on the surface of most chemically sprayed produce, even after it has been washed. Chemicals don't break down, but remain potent for years and therefore residues can also be found inside chemically sprayed produce, residues that have leached into the earth and been reabsorbed into the plant by osmosis along with the water and nutrients it needs to grow. These disadvantages to the consumer are real advantages to the grower. Neither rain nor storm can easily dislodge a chemical pesticide.

On the other hand, the benign controls I use wash off and break down into natural elements, leaving the ground untainted. This results in a fruit that is healthier for people, but in a springtime as rainy as this one, I fear that even the weekly spraying we've been aiming for hasn't been enough.

There are a number of companies nowadays that sell organic sprays for fruit trees and other vegetable plants. However, it is necessary to discover what particular insects threaten at what times and then use the appropriate infusion, which is more complicated than using the "kill-everything-in-sight" varieties. The following are a number of sprays that kill specific insect invasions, leaving the beneficial insects to thrive.

- *Dormant oil.* This is nontoxic, but smothers emerging insect hatchlings. It must be applied before blossoming.
- *Pheromone lures.* Used for both apple maggots and codling moths, these attract the sexually active moths to a trap. They must be hung in trees at blossoming time—not after—and left all summer.

- *Ryania/Rotenone/Pyrethrum.* These kill aphids, most beetles, whitefly, borers and fruit flies.
- *Imidan.* This kills curculio, codling moth and apple maggot.
- *Sulfur.* This is effective for scab infection.
- *Bt (Baccilus thuringes).* This eliminates all segmented worms.
- *Spreader sticker.* Not a killer, this helps to dissolve powdered materials and helps spray adhere to tree leaves.

This is our arsenal. The war begins.

But war and work are not all we must expect of Maytime. Remember the revelry of spring ceremonies? It's in the weather and in the air. Like peasants of the past, we too have trouble finding time away from our gardening tasks, but find it we do, to celebrate our own spring ceremonies—however quietly. It is natural that they are associated with food.

A favorite ritual is the annual hunt for the shy and elusive morel, which hides its beauty in piles of brown leaves, under old apple trees, on the edges of pastures or in a spot of sunlight in the dense forest. It seems that everyone who has an interest in morels has a theory as to the most probable places to find them. But the morel, always a step ahead of it pursuer, rarely conforms to the "word." They pop up in both likely and unlikely places, ignoring the "third-week-in-May" dictum and displaying themselves as late as mid-June. We spend a number of afternoons each May searching the edges of fields, the remnants of old overgrown orchards, the woods and the meadows until the grass is too high to see them.

After having no luck at all in these widespread areas this year, I found one tucked between two rocks at the edge of our fish pool in the backyard, another in the woods near the house and finally a small collection near a fallen apple tree by the ha-ha wall. These last were over-the-hill, too decayed to eat, but they were the largest I've ever seen and they have given me a place to search frequently next year.

It was a week later, just after a rain, that I unexpectedly discovered, in a spot that shall forever be secret, a cache of two dozen perfect morels, not too old and enough for a meal. It was a bonanza I've never found before and fear I may never have again.

Morels have such a distinctive appearance that they are one of only a few mushrooms that I am not afraid to eat once I've found them. Their wrinkled cap and hollow stem are like no other, although there are several varieties of differing sizes and hues. Remember, a mushroom guide is a must for identifying edible mushrooms one has never seen before. Never take a chance on a mysterious fungus, no matter how delectable it may seem.

Whether successful or not, "the hunt is the thing." It is really an excuse for meandering through meadows and woodlands, smelling the earthy scents of newly growing plants, spying on nesting birds and basking turtles, embracing the dappled light through pale green of young leaves, exploring rocks and ridges and celebrating the birth of columbines. And if you're very lucky, you'll find a rare king morel.

Another hunt—more popular among our neighbors—is for the furtive trout, be it rainbow or brook. After much railing about poachers this year, it seemed fitting to attempt to collect a few fish for ourselves. So, when we had a guest who had grown up fishing the streams of southern Virginia, we pulled out the old cobwebbed fishing poles, dug up a few earthworms, found a net and off we went to our stream. Since I go there frequently, the quiet beauty of the rocks and trees and the coolness of the waterfall's spray was not a new experience, but baiting a hook, casting it forth and waiting to dupe a poor fish into providing us with dinner was. Our methods were primitive—no fancy flies or masterful casting techniques—but the waiting and watching, the roar of the rushing water on its way to the Housatonic and the mystery beneath the glittering surface cast a spell that made me understand why anglers do what they do. There's a certain duality about it all. The state of waiting is almost meditative: the body, poised and silent, becoming integrated with its surroundings, the eyes gazing helplessly into the sparkling waters for any sign of life. There is a loosening, an opening of brain and breath, but also an edge, for there is always the possibility of a catch, that sudden tension on the line and then the game, the struggle between human and fish.

In our apprenticeship we lost many worms to fish cleverer than us, but we brought home enough for a tasty lunch and had entered into a world apart for a little while.

The Kitchen

May is asparagus month in Cornwall, and asparagus is the first substantial green vegetable to sprout from the garden. Slow to begin this cold and gloomy spring, now that it has, it grows so rapidly that there are ample helpings for a grand meal each day. Indeed, asparagus is noted for it speedy ascent once it breaks ground. I've never measured, but I would guess that one stalk grows several inches a day after it first appears in the sunshine.

Asparagus is actually the initial sprout of a feathery, fernlike perennial that grows to over six feet high during the summer and dies back to the ground each fall, to start all over again the following spring. It is the emergent shoot we snatch from the ground to satisfy our hunger for that crisp, fresh, earthy taste we have missed for so long.

One can pick these young stalks for up to six weeks, but to prevent the roots from giving up and dying, they must then be let go to grow, branch, bloom and reseed themselves, as their genes have taught them to do.

Asparagus takes some effort to plant and some patience to tend, for one gets no return from one's endeavor for several years. Root stocks—large, spidery, spreading affairs that look like the Medusa's head—can be bought at many nurseries. They are often advertised as two years old, meaning that one has to wait only two or three years after planting to begin picking them. The roots must be well established before they can endure having their growing stems repeatedly pulled off without giving up the ghost.

Once purchased, the roots must be carefully planted in a trench twelve inches deep and enriched with compost and well-rotted manure. Then the waiting period begins. During the first year, only a few spindly stalks will grow from each root stock, the next year a few more. If one plant has sent up a half-dozen shoots that are at least as big around as a pencil, it's probably all right to steal one, but no more. By the third year, if the plants look healthy, it's acceptable to pick prudently, but once you've tasted your first fresh-off-the-vine asparagus, you'll find it difficult to restrain yourself, for the real thing is sweeter, tenderer, juicier and earthier than anything bought from even the finest markets.

There is really no need for a recipe for asparagus. When it is superbly fresh, it can be eaten raw, unpeeled—even unwashed—and it is wonderful. The only bad asparagus is that which is overcooked, a travesty for the diner and the poor vegetable as well.

When I was newly married, I tried to convince one of my husband's aunts that the asparagus really didn't need to be boiled for forty-five minutes. I was so soundly rebuffed that I almost came to believe in her superior knowledge, that is until the dish came to the table soggy, gray, watery and tasteless. It bore no relation to the crisp earthy shoots we eat with such relish. She was of a fine character, but in her Boston-bred notion of long cooking for vegetables, she was wrong.

As I grow older, the basic flavor of fine, fresh ingredients simply and estimably prepared has become more important than the complex culinary inventions of an earlier time in my life. There was a period when achieving success with thirty ingredients was a grand accomplishment. Today, the crisp natural taste of a just-gathered pea, lettuce leaf, strawberry or asparagus stalk, unwashed and uncooked, is an experience I cherish more. Various food preparations, of course, are both delicious and necessary, but often they do not improve on that original, just-picked flavor.

During asparagus season, we eat the fresh green stalks almost every day and rarely tire of them. However I plan to prepare it, I begin by bending a stalk until it snaps, a way of ensuring the cook that he or she will be dealing with only the most tender part. The stalk breaks at the point where it begins to toughen. Peeling stalks of large diameter is a traditional procedure, but when the vegetable is very fresh, it is rarely necessary. You can judge by tasting a raw piece. If it seems tender and the stalk isn't difficult to chew through, it probably doesn't need the vitamin-rich outer part removed.

My favorite way to cook asparagus is to cut it into two- or three-inch lengths and stir-fry it in a little sesame oil in a wok. A splash of rice wine and/or light soy sauce gives the dish a Chinese flavor. A few similarly sized bamboo shoots can add a festive dash. The whole cooking process shouldn't take more than three or four minutes. The spears should be tossed about and cooked until they are a brilliant green, still crisp but cooked through. Then they must be served immediately.

My husband's favorite asparagus dish is steamed, the spears left whole, with a bit of sweet butter or hollandaise sauce on the top. This also takes very little time, but it should be watched closely for asparagus can overcook in a flash.

A third easy way to cook asparagus is to boil it briefly until it turns bright green, but still retains some of its crispness. When it appears to be done, it can be doused in cold water to stop the cooking. Then it may be kept warm or served chilled with a vinaigrette or an aioli sauce (see the March chapter).

When you grow your own asparagus, the crop comes up in all diameters, from the one-inch granddaddies to the toothpick-sized babies (which should be left to grow). An appetizing way to use the spears that are slightly larger than toothpick-sized is in an omelet. Simply chop them in one-inch lengths and toss them over the eggs for a few seconds before folding the omelet over. Salt and pepper it and serve. You'll be surprised how fresh and light the tiny spears will taste encased in the soft, creamy delectability of a fresh egg or two.

Countryside, Garden & Table

Asparagus can also be the main ingredient in a soufflé, quiche or soup (see Leek and Potato Soup in the April chapter). My own preference is to eat it very fresh in a way that requires little cooking.

Excess asparagus is easy to parboil and freeze. Simply bring a quart or so of salted water to a boil, add the asparagus and cook for a minute until it is bright green. Remove it from the heat and douse it in cold water to stop the cooking. Cool it to room temperature and freeze it in plastic bags. This is the asparagus to use in soup or quiche, for it will have lost its crunch but not its flavor in the freezing process.

Chicken and Asparagus with Fermented Black Beans

Asparagus combines well with many other vegetables and meats, so it is a natural for a more complex Chinese dish. Here is a favorite.

INGREDIENTS:
Fresh asparagus
1 handful of fermented black beans, slightly mashed and soaked in a bit
  of rice wine
2 chicken breasts
1-1/2 tablespoons cornstarch
1 teaspoon minced fresh garlic
1 tablespoon chopped gingerroot
Scant 1/4 cup corn oil
2 to 3 tablespoons rice wine
1 tablespoon light soy sauce
Salt to taste
1 cup chicken stock

PROCEDURE:
1. Wash and cut the asparagus into 2-inch lengths. Set it aside. Cut the chicken into equivalent slices. Marinate the chicken in 1 teaspoon of the cornstarch, the rice wine and the soy sauce. Put everything into a small bowl and mix it around with your fingers until all the chicken pieces are coated.
2. Mix the chicken stock with the remainder of the cornstarch.
3. Heat the oil in a wok. Add the chicken. Stir continuously. Add the black beans, asparagus, garlic and gingerroot. Continue stirring until the asparagus turns bright green and is tender but still crunchy.
4. Add the chicken stock. Continue to stir until it is a clear golden color and thickened. Adjust the seasoning if you desire.
5. Serve right away. (This dish doesn't improve with age.)

86

Rhubarb Pie

When we first moved to Cornwall, I found a leggy, unkempt rhubarb plant growing wild under a pine tree. It seemed forlorn and neglected, so I transplanted it into the big field garden when we began it. The mass of roots was mammoth and heavy, so I divided it into six plants. In a year I had six enormous, thriving rhubarb plants, enough to provide as much of the stuff as we could use. Since then I have divided two of the plants again, placing them along the edge of the garden because they keep weeds down with their spreading, elephant's ear leaves. Even leaving the required two-thirds of the plant to regenerate, we have more rhubarb than we need.

Traditionally I make rhubarb pie and strawberry-rhubarb pie when the strawberries are ripe. I also make stewed rhubarb, of the same ingredients as the pie filling, and freeze it for a quick winter dessert. Rhubarb may also be frozen raw. It can then be cooked after thawing. Conserves, marmalades or chutneys can be rhubarb-based, and even rhubarb ice cream might please the rhubarb enthusiast.

Rhubarb is best in the early spring when its stalks are new and about sixteen to twenty inches long. As the summer progresses, they become tougher and, although usable, may need to be partially peeled where they have become dry and coarse. Peeling my variety eliminates the beautiful rose-pink color, for the inside is green. However, there are newer varieties that are rhubarb-red all the way through.

An important rule when growing rhubarb is never to eat or cook the leaves. They contain large amounts of oxalic acid and are poisonous.

INGREDIENTS:

Pastry crust for a pie top and bottom (see November)
5 cups rhubarb, unpeeled, cut into 1- to 1-1/2-inch lengths
2-1/2 cups sugar
5 tablespoons instant tapioca
1/2 to 1 teaspoon almond extract (or 1 teaspoon cinnamon or nutmeg)
4 tablespoons sweet butter

PROCEDURE:

1. Place the chopped rhubarb, sugar, tapioca and flavoring in a bowl and toss to mix.
2. Roll out the lower pastry crust, fit it into the pan and prick the bottom with a fork. Bake at 500° for 8 to 10 minutes until it is slightly brown and crusted on top. This will prevent it from getting soggy.

3. Put the rhubarb mixture into the pastry crust. Place pieces of butter on top. Roll out the top crust. Place it over the pie, making sure there are vents for air to expand through.

4. Bake for about 45 minutes at 400°. It is done when the juices are bubbling nicely. Cool before serving.

Rhubarb Ice Cream

INGREDIENTS:

6 large stalks of rhubarb
1-1/2 to 1-3/4 cups sugar
1 cinnamon stick
1/2 teaspoon mace
1/2 teaspoon cloves
2 cups milk
2 cups heavy cream

PROCEDURE:

1. Cook all the ingredients together except the milk and cream for a few minutes. Stir frequently. When the rhubarb is soft and mushy, test to see if it is sweet enough. If it is not, add a bit more sugar until you are satisfied. Remove it from the heat. Set it aside to cool.

2. When it is cool, place the rhubarb mixture in an ice cream freezer. Add the milk and begin the freezing process. When the mixer is beginning to harden, add heavy cream that has been slightly whipped with a spoonful of sugar. Continue to freeze it until it is ready to eat. This should take about 20 minutes with an electric freezer.

Poached Trout

I think the best-tasting trout are those grilled over a wood fire by the stream a few minutes after they are caught. Like homegrown vegetables, fish are tastier the fresher they are; the flavors are more delicate and sweet.

Trout is a particularly delicate fish, and its flavor can be lost to the heartier tastes of garlic, onions, tomatoes and peppers. It takes little time to cook and can be braised in butter, poached in water and wine or grilled over apple wood to a fine flavor with little extra seasoning necessary if the fish is absolutely fresh.

I begin by cleaning each fish, leaving the heads on. A young trout doesn't even need scaling. All you have to do is slice open the stomach and remove the entrails, all conveniently packaged in a small space. Then the fish may be quickly cooked and either sauced or not depending on your whim.

INGREDIENTS:
1 1- to 2-pound trout per person
1 teaspoon butter for each trout
1 teaspoon minced fresh chives for each trout
1 or 2 bay leaves
1 stalk of fresh lovage or celery (lovage has a stronger flavor)
A few sprigs of fresh thyme or lemon thyme
Dry white wine and water (mixed half and half) to cover
Salt
Pepper

PROCEDURE:
1. Melt the butter in a skillet or casserole large enough to hold the trout. Add the chives and cook very briefly.
2. Add the salt, pepper and herbs.
3. Gently place the trout in the pan. Cover it with the wine and water and cook at a simmer for about 15 minutes, or until the fish flakes when tested with a fork.
4. Remove the trout to a serving platter. Serve with a sauce such as hollandaise if it is to be eaten hot or a homemade mayonnaise if it is to be eaten cold. A quick herb sauce (see below) can be made with the leftover cooking liquid.

Herbed Fish Sauce

INGREDIENTS:
Leftover cooking liquid from poaching fish
Enough beurre manié balls to thicken reduced liquid
   (These can be made and stored in the refrigerator or freezer by combining half sweet butter and half flour, blending them together into a smooth paste and forming them into balls.)
Herbs to taste (tarragon, chervil, parsley, thyme, summer savory, basil, dill or whatever combination you prefer), chopped
Splash of white wine

PROCEDURE:
1. Strain the liquid into a saucepan and boil it over high heat. Reduce it until it is the amount and flavor you desire. Add more wine if it seems too bland.
2. Add a beurre manié and stir with a whisk until the sauce is smooth. Continue adding thickeners until the sauce is of the consistency you desire. If it becomes too thick, add more wine or water.
2. Add the herbs. Correct the seasoning if necessary. You may add salt, pepper or lemon juice.
3. Serve either on fish or as a side dish to be passed with the fish.

Pan-fried Trout

Clean very fresh trout and dredge it in salted and peppered cornmeal or flour. Fry it quickly in a buttered skillet. If the trout is very, very fresh, it will curl up slightly as it cooks. Eat it this way for breakfast, lunch or dinner with whatever else is available. The experience of savoring such a fresh piece of fish in its prime outweighs saving it to adorn a more elegant meal.

Lasagne con Funghi e Prosciutto

If you are lucky enough to find a morel in the woods, eating it while it is still very fresh is a must. All too quickly morels lose their flavor and their ability to hold together. As they age, they simply crumble into pieces if they are touched.

If only one or two are found, slice them into a sauce instead of waiting to find more. You may never find them. If you have hit the jackpot and gathered a cache, simply sautéing them in sweet butter enhances their unique flavor. Use the hollow stem as well as the cap, for it is also delicious and the caps are small.

This recipe, given to me by a friend, turns morels into a feast.

INGREDIENTS:

> *1-1/2 pounds lasagna pasta*
> *4 pounds morels or shiitakes*
> *1/4 cup cooking oil*
> *6 tablespoons butter*
> *1/3 cup minced onions*
> *1/2 cup plum tomatoes*
> *2 tablespoons parsley, chopped*
> *Béchamel sauce (see below)*
> *3/4 pound prosciutto, cut in thin strips*
> *1-1/2 cups freshly grated Parmesan cheese*

PROCEDURE:

1. Clean the mushrooms. For shiitakes, cut into thin strips, excluding stems. If using morels, leave them whole, including stems.
2. In a large skillet or pan, heat the oil and half the butter. Add the onion and cook until translucent. Add the mushrooms and tomatoes. Stir over high heat. Do not burn. Add salt and pepper. Cook for about 5 minutes, until any liquid in the pan has evaporated. Turn off the heat and set the pan aside.
3. Set salted water to boil for the pasta. Preheat the oven to 400°. Make the béchamel sauce.

4. Butter a lasagna dish. Boil the pasta for only a minute or so until it is al dente. Pour off the hot water and cover the pasta with cold water. Remove the pieces one at a time, dry them slightly on a clean dish towel and place them in the lasagna pan. When the bottom of the pan is covered, spread a thin layer of mushrooms over the pasta, then a thin layer of béchamel over the mushrooms. Sprinkle the prosciutto, parsley and Parmesan cheese over everything. Repeat this process with all the mushrooms and prosciutto. Cover with a layer of pasta and spread with the last of the béchamel sauce and a sprinkling of Parmesan cheese.

5. Place the dish on a high level in the oven and bake for 15 minutes, or until a light golden crust forms on the top. Allow it to rest for 10 minutes in a warm spot outside of the oven. Serve with Parmesan cheese.

Béchamel Sauce

INGREDIENTS:

4 cups milk
1/2 cup butter
5 tablespoons flour
Salt to taste

PROCEDURE:

1. Bring the milk to a boil.
2. Melt the butter in a pan. Stir in the flour and salt. Make sure there are no lumps of flour.
3. Add the hot milk a little at a time, whisking constantly. Continue to cook and stir until the sauce is thickened to the consistency of heavy cream.

JUNE

And what is so rare as a day in June?
Then, if ever, come perfect days.

—James Russell Lowell
"The Vision of Sir Launfal"

The Land

June ... the dazzle of days that brings forth so much flourishing growth. It is a month that fills the daytime hours with new blossoms, new leaves, new faunal arrivals and a brighter higher sun. June pushes in on you—a kaleidoscope of colors, smells, temperatures and sounds—almost too much to take in, if that is your aim. It is a time when one needs a bit of solitude to contemplate the explosion of the natural elements. All of nature is now in the fray, competing for food, space and air, struggling for a secure spot in the environment: the proper plants are growing with pale decorum while the rambunctious weeds are elbowing their way up and past them; both wild and tame animals are birthing, tending their newborns and searching for sustenance in the new growth and gardeners are aligning themselves with the tamed to prevent the encroachment of the feral. This is surely a time that confirms the adage about the early bird getting the worm, for no meek young hatchling is likely to be the heir of its biota.

Birds of all colors and songs are everywhere around our fields, nesting, singing, preying and being preyed upon. We missed our beautiful bluebirds for several days and went scouting around their house for a sign of life. We didn't find it. Their nest was empty, and there were telltale blue feathers and a blue egg on the grass below. I returned the egg to its nest in hopes that what appeared to be was untrue, and that the parents would come again to claim it. It was gone later, found by either the original culprit or another contender in the game of life. I have mourned the bluebirds and plan to reinforce the pole with metal next spring to make invasion of their house more difficult, but I learned when we first began our pilgrimage into this natural world that it cannot be consummately controlled. We may try by digging our weeds, spraying our trees and protecting our livestock, but it is Mother Nature who has the upper hand.

Along with the rest, the insect population explodes this time of year. Mosquitoes, deerflies and gnats attack both humans and animals, drinking their blood and leaving itchings and swellings. Flea beatles, cucumber beatles, gypsy moth caterpillars, codling moth caterpillars, aphids and others attack our garden plants, ignoring the pigweed and selecting cabbage or apple pippins for their daily meals. Carnivorous insects, such as ladybugs and preying mantises, become our heroes as they attack the slower moving vegetarians, and we commend their grand appetites and ferocious ways, even purchasing them by the bag to reinforce their natural numbers. When we find it necessary to use such natural toxins as rotenone or pyrethrum, we hope they will kill the vegetarians and fail to intimidate the carnivores.

A particular scourge this season has been the flea beetle, which arrives in multitudes, eats pinhole patterns in the most delicate seedlings, lays its eggs and then vanishes until the next wave of hatchlings some weeks later. This year extra rain has meant extra flea beetles, and lack of sunshine has meant less growth by the plants that flea beetles love, like eggplants, arugula and the brassicas: cabbage, broccoli and Brussels sprouts. My eggplant seedlings have been so stunted by beetle bites and weather that I have succumbed to buying some nursery plants, not my favorite Oriental ones, but the larger Western variety. They were sizable when I bought them, so they should survive a few lacy leaves.

Another yearly plague that comes to remind us we are not really in heaven is the gnat or no-see-um, a small black fly that resembles the flea beetle from afar. However, the object of this small soul's voracious appetite is not our immobile cabbage crop but rather our own blood and the flesh before it. Gnats love to buzz in large groups around a person's head, ready to attack at any moment. Fortunately their brains are not large, and they threaten more often than they bite. Wearing a wide hat keeps them circling mainly above the brim and generally out of harm's way, but when they do find their mark, the result can be unpleasant. The first bites of the year can produce welts the size of half an orange, even closing off an eye if near enough. As the season goes on, the wounds are less imposing, perhaps because the previous bites have created a certain immunity. Nevertheless, a frequent conversation heard in Cornwall is about effective deterrents to these minibeasts.

Recommendations include ingestion of vitamin B1 (said to make the person as nasty-tasting as the pill) or external slathering with vanilla extract, Vick's Vaporub or citronella. I have found a couple of natural commercial deterrents that smell mostly of citronella and pennyroyal work effectively—if briefly—and make the user fragrant indeed. Remedies for after-the-fact swelling and itching are Adolph's meat tenderizer (its active ingredient is papain, a papaya extract, recommended by the Red Cross to reduce swelling), ammonia, alcohol—and scratching.

If the above descriptions make June seem less than ideal, it still comes closer to a paradise than most months in New England. It is the best of times. For every obstinate weed there are a hundred blossoms, tamed and wild, to enhance a moment or an hour. For every biting gnat or deerfly there are butterflies, birds and dragonflies to observe with pleasure rather than pain. Flowers bloom and die in a profusion of color and sweet aroma. Trees provide greening shade. Grass makes a soft and cool mattress. And each morning offers a bright revision of the day before.

Even our growing poultry population provides daily diversion. Its numbers have changed in the last few weeks. The larger and more powerful of our last two adult roosters has been beheaded. In his authoritarian role he had become a belligerent and fanatic ruler of the roost. He so mauled the hens in his tyrannical enthusiasm that their backs were pecked or clawed clean of feathers, and when he threw one down, breaking her leg in front of us, he sealed his fate. Now the meeker of the original horde is reigning for the first time. I hope his newfound power will ease the memories of his love for the broody goose but not turn him into a tyrant.

To add to the poultry stock we bought eight day-old laying hens and twelve day-old broilers (bred for eating) on the first of June. We also purchased three baby turkeys, although we were told they were difficult to raise. We hope one will survive until Thanksgiving.

We have raised chickens for the last five years, mostly those hatched by our own hens (hence the multiple rooster problem). This year none of the older hens became broody, so reinforcements for the aging and unproductive layers had to be bought. The success of the roosters as food encouraged us to try raising fowl for that purpose as well.

We have raised this group together, first in a large wooden box heated with lights, then in a cheerless but safe and draftless room in the barn. Chickens observed from afar seem all of a cut, hardly expressing much individuality, but on closer scrutiny they are not so much the same. The "broilers" after three weeks of life are at least double the size of their peers, the "layers." They seem to eat constantly, and when they are satiated they loll about, engaging in none of the endeavors of our other chickens such as scratching, pecking at the ground and each other, chasing each other, cackling and roosting. Marked for the roasting pan, these do nothing but digest as quickly as possible so they can begin eating again. They have no energy to stand up and simply sit or lie in huddles of lethargy. They rarely even peep, conserving all their energy for the task of growing quickly to oven-ready corpulence. Of course they are bred for baking, but I would like to see one rebel, one individualist among them, an avian Ferdinand that would beat the odds by remaining skinny and showing some spunk.

All of our new chickens and turkeys are orphans, emerging in incubators somewhere far from their progenitors. Even those born under a soft, warm brooding hen's bottom must soon be removed, for our nesting cubbies are high off the ground to prevent mice, chipmunks or skunks from entering and feeding off the eggs. Baby chicks have no means of exit and soon they must eat and drink, a requirement nonmammalian mothers cannot handle alone. We must take them, avoiding as we can the agitated pecks of their parents, to our homemade incubator with its electric warmth and commercial food.

The geese and their passel of eggs have become another matter altogether. A bit more than halfway through June, I found a yellow, fuzzy peeper peering from beneath its mother's down. Since her nest was on the barn floor, since infant geese are considerably bigger than infant chickens and since the gander would have taken my arm off had I tried to remove the baby, I put food and water nearby and let the parents show their inherited expertise in rearing their young. Soon they produced three more squawking infants and have become vigilant and resourceful caretakers, prodding their progeny to eat, drink and eventually bathe in the plastic pool in the yard. The gander—usually a wanderer—stays resolutely by, never letting a little one roam far from its three protectors. All three adults express their innate distrust of us by hissing when we approach, even when we have food in hand. This instinctive intelligence, this suspicion of the "other," now prevails over their learned knowledge that we are indeed their custodians.

Other June births, seen but unattended by us humans, include fox kits, baby robins, frogs, toads and that plethora of uninvited seeds that sprout and grow vigorously, routing one's favorite plantings if allowed to do so.

The weed—that pejorative word—is really in the eye of the beholder. The edges of our lawn and woods for example, are full of such edible but little esteemed greens as pigweed, lamb's-quarters, purslane and wood sorrel. They make delicious salads, although they wilt quickly after picking. They are easy to grow, certainly. Are they weeds? The unopened flower buds of the milkweed taste like asparagus and can be sautéed in butter for an exotic wild-vegetable course. The succulent jewelweed is a favorite food of the chickens and geese, and for us it is a soothing balm to slather on a nettle sting. A medicine? On the negative side quack grass, crabgrass and plantain are nuisances, but they can be dug out or mowed over. Dock sends roots to the middle of the earth, but it doesn't spread rampantly. And then there is bindweed.

I once read an Agatha Christie story in which Miss Marple spent most of her time pondering a mystery while digging away at some bindweed struggling up through the stones of her garden path. By the end of the novel, the mystery was solved and all the bindweed had been uprooted from the path. Now, I admire Agatha Christie and her way with a story, but either English bindweed is different from American or Dame Christie doesn't know as much about gardening as she does about solving mysteries. Bindweed is so insidious that to eradicate it simply by digging in one small area within the time span of a simple murder case is a feat too preposterous to imagine.

Bindweed is a faintly pretty vine, if one can overcome one's prejudice about it. I once saw a very elegant china pattern that featured bindweed around its perimeter. It has pale pink blossoms, smaller than but similar to those of its domesticated relative, the morning glory; heart-shaped leaves; and flexible tendrils that grow quickly and twist themselves around any available plant or stem, sometimes bringing it to the ground in an unyielding embrace, sometimes choking its leaves and flowers. Its aboveground tenacity is irritating when it settles in among the raspberries or the cucumbers, but its infrastructure represents survival adaptation at its best, much to the dismay of the gardener. The root system of the bindweed is a masterpiece of guerrilla strategy. Each vine grows off of a seemingly endless lateral root that, according to my books, can extend for as much as sixty feet, something like a water main traveling along under the street sending up pipes to each house it passes. I believe that sixty feet is an understatement, however. This root is of a single piece, as brittle as its aboveground counterpart is pliant, and difficult to find because it often grows a foot or more below the surface. If one is lucky enough to get at it, it breaks so easily that pulling out a long portion is impossible, and to top it off, any broken bit—no matter how small—can and will produce with alacrity a whole new bindweed plant. If you throw your findings in the compost, yes, you'll have a pile full of incipient bindweeds. If you break it up by rototilling, you simply multiply what was there before.

I have spent many hours on my knees filling buckets with bindweed root that I scrupulously dug out, following it along its path and removing it piece by piece. I still have the stuff in the garden, not so much as I once had, but it is not vanquished.

By mid-June, bindweed and I have reached a curious détente. I pull up the tendrils, leaving the underground structure alone, since extracting it would disturb nearby vegetable plant roots. My hope is that it will weaken from lack of sun and its need to repeat the growing process, and finally give up the ghost. So far it has not.

The Garden

By the end of the first week in June, planting should be done for a time, but the sower must not be misled into relaxing vigilance over the garden. Plants are newborn babes and need the nurturing and tending that a child would demand. Their silence is no indicator of their needs. They can only tell you of those by withering, browning, refusing to grow or simply dying.

Different sorts of plants have different needs, and when subjected to the same environment in a garden, it is up to their keeper to make adjustments in their individual areas. Tomatoes need warm earth to grow well, so mulching with leaves can be put off until the ground is thoroughly heated by the summer sun. Eggplants need lots of fertilizer and water, so a can of water with a bit of fish emulsion added should be on their agenda. Peas like cool, humid days, so they can be mulched high with leaves to keep the earth under them chilly and moist. Potatoes can be plagued by the Colorado potato bug, which concentrates only on them and their eggplant relatives and must be either plucked off and destroyed or sprayed with an organic potato-bug killer. Every species of plant is susceptible to its own pests and bacteria, which is another reason for interplanting many species. No pest is then likely to ravage an entire crop.

There is an old Wall Street rule of diversifying investments—buying many different sorts of stocks and bonds—so if one kind does poorly, another will probably not and pick up the slack of the underachiever. The gardener's investments are plants, and diversifying them allows the garden to grow more securely. One year may produce poor broccoli, peas and lettuce but great melons. A cool, rainy summer is likely to intimidate the tomatoes, but their cousins the potatoes will be wonderful. A drought may stunt the corn but leave the beans unaffected. A beetle infestation may undo the cucumbers but ignore the cabbage. These caprices of nature can't be wholly compensated for, but diversification, as well as forethought and daily observation of the garden, may divert calamity.

By June the seeds and seedlings we sowed in April and May are big enough plants that they can be mulched. Mulch, related to and second only to compost, is another basic requirement for the organic garden. Its primary use value is to cover the area around the growing plant, deter moisture evaporation and keep down weeds. It can be made of anything from old pieces of carpet or black plastic to such natural materials as dried leaves or straw.

In our first year of gardening, I attempted to down the quack grass with black plastic. The grass grew right through it, pulverizing the plastic, which—twelve years later—I still dig out of the ground on occasion. It was then that I began collecting leaves, which have been my standard mulch material ever since. I supplement with salt hay or straw, but leaves from our own trees are my elementary garden cover.

For most of the garden I use leaves that were raked last fall and earlier this spring and lie in a vast pile in the north corner by the fence. They are the remnants from maple, willow, beech, apple, pear, linden, ash and birch trees. Over the winter they have compacted into layers that are wet, heavy and stuck together, but once out in the air and light, they will dry and allow moisture through. These simple leaves keep weeds at least partially in abeyance, prevent moisture from evaporating too rapidly, keep earth from eroding in a rainy time and, in their slow but steady disintegration, return the nutrient elements to the earth that they usurped in their initial growth.

Since our leaves are never enough to cover the whole garden, this year we invested in a wood-shredding machine to grind up some of the rising accumulation of branches and prunings. The machine, a great gas-powered behemoth, is gardening's answer to the food processor. It has managed to chew up a small mountain of dead shrubbery and turn it into a heavy and slowly decomposing mulch that covers the garden paths and contributes chips for the raspberry patch, fruit trees, blueberry bushes and various other shrubs—treasure turned out of a smoking, gulping mechanical monster.

Although mulch is a primary weapon in the war on unwanted weeds, it does not present a cure-all. The patch must still be watched and weeded. Luxurious weeds pop up a half-inch from many a vegetable root, threatening to overthrow it. These must be carefully extracted, disturbing the goodly plant as little as possible. Aphids and flea beetles are lurking about. A few of them can never destroy a healthy plant, but it is the business of the caretaker to be ever on the alert to possible problems.

When transplanting seedlings into the garden, any specimens left over at the end of a row are heeled in around the labeling stake to be transplanted, if necessary, in the place of dead kin. This year these extras have come in handy because cutworms, not usually a serious problem, have destroyed several baby plants. Cutworms hide in the ground during the day, come out at night and gnaw through any stem that is tender enough for the worm's mastication. I deflect them with collars made of paper cartons or plastic bottles cut into one-and-a-half-inch pieces and placed around new seedlings. This is usually ample discouragement, but this year I didn't have enough collars to go around, and a few collarless representatives were annihilated and have had to be replaced.

Replacing these is a task I prefer to do in the evening, just before sunset. A sunny midday is never a good time to transplant anything, for the hot sun wilts the disturbed plants as they struggle to reorient themselves. Shading them with old newspapers or overturned clay flowerpots after transplanting is a good move if midday work is necessary, for then they can concentrate on realigning their roots and gathering the earth's nutrients rather than on photosynthesis, an essential role for a plant, but often too much for it after a transplanting occurs. I also try to keep as much earth as possible around the roots during transplanting. Never expose roots if you can help it. Keep them covered with earth and be gentle but firm when you insert them into their newly watered home. Also try to find (and kill) the cutworm that did the dirty deed to the previous resident. It is often waiting within a few inches of the plant it beheaded. Once you've gotten rid of it, put a collar around the new plant just in case the worm has a friend.

All of this may sound complicated and excessive, but it isn't. Transplanting properly takes no more time than doing it crudely. It simply responds to the needs of a young plant, which is as sensitive and alive as any animal life-form responding to its surroundings and trying to survive.

Not all plants are equally successful at beating the odds in the survival game, but the examples of those that have made it are a formidable number. When you see plants growing out of crevices in the middle of a major New York City highway, try to imagine what a struggle they have had to endure and how determined they must be to do so.

My peppers, broccolis and eggplants are not made of such hardy stuff. Rather than evolving in such a way as to best adapt to a specific biota, they are bred by us to fulfill a different role: to be eaten. We develop seeds not for their ability to procreate and spread, but for their food-producing capacities. Seeds cultivated in one climate are planted in many others, each different in a hundred ways from the original. Adaptation to site has no time to occur naturally, so seeds may have less stamina and genetic will to survive. We made them, so it is up to us to help them along.

Our vegetable garden isn't the only site of growing things around the yard. There are perennial borders, a row of daylilies, a plot of peonies, a bed of azaleas and a kitchen herb garden. It is this latter spot just outside our kitchen door that I must now consider. It is in a small, rectangular area fenced to accommodate the two espaliered peach trees, a lurid purple clematis vine, a never-blooming wisteria and a clothesline. Beneath this high-flying assortment is a bit of grass and our herb garden. Part perennial, part annual, this small space is a mainstay of our kitchen endeavors. After thirteen years I still glory in the extravagance of being able to walk ten steps to pick the freshest of herbs for cooking, drying or freezing, or for making a potpourri to perfume a closet or drawer.

The luxury of herbs has come to me only in adulthood, for my childhood family rarely used them. Many of the basics we cook with today were unheard of in west Texas around 1940. Basil, oregano, marjoram, tarragon and cilantro might as well have been produced on Mars. Parsley, mint and musty boxes of powdered thyme and sage were all I knew about then. When I first discovered fresh basil as a bride, I put it in so many dishes that my new husband cried for help.

Today I have more than one or two herbs with which to garnish meals. Sorrel springs forth as early as April, followed by three sages, thyme of several kinds, peppermint, spearmint, marjoram, chervil, tarragon, winter savory, oregano, chives, lemon balm, tansy and lovage. Later I plant the annuals: basil, summer savory, coriander (cilantro) and parsley (actually a biennial) as well as nasturtiums, which can be used in salads or as "false capers" by preserving the unopened flower buds in vinegar or salt.

Also summering just outside the door are four of my most valued belongings: a twelve-year-old rosemary bush, two huge pots of bay laurel (two varieties) and a bedraggled lemon verbena. Not hardy in this area, I drag them into a south window for the winter and back out again for the summer. They provide year-round flavors that can't be duplicated in a jar.

I feed these aging potted herbs fish emulsion in the summer but a seaweed fertilizer in winter, since fish emulsion can be redolent in a closed room. I have transplanted them over the years until now the bay laurels are in the largest clay pots available. They are well over seven feet high and provide more bay leaves than a family could ever use. The rosemary, also in an outsized pot, is a dense bush that fills a room with fragrance as one brushes past it. The lemon verbena is tough. On occasion it loses all its leaves, plays dead and then revives to bloom and produce again. Its rough, narrow leaves are a quick substitute for lemon flavoring in tea, ice cream or Veal Marengo.

Raising herbs can be one of the easiest of gardening tasks. Most of them flourish in less-than-perfect soil and with less-than-plentiful sunshine. They may be grown almost anyplace, whether in pots on a windowsill or in garden knots of ornate topiary design that must be pruned and patterned to keep them in the showcase condition they require. The only place they shouldn't be kept is in the kitchen, or at least not near the stove, for the residues from spattering grease are never good for a living, breathing plant.

A hardy and problem-free herb I have used more and more over the years is the stately lovage. A relative of celery, but with a more pungent aroma and flavor, it gives a stew, stuffing or soup a distinctive, earthy flavor. It grows rampantly, so I plant it in a large plastic flowerpot buried in the ground and cut out at the bottom. This way it receives the drainage it needs but cannot spread. By now my lovage plant has filled the pot's fourteen-inch diameter and will be ready next spring for a subterranean repotting. I shall put the extra divisions along the edge of the field and let them prosper there if they will.

The Kitchen

By June there is no need to search the larder for a can of this or that left over from last year in order to claim homemade fare at the table. Our June dinners are fresh and green, plates piled high with an abundance of tender young lettuces dressed in fresh vinaigrettes, barely cooked Oriental greens misted with rice wine and chicken broth or buttery, sweet spinach without that harsh grocery store taste that has given it such a bad reputation among young children. This is the best time for greens, before the summer heat toughens and embitters them, and all of our dinners include them in some form. Herbs from the kitchen patch all add their unique scents and flavors to everything from fish to pasta. The ripening of the first snow peas mitigates the pain of the end of asparagus season at midmonth. If anything can equal that first pure taste of a newly surfaced asparagus, it is the first crunchy sugar snap pea just picked from the vine.

Strawberries, too, bring the sugars of the earth to the surface for us. The crop from our four-year-old bed has been lavish this year, providing quarts for neighbors and friends and full freezer jars to remind us of such beneficence next winter. Rhubarb continues to supply us with another distinct flavor and, combined with strawberries, is a lively treat fitting for its singular time in June.

Many of our meals this month shift between Occident and Orient in their focus and flavors. The herbs, lettuces and fruits create the tastes of Europe and America while the delicate snow peas, Oriental cabbages and greens create those of the East.

I have been to the Far East several times now, eating my way from place to place through China, Japan and Taiwan. My interest in Asia has not diminished since I tried to dig a hole to China when I was a child. My interest in Asian cuisine grows steadily. Despite its lack of the grape, milk and maize, it is the most varied and intriguing of cooking processes. It harbors fewer food taboos, more economical cooking methods and a wider range of resources than any cuisine I know. Done at home with fresh ingredients, it is unsurpassed.

Ten years ago our daughter spent some months studying Mandarin Chinese in Taiwan. I visited her there in the spring, a comfortable time to be in that sometimes steamy place, and a time of numerous freshly ripened foods, all beautifully arrayed in outdoor markets. Fresh lichee nuts, purchased on the stem they grow on, are unforgettable. Other fruits with no Western names are also memorable for their succulence and flavor. These are for the most part unavailable in the northeastern United States, but many of the vegetables are not, and some are now ripening in the garden to be made into dishes good for both your health and your palate.

My Chinese cooking larder is supplemented periodically by a trip to Manhattan's Chinatown, where I buy soy sauce, hoisin sauce, rice wine, bamboo shoots, fresh gingerroot, water chestnuts, fermented black beans, tiny dried shrimp, sesame oil and such spices as Szechuan peppercorns and five-spice powder. Many of these essentials to Chinese cooking are more widely available these days, as are Chinese kitchen utensils like the wok and the cleaver, which, of all my array of kitchen equipment, are the two items I would be most loath to give up. Once you have mastered it, the cleaver is a five-dollar food processor with no extra parts to wash. It minces, pulverizes, juliennes, dices and serves as a spatula for transporting the chopped foods to the wok. The wok stir-fries vegetables in seconds, deep-fries in a perfectly shaped space and, with the help of a bamboo steamer, can steam layer after layer of whatever needs it. I use an eighteen- or twenty-inch wok even for small amounts of food because it has room for stirring about without spilling or splattering, and washing a large pan takes no more effort than washing a small one.

Soup Taipei

In Taipei in 1981, the streets contained abundant fast-food counters, different in every respect from those in the United States except for speed. My favorite fast meal was concocted in stainless steel booths the size of a closet and open to the street. These were Taiwanese soup kitchens. For a few pennies one could buy a large bowl of soup to order. Its base was chicken broth, and it usually had noodles and vegetables, but one could specify pork, chicken, beef, sausage, tofu or any combination of the above to be plopped on top of the basic dish. One simply stood on the street and slurped it down, a reviving and delicious nosh.

My homemade version of this snack is a nightly supper in Cornwall when I'm there alone in June. The Oriental greens are up and begging to be eaten, and what better low-calorie, high-flavor meal than Taiwanese soup.

I used to shop in a small store in New York's Chinatown frequently. Whenever I asked the grocer what a particular unfamiliar vegetable was used for, he always said "soup." Then I thought he was joking. Now I believe he was correct.

INGREDIENTS:

Rich chicken broth
Rice noodles or wheat noodles
Tofu
Greens, Bok choi, Taisai, Chinese cabbage or other vegetable
Scallions or chives
Diced pork, chicken, beef, shrimp or other meat
Soy sauce

PROCEDURE:

1. Bring the broth to a boil.
2. Add the noodles and boil for 1 to 2 minutes.
3. Add remaining ingredients. Heat through and serve.

Green Chinese Vegetables

INGREDIENTS:

Asparagus
Small Bok chois (Qing type, left whole)
Dried Chinese mushrooms or fresh mushrooms
Immature Chinese cabbages, left whole or large leaves sliced
Soy sauce
Salt
Cornstarch
Chicken stock
2 to 3 tablespoons vegetable oil
Rice wine

PROCEDURE:

1. If using dried mushrooms, soak them in boiling water. When they are tender, remove the tough stems. If using asparagus, cut it into lengths that

will be compatible with the lengths of the Bok choi and Chinese cabbages.

2. Pour about 2 cups of chicken stock into a wok. Add salt if necessary. Cook each green vegetable in the stock for about 2 minutes until cooked through but still crunchy. When each vegetable is done, remove it with a strainer and place it on a round platter in a pattern radiating out from the center. Leave a space in the center.

3. Remove the stock from the wok and add the oil. Fry the mushrooms in the oil. Add 1/2 cup of the mushroom water or chicken stock and a spoonful of soy sauce. Thicken it with 1 teaspoon of cornstarch. Place it in the center of the platter.

4. Return the remaining chicken stock to the wok and boil it with another spoonful of cornstarch, salt if needed and a splash of rice wine. When it is thick, pour it over the vegetables and serve.

Whole Peas with Butter and Herbs

Sugar snap peas are a Western invention derived from the Asian snow pea. Both are eaten whole. Aside from saving the cook the trouble of shelling, these crisp, sweet peas enhance any garden or kitchen. They are infinitely versatile, tasty raw or cooked, mixed with other ingredients or served by themselves. They may be cooked Chinese style, Western style or simply piled in the middle of the table, freshly picked and raw, to be dipped in an aioli and eaten with a wine accompaniment. As usual, the key to these recipes is the freshness of the vegetables.

INGREDIENTS:

Sugar snap peas, strings removed
Fresh sage or thyme, chopped
3 to 4 tablespoons sweet butter
Salt
Pepper

PROCEDURE:

1. Melt the butter in a skillet. Add the chopped herbs (sage is especially good, but only if fresh), then the peas. Cook quickly, stirring to prevent them from burning. Remove them from the heat when the peas are bright green and still a bit crisp. Salt and pepper to taste.

2. Serve immediately.

Snow Peas with Mushrooms

INGREDIENTS:

1 pound snow peas, strings removed
3 to 4 tablespoons corn oil
Mushrooms to taste (Chinese straw mushrooms are delicious and can be
*   used whole; shiitake mushrooms may be sliced and have a meaty*
*   flavor that combines well with the peas.)*
2 to 3 tablespoons rice wine
Salt

PROCEDURE:

1. Heat the corn oil in a wok or skillet. Add the snow peas and mushrooms. Cook, stirring continuously for 1 to 2 minutes until the peas are bright green and still crisp. Add the rice wine and salt.
2. Serve immediately.

Glazed Fresh Strawberry Pie

This first fruit of the season comes in with a bang. We eat strawberries for breakfast on cereal, plain for lunch and as ice cream, pie or shortcake after dinner. I make jam and freeze crushed berries with a little sugar to be used in ice cream or sauce later in the year. I invite people over to pick.

Strawberries are one of the fruits that retain the highest pesticide residues, so access to unsprayed ones is a benefit for the cook. If you don't raise your own, try to find a local farm that grows them organically.

This recipe makes one large (11-inch) pie or many tarts, the number depending on the size of the tart pans.

INGREDIENTS:

2 quarts whole, fresh, ripe strawberries, washed and picked over
8 ounces cream cheese, room temperature
1-1/2 cups superfine sugar
2 tablespoons lemon juice or 1 teaspoon almond extract
1 teaspoon grated lemon rind
2 tablespoons milk
3 tablespoons cornstarch
1 baked pastry crust (see November) or 8 baked tart crusts (or 16 if the
*   tart pans are very small)*

PROCEDURE:

1. Mix 1/2 cup of the sugar and the cream cheese, lemon juice or almond extract and lemon rind. Add the milk, if necessary, until it is the

consistency of whipped cream. Make sure to beat it until the sugar is no longer granular to the taste.

2. Spread this mixture evenly into the baked pastry crusts.

3. Place the fresh strawberries on the cheese mixture stem side down, as close together as possible.

4. Mash or put the rest of the strawberries through a food processor. Add 1 cup sugar and the cornstarch. Cook until the mixture is thick and the liquid has become clear. Cool.

5. Pour the mixture over the berries in the pie. Chill.

Fruit Ice Cream

This recipe may use strawberries, raspberries, blackberries or peaches. Whatever the fruit, the result is far removed from even the best commercial ice cream.

INGREDIENTS:

1-1/2 quarts ripe strawberries or other fruit, washed and picked over
  (If peaches are used, they should be peeled. If raspberries are used, they should not be washed.)
1 cup superfine sugar
2 cups light cream or milk
2 cups heavy cream
1 teaspoon vanilla extract
1/2 teaspoon almond extract

PROCEDURE:

1. Thoroughly mash the fruit so that large, hard, frozen bits of it will not settle in the ice cream. A food processor can do the job in seconds, but you must be careful not to overdo it and end up with a puree. Sprinkle half the sugar over it and set aside.

2. Mix the remaining ingredients and put it into an ice cream freezer. When this cream mixture is fluffy and partially frozen, add the fruit and continue to freeze until the ice cream has reached the consistency you like.

3. If you are making this ahead of time, you may reserve it in your freezer. It will, however, get very hard. (I prefer to prepare the ingredients ahead and then pop them into the ice cream freezer at the last minute. Then I serve the ice cream immediately when it is done.)

Frozen Strawberry Jam

Because it isn't cooked, this jam tastes quite different from the boiled variety. It is kept in the freezer until time to use it. Then it can be stored in the refrigerator.

INGREDIENTS:

1 quart ripe strawberries, washed, picked over and mashed
2 to 4 cups sugar, depending on how sweet and how stiff you prefer jam
Lemon juice to taste
1/2 bottle of fruit pectin

PROCEDURE:

1. Combine the mashed fruit and sugar. Let it stand for a few minutes.
2. Add the lemon juice and fruit pectin. Stir it for 3 to 5 minutes until the fruit is set.
3. Ladle the jam into small freezer jars. Allow it to set at room temperature for 24 hours. Store in the freezer until ready to use.

Strawberry-Rhubarb Pie

INGREDIENTS:

3 cups sliced rhubarb
3 cups strawberries
2 cups sugar
5 tablespoons instant tapioca
1 teaspoon almond extract or 1 teaspoon nutmeg
Dash of salt
4 tablespoons sweet butter
1 prebaked, 11-inch pastry crust, plus enough dough for an upper crust
  (see November)

PROCEDURE:

1. Heat oven to 400˚.
2. Stir together all the ingredients except the butter, and place in the crust.
3. Cut slices of butter over the pie mixture. Cover with the upper crust, cutting holes in it to vent escaping steam.
4. Bake for 45 minutes or until the fruits are soft and bubbling and the crust is nicely brown. Serve while still warm or at room temperature.

JULY

*Summer afternoon—summer afternoon; to me those
have always been the two most beautiful words in the
English language.*

> —Attributed to Henry James by
> Edith Wharton

The Land

I prefer summer morning, because it suggests a beginning, an opening out into brightness. Picture it: the early morning of a sunny summer day, long rays of light filtering through the pine trees, reflecting in the motes of dust that float languidly on their way to nowhere. There is still dew on everything, for the sun is not high enough to send it back into the atmosphere. It is sprinkled over leaves and grass in sparkling prisms of light, droplets collecting in the centers of the spiderwort flowers and the saucered leaves of lupine and nasturtium. Dew soaks through the tired gardening sneakers as they move across the grass to the chicken barn to open the doors, change the water and enjoy the rooster's preening crows and the geese's honking cacophony as they herd their growing offspring down the ramp and into the yard. The goslings are big enough to wander now, but they do so in a close-knit group, the young ones never allowed more than a few feet from their polygynous elders. They rarely eat the commercial feed we provide during this season, but keep the lawn closely mown by ingesting enormous amounts of grass, which promptly emerges as another kind of green manure.

To me, summer mornings are the best time to be in the garden. Remnants of the coolness of the night touch the skin and give the lungs stamina for hoeing, weeding and watering. Birds circle vigilantly, waiting for a back to turn so they can filch a pea or bean. Butterflies bask on milkweed blossoms. Clear colors abound until the sun rises higher and casts its whitening rays over all. Summer mornings, summer afternoons … All are summer's pleasures.

With spring planting over and weeding slowing a bit, July gives us time for the vacationer's pleasures. We swim at the lake, play tennis, take in one of the movies in town and read the sorts of books that can be finished in a day or two. Sometimes we lure friends into going on a picnic, taking a basket of cold chicken, potato salad, fresh raspberries and wine and trudging to the brook, or even taking a tray of food to the table under the willow trees to eat, swat bugs and gaze at the distant mountains and nearby flowers.

One member of our family doesn't particularly like picnics. Long ago, when we traveled across a bay to get to a beach on Fire Island, a picnic was acceptable to him, for it was necessary accompaniment to surfing and lying in the sand. Nowadays, with no beach to pull us, an alfresco lunch under the willows or by the waterfall has little appeal for him. He thinks carrying dishes and food in and out is a waste of time and energy, if not a pain in the neck. The beauty of the garden or the forest, the cooling breezes, the bird songs, the ever-different dapple of sunlight, the earth smells—simply the change of environment—are of no consequence to this extreme pragmatist. On the other hand, to me a picnic is an excellent idea in every sort of climate save a tornado, thunderstorm or blizzard.

I love the planning, preparation and packing, the pilgrimage to a different place to have a new eating and living experience. To me, cold chicken always tastes better on a rock by a waterfall, never mind the ants or mosquitoes. Wine has a fragrance that meshes with the aromas of wild mint, pine woods and earthy bogs, changing it in a positive way. I guess I'm a sucker for surroundings.

Once, at least twenty-five years ago, when we were young and newly mortgaged to our house in Brooklyn, we went off to Canarsie in southern Brooklyn to find inexpensive bushes for our little back garden. We found a nursery down near the ocean with acres of rhododendrons and azaleas but also tomato and eggplant seedlings and basil plants. After we had made our few modest purchases, the elderly Italian owner invited us to have a glass of homemade wine under a grape arbor at the back of the nursery. I shall never forget it. A few dozen yards from a four-lane major thoroughfare in the midst of a metropolitan area, the world changed. We sat around a rustic table covered with oilcloth beneath a bower of infant grapes, drinking wine from a carafe, chatting idly and enjoying a peace we would leave behind only a few yards away. The wine was fresh and fruity, the conversation friendly but not memorable, the setting a fragment transplanted out of another time and place. It couldn't have been better, and it was the *all* of it, not merely the wine.

The next spring we returned to find a bulldozed scar and the beginnings of an apartment complex, the end of a bit of heaven in the bowels of Brooklyn.

My earliest picnic memories are of a place that still exists, called Buffalo Gap, Texas, at the state park just south of the town. Buffalo Gap is a village about fifteen miles south of my hometown, so named because buffalo herds once ranged between the two mesas that flank the present town. It was settled before Abilene and was once the county seat, but all that changed when the east-west railroad was built and came through Abilene instead of its more prosperous rival. There was discussion among Abilenians that, what with the railroad bisecting their town and bringing in the advantages of a mass transportation system, it should surely be the new county seat. The issue came to a vote and, as the story goes, on election day the citizens of Abilene stopped a westward moving train and at gunpoint (with the added incentive of a keg of whiskey) obliged the passengers to get out and vote—for Abilene, of course—thus swinging the election in their favor. With both the railroad and the mandate, Abilene became the largest town of Taylor County, growing to a population of about twenty-five thousand when I was young, and today about eighty thousand or one hundred thousand. Buffalo Gap has only a few hundred residents, but it has a natural richness that relieves the monotony of the surrounding area.

My part of Texas is a vast extended plain, flat and almost treeless to the horizon. We lived at the southern end of the Great Plains, an area called the Edwards Plateau. At Buffalo Gap there is an area called the Callahan Divide, a large gully or gulch in the otherwise level tableland, with crevices of red, iron-filled earth spilling into a low area filled with live oaks and dusty reminders of long dried-up streams. Here was the state park, and to me it was surely the Garden of Eden—of which I had heard much at Sunday school—returned to the planet.

We would go there from time to time, taking a picnic basket with fried chicken, potato salad, fresh coconut cake and fruit punch. Mother would spread a tablecloth on a wooden picnic table in the shade of a tree and lay out the food. We were usually there alone as I remember, so we probably went in the fall or early spring. My parents would sit and talk at the picnic table under the oak trees, hardly noticing me, absorbed in their own reflections while I for those few hours felt a freedom I did not otherwise know. I ran willy-nilly down the iron-red fissures, my legs barely able to keep up with my flying body. I imagined I was hurtling down Mount Everest, the height immense to a young mind so accustomed to the horizontal. I explored gullies and creek beds, never fearing the rattler or the scorpion. I noted the instant cooling that a live oak afforded when you came under its branches out of the simmering southern sun. I breathed the freedom of the uncivilized. I was the wind, the bird's song.

I even returned to the table to eat the elegant repast served up by my mother, a lady who never dreamed of being a wild thing, but whose culinary instincts brought me back to the polished world of people.

Now it is our grandchildren who fly recklessly down our own grassy back hill in Cornwall while we sit applauding their daring, sometimes even entering into the action. I have taught them how to roll down the incline sideways with arms extended above their heads, preferably holding onto the hands of a partner. Though their two- and three-year-old arms are a bit short for such stretching, it has become a popular after-dinner sport. Even a few of us grown-ups engage in a healthy tumble, using the babies' need for a partner as an excuse.

I recently spoke on the telephone to one of our granddaughters. She talked about "tumbling down the hill," and I hope this memory will stay with her as mine has and that our little hill will grow in stature for her as the red gulches of Texas have for me.

The Garden

Local lore has it that corn must be "knee high by the fourth of July," and ours just made it. Actually, the replacement seed we put in to succeed that which failed to germinate in the cold days of early June is a bit puny, but the rest is flourishing, a sign of many golden-grained meals ahead.

Another maxim, this one heard in the Southwest, is "Never buy a melon before the fourth of July," for it will not be sweet enough. Our melons, a month in the ground and a month in pots before that, are olive-sized, green, fuzzy infants, a laughable sight to a Texan thumping her first watermelon of the season. Although a New England melon could never compete with a southern one, this is slow even for our northern climate.

The rest of the garden, however, is thriving. It puts on a great show of growth this month, visibly changing from day to day. Weed-whacking generates mounds of developing compost that steams as it "cooks" bolted lettuce and pigweed into primal soup. Winter squash invade the whole area, spreading their prickly leaves into the asparagus patch and the strawberries, crawling over the fence and out into the open field. Zucchini and yellow squash are doing their thing, which means producing almost too much to deal with, even though we planted only one mound of each.

Carrots, peas, beets, broccoli and green beans mature in abundance. By mid- to late July, new potatoes may be "stolen" and are wondrously delicate and sweet when cooked and eaten within an hour of digging them up. Stealing potatoes is defined as digging around the stems of a potato plant with considerate fingers—never trowels—until a sizable spud is felt. It may then be gently extracted without disturbing the rest of the growing plant. These early forms have thin skins and a delicate grain. We cook them skin and all after a good scrubbing.

Toward the end of the month, our Chinese greens and cabbages and most of our lettuces and peas are finished. In the raised bed the slow-growing parsnips, carrots, salsify, kale, fennel and Brussels sprouts lop over into the rows that housed these greens, filling the space with their own greenery.

As one crop is finished, I replace it with new Bok choi, Chinese cabbage and several new lettuces. I try to do this during a patch of cloudy, cool weather, for these species don't germinate well in the heat. If there are no cool days, autumn greens may be germinated indoors and then transplanted outside, protected them from the ravages of the midsummer sun by a shade of lath or cheesecloth. They may languish during a very hot spell, but if kept well watered, they will survive to flourish through the cooler autumn days and provide tougher but still tasty greens for the table.

Outside the walls of the vegetable garden, our cherry tree and our three rows of raspberries ripen to give us our second and third rounds of fresh fruit. Both of these succulent sweets establish an environment of avian nirvana, so each tree and bush must be netted to deter an onslaught of robins, swallows or jays. I've found that birds can get their wings or necks hopelessly caught in the large gridded, black plastic netting, so now I use a smaller gridded, white cotton or nylon sort.

The greatest amount of time spent in the vegetable garden this month is in maintenance and harvest. Maintenance requires weeding, watering and fertilizing if need be, and daily checking for pests and problems.

Because most of the garden is mulched, I weed by pulling up any invasive plant by the roots. This sometimes requires a great deal of bending, but it is a permanent rather than cosmetic solution to a particular weed problem. Weeds growing through a heavy mulch are easy to extract, and their numbers are few. In the raised bed, growing vegetables have formed their own protection, the leaves of each row merging with those of the next. Only rarely does a weed find its way through this dense cover.

Extensive watering hasn't been necessary this summer, but I have watered nonetheless during a dry spell. I use a system of drip hoses that seep water through an entire length of plastic tubing. In the morning I spread them around and leave them to drip away in each location for several hours. I avoid spraying the tops of plants in the midday sun and always try to water each area until the earth is thoroughly soaked. Superficial watering compels roots to reach for the damp earth surface. Once they are there and the earth dries out again, they can die. Again, mulching helps prevent moisture from evaporating from the earth.

I have fertilized nothing this year since its initial planting save the eggplants and melons. All else is growing apace and seems not to need it. It is even possible to overfertilize, but your plants, if you attend them, will tell you what they need.

Daily checking of the garden isn't always possible, but it is the surest way of averting disaster for cultivars. These daily checks can mean the difference between survival and death to a group of plants that is being attacked by some outside force. This summer, with frequent wet weather, has been a paradise for insects and microorganisms both good and bad for plants.

Slow and stodgy Colorado potato beetles in both their forms, larval and imago, can be found on the potato plants. I pick them off easily and by doing so each day avert any infestation. A few squash beetles hop about the squash and melons, perforating their leaves but ignoring the growing fruits. I sprinkle sabadilla and rotenone powder, and their numbers are reduced even further. The cucumbers are affected by a bacterial wilt that is common to them, in the same spot where they were infected eight or ten years ago. In the future I must remember to avoid that place when I plant them. I dust rotenone and sabadilla again and water the area thoroughly to soak these disinfectants into the ground. I continue this every few days, but still the plants wilt. Finally, all but four or five die completely, leaving me with only a few stunted cucumbers. Fortunately I have a friend who has excess cucumbers and I have excess everything else, so we trade.

Cabbage loopers, those charming green worms that remind me of Danny Kaye singing, "Inchworm, inchworm, measuring the marigold," are busy decorating the broccoli, cabbage and Brussels sprouts. I squash their bunches of eggs if I find them under a leaf, but I dislike putting even organic poisons on vegetables with crevices that can catch the toxins and prohibit them from running off in the rain. The loopers, or inchworms, do damage only to broccoli leaves and the outside of cabbages—the leaves you discard anyway—so I don't bother too much about them unless they become pervasive. Often when I am parboiling broccoli for the freezer, a dead green worm will float up to the surface of the water from among the tight flowerets. I wonder what happens to such specimens when I stir-fry or steam broccoli? Do we eat them unwittingly, adding a bit of extra protein to our diet?

Similarly, we found the same sort of protein in some of our cherries when we were pitting them to make pie. Even though the cherries in question were sour ones, we had enjoyed eating them raw as we picked. They are juicy, tart and fun to pop in our mouths as well as our baskets. While I was preparing the pie, someone else was using the cherry pitter, so I used my thumb to do the job. It was then that I found an occasional small white larva—a cherry maggot—nestled in just by the seed. The outside of the cherry seemed perfect, unsullied by faunal life, yet here was a potential insect encased in a lifetime's nourishment. When I confessed my findings, there was a sudden decline in the enthusiasm for the forthcoming pie and for munching cherries straight off the tree. We served the pie to guests without mentioning our discovery, and it was a success. If it included a stray white worm it most likely added to the pungent flavor and the vitamin content. Yet most of us do feel repugnance or queasiness at the idea of eating a worm. Remember the childhood riddle, "If you're eating an apple, what would you rather find in it, half a worm or a whole worm?" The right answer, of course, is a whole worm, assuming that the other half of worm would be residing in your stomach. And what is so bad about that? As a wise friend of mine once pointed out, a worm that is born in an apple consists primarily of apple. Why is it so loathsome? At worst, consider that you can at least *see* the odious worm, whereas chemical residues, which are much worse for your health than a cherry or apple maggot, go undetected.

All of us the world over have food taboos of one kind or another, some rational, some mysterious. There are cultures that welcome the addition of insects in various stages of life to their diet. Aztec peasants depended on a slimy lake alga for protein in a meat-deficient culture. Even modern Westerners consider snails a delicacy, though slugs, their relatives, are viewed with disgust. Many of us enjoy pork and shellfish, while to Jews and Muslims they are considered an abomination, something that would turn the stomach.

We have a Muslim friend from the far north of India. When he came to the United States for graduate school, he was dismayed by the widespread consumption of hamburgers, the very smell of which repelled him. Later, when he discovered they were made of beef, not ham, their flavor much improved. For a Hindu the opposite would have been true. I have known Americans to be equally repelled — indeed nauseated — when faced with the possibility of eating dog, horse or monkey, all acceptable foods in other cultures. Among Bedouin groups, the sheep's eye is the prize tidbit and is reserved for the most honored guest. It would be the most discourteous of acts to refuse it. What would you do if such a tidbit were offered you?

I was brought up by a shameless mother when it came to discouraging me from eating items she disapproved of. She told me blatantly that hard candy was made from the sweepings on the candy-factory floor and contained not only dust and dirt but bits of dead cockroaches and mice. The ingredients she attributed to bologna were hog's eyes, intestines, hairs and unnamed horrors that she only shuddered at. Despite this background of repression, when it came to alien foods I was undaunted. I have eaten hippopotamus, bull's testicles and fish eyes. They didn't bother me. I find the food preferences of other societies of great interest. Still, I don't relish worms.

When I was five or six, I slipped away sometimes to play with a girl across the street. We moved away just after I started first grade and I never saw her after that, but I remember that her name was Charlotte Sloan and her hair was that barely wavy blond that falls softly over the shoulders. Her family, like most depression families, kept chickens in the backyard in a coop of corrugated tin surrounded by the usual dusty chicken yard. A climbing rosebush grew up and over the tin roof, hiding it from the house and the eyes of watchful adults. We could reach the wavy roof by scaling the chicken-yard fence and then heaving ourselves up. We sat on this roof, hidden behind the roses, doing little but feeling the excitement of concealment, talking in low whispers and nibbling at the sweet, velvety petals of the roses. I still remember the soft texture of those pink circles on my tongue and their heady fragrance in my nostrils. I also remember in detail a story Charlotte told me while we were sitting up there on a warm summer day:

> You gotta be careful when you eat a petal that you don't eat a worm's egg by mistake. These big worms lay their eggs on roses. The eggs—they're real small, too small to see even—and they can hatch out in your stomach.
>
> My mama knew this lady who loved to eat rose petals, but she kept getting stomachaches, and one day she could feel something moving around in her stomach. Well, she went to the doctor, and he figured out what was wrong right away, so he told her to go home and not to eat anything for three days. That would make the thing in her stomach real hungry. Then she was supposed to come back to see him again.
>
> When she came back, he told her to sit down and keep her mouth open. He put a plate of food that smelled real good right there in front of her, told her not to eat any no matter how hungry she was, but just sit there and wait. Well, it happened just like he thought it would. Up out of her stomach and out of her mouth crawled this great big white worm looking for that food. It was as big as a snake—a big snake—and all white because it had been living in her stomach, and it crawled up through her throat and out her mouth all slimy against her tongue and all. She was lucky, because if it hadn't crawled out, she could have starved to death because it was eating all the food that she swallowed.

I never munched a rose petal after that, and I've never told anyone this strange story until now. At the time I didn't dare tell my parents for fear of punishment, but I lived for a while with the fear of a snake-sized worm growing in my stomach. From what sources Charlotte Sloan put together her story I do not know, probably from talk of tapeworms and Sunday school "Jonah and the whale" lore, but she was a great storyteller. And I still do have an aversion to white worms.

The Kitchen

There probably should be no recipes for this plentiful time of year. Each new mellowed product of the earth arrogantly sings its own praises to one's tongue and taste buds as it arrives straight off the vine. What sauce could improve the freshest haricot vert or broccoli bud? Our granddaughter eats them both while standing in the garden, the object just picked, with a two-year-old's excitement at finding food in "the wilds," choosing for herself one bean over another and popping it straightaway into her mouth. There is no middleman here, no authority figure imposing rules of etiquette or nutrition, no culture-bound objects like plates, spoons, napkins or recipes between the edible and the eater.

It isn't only two-year-olds who enjoy this rare experience. Once some years ago when I was entertaining a sophisticated urban friend, we found a wild raspberry patch on the edge of a meadow. We lay on the grass, laughed and ate seedy raspberries until we were satiated, so impressed were we with our discovery—food for the asking, food as it always used to be but rarely is anymore, just plain, fresh and there growing, waiting to be unearthed.

The July garden provides a multitude of flavors and flavor combinations straight from the earth. The herb garden gives us oregano, basil, parsley, dill, lovage, sage, savories, cilantro, thyme, rosemary and tarragon, all fresh, tender and waiting to be combined with the peppers, green and wax beans, green onions, shallots, beets, zucchini, cucumbers, Chinese cabbages, new potatoes, early broccoli and carrots. Cherries replace strawberries, which are replaced by raspberries and then blackberries. None of it needs much help to create a taste paradise.

These recipes make use of the flavors of July in various combinations. Singly, each vegetable stands on its own.

Pan Bagnas

Although in general the French are not noted for their treatment of the sandwich, there is a creation from the south of France that incorporates the flavors of the province between two pieces of bread. These ingredients are not all available in our New England garden. However, the idea of it is to combine flavors. A mix of local produce may combine in an equally palatable way, leaving only the fish and olive components to foreign manufacture.

INGREDIENTS:

1 large, hard-crusted Italian-style roll for each sandwich
Garlic cloves, peeled
Good olive oil
Tomatoes, sliced
Pickled onions (see below)
Sweet peppers, sliced
Sardines or tuna, packed in olive oil
Anchovies
Pitted olives
Hard-boiled eggs, sliced
Fresh basil
Faux capers (see below)
Lettuce
Salt
Pepper

PROCEDURE:

1. Slice the rolls in half. Remove a bit of the bread in the middle and rub the bread with garlic.
2. Put 1 or 2 slices of tomato and sweet pepper into the bottom of each roll. Sprinkle with the olive oil, salt and pepper. Build up each sandwich with any or all of the listed ingredients. When the mound seems as high as is possible to bite through, sprinkle with a bit more olive oil, salt and pepper and put on the top half of the roll.
3. Place the finished sandwiches under a weight, cutting board or platter to condense them and allow the flavors to mesh and the bread to soak up the juices and olive oil.
4. After the sandwiches have marinated for an hour, they are ready for serving or packing into a basket to take on a *pique-nique*.

Pickled Onions

This is an old Brown family method of rendering raw onions "burpless" and "onion breath-less." There were never any measurements.

INGREDIENTS:

New sweet onions
Ice cubes
Dash of sugar
Salt
Freshly ground pepper
Red wine vinegar, preferably balsamic

PROCEDURE:

1. Slice the onions into the thinnest rounds possible. Place them in a bowl and cover with ice cubes.
2. Sprinkle the sugar, salt and pepper over the ice cubes. Pour the vinegar over everythng. Marinate them for about an hour.

Faux Capers

INGREDIENTS:

Fresh unopened nasturtium buds, washed
White wine vinegar
Salt

PROCEDURE:

1. Cover the nasturtium buds with the vinegar and a little salt.
2. Refrigerate them for several days until they pickle. They will keep for several weeks.

Squash Blossoms with Capers and Mozzarella Cheese

Fresh squash blossoms are easy to find in season in the markets of Rome or Siena. In the United States they are rarely found outside the home garden, which is reason enough to raise squash. Any variety of squash or pumpkin will do so long as each blossom is open and at the peak of its vigor. Pick them when they are open and reserve them as you would a flower—the stems in a glass of water—until they are ready to be used.

INGREDIENTS:

Squash blossoms with a bit of stem on each, at least 3 for each diner
Mozzarella cheese
Capers, cured in vinegar
1 cup flour

1 cup water or milk
Salt
Pepper
Cooking oil

PROCEDURE:

1. Mix the flour, water, salt and pepper into a batter. Reserve.
2. Do not wash the blossoms, but check to make sure there are no insects lurking within the petals. Slice the mozzarella cheese into 2-by-1/2-inch wedges. Place a slice of mozzarella and 3 or 4 capers in the middle of each blossom. Close the petals around the cheese and capers. Twist the ends of the petals to keep them closed.
3. Heat the oil in a deep skillet or wok.
4. Dip each stuffed blossom into the batter and then place it immediately into the hot oil. Cook until lightly browned on the outside. This should take no more than 1 to 2 minutes.
5. Serve immediately. These can be simply piled on a plate for everyone to help themselves to. They are so delicious that no one will mind the lack of formality.

Fried Chicken Anita Perez

Anita Perez is a Haitian friend and one of the best natural cooks I know. I once showed her how I made southern fried chicken, and she has often made her own version for us since, a version that combines the grease of Texas with a creole flavor.

INGREDIENTS:

2 or 3 chickens, cut into pieces
2 or 3 garlic cloves, chopped
1/4 to 1/2 cup olive or corn oil
1/4 to 1/2 cup good wine vinegar
Salt
Freshly ground pepper
Fresh herbs (such as oregano, thyme, rosemary), chopped
Flour
Cooking oil

PROCEDURE:

1. Wash the chicken pieces and place them in a large bowl. Combine the garlic, oil, vinegar, salt, pepper and herbs. Pour it over the chicken, making sure all pieces receive the marinade. Let it sit for a while, occasionally turning the chicken with your hands.

2. Heat the cooking oil in a large skillet or wok. Put a few cups of flour in a large paper bag. Put the chicken pieces 2 or 3 at a time into the bag and shake vigorously until they are coated with flour.

3. Place the chicken pieces in the hot oil and fry them, turning when necessary, until they are browned on the outside and cooked but still juicy on the inside. Serve either hot or at room temperature.

Cherry Pie

Assembling this pie takes minutes. Pitting the cherries is another matter. This task should be approached in a relaxed and unhurried way, anticipating the grace of the end result. I have used a cherry pitter and a thumbnail. Both function equally well.

INGREDIENTS:

1 11-inch pastry crust (see November)
1 quart ripe sour cherries, washed, pitted and picked over
3 tablespoons instant tapioca
3/4 to 1 cup sugar, depending on sourness of cherries
1/2 to 1 teaspoon almond extract

PROCEDURE:

1. Prepare the pastry crust. Roll out half of the crust and fit it into the bottom of the pie pan. Bake it at 500˚ for about 8 minutes or just enough to dry the outside of the crust.

2. Combine all the other ingredients. Put the filling into the pastry shell and cover with the other half of the crust. Cut air vents into the crust. Bake at 400˚ for about 45 minutes until the pastry is browned and the cherries are soft. Serve at room temperature.

Blackberry Cobbler

I have been picking blackberries, wild and cultivated, all my life. We called them boysenberries in Texas and picked them at a farm outside of town. We also found them, plump and juicy, in overgrown, vacant lots on Long Island when we summered there. We have small, seedy wild ones in our fields in Cornwall, but we grow the garden variety. Unlike raspberries, they seem to gain in flavor when they are cooked. However, they are tasty raw as well. They may be substituted for raspberries in ice cream, jam or pie, but they are best in a cobbler.

INGREDIENTS FOR FILLING:

5 cups fresh blackberries
1 cup sugar
3 tablespoons sifted flour
6 to 8 pats sweet butter

INGREDIENTS FOR CRUST:

2 cups flour
2 tablespoons sugar
4 teaspoons baking powder
1/2 teaspoon salt
1/2 teaspoon cream of tartar
1/2 cup sweet butter
1/2 cup milk

PROCEDURE:

1. Preheat the oven at 400°.
2. Toss the blackberries with 1 cup of sugar. Pour into a 1-1/2-quart baking dish or soufflé dish. Sift the 3 tablespoons of flour over the berries. Dot the top with the butter. Set aside.
3. For the crust, sift the flour, sugar, baking powder, salt and cream of tartar into a bowl. Cut in the sweet butter until it is in small lumps and the mixture resembles a very coarse meal. Stir in the milk. Form it into a ball. Roll it out on a floured board to make a circle to fit the baking dish. The dough should be about 1/2 inch thick.
4. Cover the berries with the dough, attaching it to the rim of the dish so that it won't sink down. Cut a vent in the top. Sprinkle it with the sugar and bake for 40 minutes or until the crust is golden brown and the juice is bubbling.
5. Serve warm with whipped cream if you like.

Cherry Frozen Yogurt Sundae

On a ninety-degree day, the motherly offering of freshly baked pie is not worth the sacrifice. Here are two cooler ways to deal with fruit. If anyone complains, let them light the oven.

INGREDIENTS:

1 quart nonfat yogurt
1 large or 2 small egg whites, lightly beaten
1 cup sugar
1 teaspoon vanilla extract
1/2 teaspoon almond extract
1 quart fresh sour cherries, pitted
1 cup sugar (or to taste)
1 tablespoon cornstarch
Splash of dark rum

PROCEDURE:

1. Combine the yogurt, egg whites, sugar and seasonings. Stir until the sugar is dissolved. Put the mixture into an ice cream freezer and begin to freeze it by whatever process your freezer demands.

2. Put the cherries, cornstarch and sugar into a saucepan. Cook over medium heat until the liquid comes to a boil and the cornstarch clarifies. Set the pan in cold water. Add the rum.

3. Just before the yogurt is entirely frozen (when it is at the soft ice cream stage), add about 1 cup of the cherry mixture. Finish freezing. Serve with the rest of the cherry sauce as a topping.

Raspberry Granite

INGREDIENTS:

1 quart fresh raspberries, unwashed and picked over
1 cup water
1/2 cup sugar
2 tablespoons raspberry or strawberry jam
2 tablespoons kirsch

PROCEDURE:

1. Combine the sugar and water in a saucepan. Simmer until the sugar dissolves. Set it aside to cool.

2. Set aside a few raspberries for garnish. Puree the rest. Add all the other ingredients and mix together.

3. Pour the mixture into ice cube trays and cover. Freeze them until hard. Remove and blend the cubes in a food processor until they are the

consistency of ice cream. Return the mixture to the freezer for a short while. Serve with fresh berries as a topping.

Cornichons

By mid- to late July, there are more vegetables that can be eaten fresh from the garden. Canning, freezing or drying a few of them is a satisfying way to fill a rainy afternoon. These cornichons are made from the smallest of gherkin-type cucumbers. Ideally, they should be no more than two inches long when they are picked, but in reality it is difficult to find enough that are all the same size. I try to pick every day, and make a jar of cornichons when I have enough for a half-pint jar.

INGREDIENTS:
1/2 pint gherkin or cornichon cucumbers
A few small onions or the tops of the Egyptian onions, left whole
Pickling salt
1 large sprig fresh tarragon
3 or 4 peppercorns
1 bay leaf
White wine vinegar

PROCEDURE:
1. Wash the cucumbers and wash and peel the onions. Place them in a ceramic bowl and sprinkle them with the pickling salt. Let them stand overnight.
2. Wash and drain the cucumbers and onions. Pack them in a sterilized canning jar, filling it to within 1/2 inch of the top. Add the tarragon, bay leaf and peppercorns to the jar. Fill it with boiling white wine vinegar. Store in the refrigerator.

Dill Pickles

For the gherkins that seem to grow from 2 to 6 inches overnight, the answer is the dill pickle barrel. These pickles do not last forever, since they get saltier with each day of pickling, changing from half sour to sour to terrible. However, if one's family is about, they are usually gone before the last stage.

INGREDIENTS:

> *15 to 20 6- to 8-inch unwaxed, washed cucumbers, enough to line a*
> *ceramic crock standing upright*
> *Several garlic cloves, unpeeled and slightly crushed*
> *Spoonful of whole coriander seeds*
> *Spoonful of whole mustard seeds*
> *Spoonful of peppercorns*
> *2 or 3 dried hot peppers*
> *2 or 3 bay leaves*
> *12 sprigs of fresh dill with seed heads*
> *Water*
> *1/3 to 1/2 cup kosher salt*

PROCEDURE:

1. Stand the washed cucumbers on end in a ceramic crock. There should be enough that they stay in place without crowding.
2. Add all the other ingredients except the water and salt.
3. Mix several cups of water with the salt. Stir until the salt is dissolved. Pour the salted water over the cucumbers. Continue to add water until it rises several inches above the cucumbers. Jiggle the crock a bit to remove any possible air pockets. Place a heavy plate directly over the pickles to prevent them from rising to the top of the water.
4. Place the crock in a cool place. A perfect temperature is between 65° and 70° Cover the crock with a cloth to prevent bugs from entering.
5. Check the pickles every day. Remove any foam that forms on the surface. Add more spices if the brine seems bland. They should be half sour after 4 or 5 days and very sour within 7 to 10 days.

Dilled Green Beans

INGREDIENTS:

> *4 pounds green beans, or enough to fill 8 pint jars or 4 quart jars*
> *1 bunch fresh dill seed for each jar*
> *1 dried chili pepper for each jar*
> *1 garlic clove for each jar*
> *3 or 4 peppercorns for each jar*
> *5 cups cider or white vinegar*
> *5 cups water*
> *3 to 4 tablespoons salt*

PROCEDURE:

1. Sterilize the canning jars and lids. Wash the beans, leaving them whole but removing the strings and stems.

2. Put the dill seed, chili pepper, garlic and peppercorns into the jars.

3. If the beans are very young and tender, put them directly into the canning jars. If they are older and tougher, parboil them for 1 minute, then pack them into the jars. Stand them on end and try to have fairly uniform lengths.

4. Bring the vinegar, water and salt to a boil. Ladle the liquid into each jar, covering beans and filling each to within 1/2 inch of the top. More or less liquid may be needed, depending on how tightly the beans are packed.

5. Place lids on the jars. Cook the jars in a boiling water bath for 10 minutes.

6. Remove the jars from the water and let them cool. Once they are thoroughly cooled, test the seals. If a jar has not sealed properly, put on another seal and rebathe the contents.

7. Store at room temperature (do not freeze). Don't open them for a few weeks. Give the contents a chance to "marry," to mesh their various flavors.

August

... Butterflies, off Banks of Noon
Leap, plashless as they swim

—Emily Dickinson
"No. 328"

The Land

Spiders and butterflies, ferns and flowers hover silently in the sultry air as we harvest and play and count out the remaining days of summer, marking the dog days of August.

Our New England summers surprise us each year by the number of those heavy, wilting days they dole out. You know the kind—when clothes stick to the skin, bodies stick to the furniture and book pages and playing cards stick to the resting arm or hand. This year has given us fewer of these days and included more rain and cooler temperatures on its August agenda. The rain has been acidic, 10 percent higher than normal according to the local paper, and ferns and flowers have an unseasonal pallor and a dry, dappled bronzing at the edges of their petals. Our little backyard fish pool, which catches the overflow from the well, has suffered greatly from some unnamed blight, perhaps the acid rain. Fish have died, water lilies have not blossomed and the lotuses have never sprouted, although their roots were healthy when I transplanted them in the spring. The water continues to flow through, transparent as it should be, but it seems to carry a secret weightiness that impedes vigor.

Water ... Its purity was rarely an issue for people in the past. If water was polluted and caused disease, no one knew it and the gods were blamed for the pestilence. In Texas we blessed the redolently chlorinated stuff that poured from the kitchen tap, thankful it was there at all. In an area where drought was more common than rain and rivers were habitually dusty, dry beds, exposing the ancient strata of Stone Age encampments, we were grateful for the manmade lakes and tanks that provided our town with a means of survival, chlorinated though it had to be. For years we thought a little chlorine would fix up anything and that earthen sediments filtered out the contaminants that accumulated in surface water. Now we know this is not always true. We may gaze at water that shows no sign of murkiness, no smell of pollution, and wonder at what indispositions it hides.

My first unwitting encounter with the mysteries concealed in the depths of impure waters was at an August summer camp in the Texas hill country the year I was thirteen. I was old for a first-time camper and inept or unschooled in most of the competitive activities offered there: archery, riflery, tennis, canoeing, horseback riding and swimming. Since everything that one did well gained points for one of the two competing "tribes," the pressure was great to improve one's competitive position. My cabin mates—all practiced campers—rolled their eyes suggestively and assumed leaden expressions at my inability to amass points for the Kiowas and serve the tribe in winning prizes at the end of the term. I could have concentrated on arts and crafts, an easier area in which to gain distinction, but I was determined to achieve something in the more prestigious rivalries—sports. I had never taken swimming lessons before but could keep afloat, and after watching at the initial placement tryouts, I had copied the others and gotten myself into an intermediate class. I couldn't be that bad.

I became a water animal, spending as much time as I could practicing the backstroke, the crawl and the butterfly kick back and forth across the river in which we swam.

On the day of the tryouts for the intertribal contests, I waited anxiously on the shore, a skinny, awkward kid in her mother's twenty-year-old bathing suit, a scratchy, pea-green, woolen, college swimming-class number (Mother rarely threw anything away). Our group was called in to the water and told by the older tribal leaders to do our strokes when our names were called. I waited, hanging on to a raft, until all the rest had exhibited their skills. I continued to wait, shivering with cold and anxiety, while the leaders sitting on the raft discussed the possibilities of various other swimming Kiowas. I would like to say that I was bold, but I was not. After what seemed like a long time, I timidly asked if I might try out. They took only casual notice of me. I did a few strokes and heard a disinterested voice say, "Naw, you're not good enough," and then resume the conversation. I had failed.

Later, when my ear began to ache, ooze and plug up, the camp nurse poured peroxide into it and suggested that I had gotten the usual otitus from the bacteria-laden river water. She ran off with the tennis instructor shortly thereafter—with her peroxide—and the ear grew steadily more painful until I received some medical attention at home after camp was over. The ear has been vulnerable ever since.

That year another camper from our town was not so lucky as I in her encounters with the river. Its water carried the germs of polio into her young body and transformed it irretrievably into a motionless mass.

Water is a necessity for our lives and the lives of plants and insects. Yet water can conceal elements of devastation.

Egypt is a land that would be uninhabitable were it not for the Nile and the massive and intricate canal system that depends upon it. Yet, since the advent of the Aswan Dam, those waters, no longer flushed out into the sea by annual flooding, harbor a microscopic parasite that burrows through the skin and into the blood of humans and fish alike, slowly eroding health and life. As the tourist sails up the shimmering Nile past mud-brick villages, fields fed by ancient canals, water wheels turned by blindfolded donkeys, past children bathing and women carrying pots of water on their heads or washing vegetables, one observes that the ageless river is still—after five thousand years—the heart of a culture. It is lamentable that what brings life there also brings degeneration.

There is no place better than Egypt to observe the dependence of a society on a single source of water. There are some who believe that such mighty civilizations as those of Egypt, Mesopotamia and China could originally be controlled by a central force only because that force controlled the accessibility of water. This is a controversial theory, but there is indication that the earliest authoritarian states may have been irrigation cultures, and where there is irrigation, someone controls who gets water and when.

In the sparsely populated state of Ladakh, high in the Himalayas where rain does not fall, subsistence farmers depend on the water that melts off the high mountain slopes and flows down into the infant Indus River. Everywhere you walk in the river valley there are canals less than three feet wide that carry water to fields and cisterns. To be downstream from a neighbor who overuses this limited resource is not a position to be coveted, and even in tiny, pious Ladakh disputes arise. Similar conflicts undoubtedly arose five thousand years ago in Sumar and Egypt, and as populations grew, the need for controls over angry people demanding their share of a scarce commodity may have changed the social organization of these areas into authoritarian states.

Clean, usable water is something we all take for granted until it becomes unavailable. Only then are we reminded that it is indispensable. A sign in a Mexican hotel that says, "Do not drink, not potable," is a reminder, as is a young waiter in a Delphi restaurant who takes each half-filled water glass from an abandoned table and feeds the pots of basil on the terrace. The residents of Love Canal remind us. Searching for water on our own watershed of a hill has recently reminded us.

A year ago we decided we would build a guest house on our property, a small cabin of simple construction that could be used when our growing family overflowed the main house. Originally we planned no basement, insulation or central heating, but only a large wood stove that could be brought into service when needed. The local housing board dashed our economical hopes, and after many delays, we began to dig a cellar, a septic tank, a leaching field that could accommodate the Waldorf Astoria and a new well. The cellar came first, complicated by its location on the hill near a stream. Shortly after digging began, the bulldozer uncovered a spring about ten feet down, and soon after that another one, both dispatching steady streams of water that moistened and weakened the sides of the excavation and settled in stagnant pools on the clay floor of the pit. Several weeks of rain added to our problems by eroding the site even more and creating a topsoil so soft that the bulldozer couldn't function. The architect, contractor and consultants were daunted, and work stopped for more than a month. The springs continued to flow. Finally, an inspector approved a complex and expensive plan for drainage pipes, drainage gravel and more. I believe we could have built our original cabin for less than it cost, but we were in too deep to turn back—literally. It took modern, state-approved, engineering technologies, much time and much money to achieve what has been going on in our old house for two hundred years. We now have two structures with foundations of substantial proportions and in each a rivulet running from one corner to the other and then out and down the hill. The difference is that in one the water simply runs naturally out of the fieldstone foundation wall, across a dirt floor and away; in the other we have a profusion of plastic to guide it.

The next effort in our building venture was to find water where we wanted it, a well. The state's parameters were narrow, yet we wanted to pick the best possible spot. We heard that a new well in our town was producing over a hundred gallons a minute. At a friend's new house, the well came in at twenty-five gallons a minute. A well in Cornwall can't miss, for it is a labyrinth of underground water. Just to make sure, I hired a dowser, a friendly young man who had learned the craft from his father and had found a fine well just up the hill from us a few years before. He arrived with the tools of his trade: two pliant plastic sticks attached to each other at one end. (I was a little apprehensive about their material content. I expected an ancient, much-used iron or wood arrangement.) He explained his methods carefully and with good humor. (My apprehensions waned.) He walked the area with great concentration, eyes closed and face turning red, holding an end of each stick in toward his chest, the attached ends meeting in the middle to make an M shape. When the mechanism felt the pull of water, it was to turn downward, forming a W. He—or it— felt water almost immediately. The site was retested to make sure of it and then marked carefully. A set of brass weights told him we could expect to get about six gallons a minute at two hundred feet. This wasn't an extraordinary amount, but more than we would need for a small cabin with no washing machine and only one bathtub. Two hundred feet is deep, but we were told that a deeper well is less likely to be polluted, an important concern with farms nearby. Money crossed our palms (with a money-back guarantee) and we settled down to await the well digger.

A man of great experience, he arrived with equipment that looked like a toy-sized model of an old wildcatter in Texas. The process of digging came back to me in a flash of recognition. The way the pipe was added, the sound of the grinding drill, the gray clay slush that ran out of the deepening hole and the jocular stories about wells and water were all of the same ilk, and all added to our apprehension and expectation. The drillers knew the dowser and trusted him, so the two-hundred-foot depth was awaited eagerly. The driller said again and again not to worry, that ten or twenty feet on either side of the estimate was to be expected. When we hit 240 feet or thereabouts, a bit of water bubbled up, different from the water that was being pumped into the hole to cool the drill. Drilling stopped and the amount coming forth was timed and measured in an ancient gallon bucket whose dents must have diminished its holding capacity by a pint. The measurement showed about three-quarters of a gallon per minute, not enough for a state-approved well. The drill pressed on downward. The sun began to set. Work was halted for the night. It wasn't until the following afternoon that we hit water again, this time at 420 feet and only a gallon and a half per minute. The well digger recommended quitting, though the amount of water was not praiseworthy, and pointed out that 420 feet of accumulation would make it an adequate well for our limited uses, and any more drilling might make it the most expensive well in the county.

It will probably go into his lore as the worst of all possible well sites, for a week later the bulldozer hit another spring while digging for the septic tank. We are all convinced that the well passed through the only twelve-inch piece of waterless land on the whole hillside. Water ...

The Garden

In our family August is a time of congregation—parents and children, grandchildren and friends—vacation in the country, dinners for twelve, staggered breakfasts that last until lunch, unmatched tennis matches, hikes through the woods. It is a time of trips to the lake for a swim, to the barn for eggs or to the garden—surely a dozen times a day to the garden.

The paths there are now disappearing under an inundation of squash and melon vines. The spaces between rows have vanished under thick foliage. Branches are heavily laden with tomatoes and peppers and corn. A surfeit of food is everywhere before us. Our only problem lies in the choosing.

To keep back this formative jungle we prune the lengthening tendrils of the pumpkins, hoping to direct the flourishing growth into fruit rather than leafage. We continue to pinch back tomato suckers, knowing that blossoms forming in August are unlikely to ripen before the first frost. We try to keep pole beans from winding themselves around the neighboring tomatoes, and the squash trained into available open spaces rather than over the potatoes. Kale is discouraged from choking the runner beans on the fence. Dill discovers its name and, weedlike, spreads beyond its bounds. We allow much of it to remain. We become less weeders than abbreviators. Weeding is no longer a primary occupation.

There are gardeners around these parts who maintain that there is no need for weeding after the middle of August, and indeed, few of our flourishing vegetables are likely to be pushed under by a newborn pigweed. However, I do like to keep the foreign population under control, if merely as preventative medicine. Each pigweed, for example, produces a hundred thousand seeds that, if allowed to develop, can work their magic on next spring's garden and add to future hours of pulling and digging. I also continue my silent battle with the patch of bindweed that persists as valiantly as Sisyphus to push up yet another new tendril, but that is little enough. Weeding is a minimal activity these August days. Attention turns to water, harvest and, as always, attending.

In our climate, irrigation is a sometime thing, one year essential, another year needless. There has been little necessity to irrigate this year, as rain has been the superstar, making more appearances than its audience really cares to witness. In other years we seem to spend each morning and evening dragging the hose, deciding which plot needs it most because we can't cover everything, and hoping that our well won't run dry. It hasn't, but there have been summers when our neighbors were less fortunate. Why one well and not another? The underground system that supplies our hillside continues to be a mystery.

The one gardening principle that doesn't change from crisp spring mornings to languid summer days is the requirement for vigilance. A single hornworm can decimate a tomato plant in a matter of hours. An infestation of aphids can wither a pear tree. A flock of crows can eat the hearts out of every cabbage. A family of chipmunks can take chunks out of carrots and beets as well as one's broccoli roots, actions never observed until the unfortunate carrot is pulled, or the broccoli suddenly droops and dies. Meals for the adversary ... Well, we can afford to be charitable this year.

While in the process of attending, all garden hands now turn more and more to the assignment of greatest import: reaping, organizing, cooking, preserving and eating the growing mountain of food at hand.

One soon learns to differentiate between the produce that can remain in the ground to no detriment and that which too quickly overgrows and becomes an unwieldy nuisance. Carrots, beets, potatoes, leeks, parsnips, salsify and even kale can be left growing until needed, but there are other vegetables that need consideration, and they should be picked at the magic time when they are freshest, sweetest and tenderest. Zucchini and yellow squash are infamous for their ability to grow, seemingly overnight, to elephantine proportions with large, unappetizing seeds and tough exteriors. Zucchini is more elusive than the yellow squash, since its green exterior may allow it to hide under a group of leaves until it is three feet long, ten pounds in weight and usable for only the most imaginative and determined cook. Mine now go straight into the compost heap, for even the chickens shun them. Cucumbers, too, can camouflage themselves as leaves until they become bulbous, bitter and full of large seeds.

Lettuce becomes bitter, harboring a milky secretion in its leaves and roots as the weather warms. It bolts soon thereafter into a tall, conical, single-stemmed unit, a floral dunce's cap with tiny yellow blossoms sprouting out of the top. These you may leave to produce the seeds of next season, or to compost or feed to chickens, which seem not to mind the musty, bitter flavor and tough leaves.

All the varieties of broccoli in our garden must be watched for the right moment to pick their unopened blossoms—which constitute the broccoli head that one eats—for each small bead will continue to grow, adding stem and flowers if not removed at the appropriate moment. While the Romanesca variety produces only one monumental, glorious head, crowning each plant with a diadem of pale green, beaded cones, most other varieties make second, third and fourth contributions by sending out side shoots of smaller but equally delicious heads after the initial one has been sliced away. The more shoots one picks, the more shoots the plant produces. This process continues until winter, as each plant becomes an ever larger, denser bush.

Green beans, which we have been picking since mid-July, become tough and stringy when left too long on the vine. They too are best young and tender. Snap beans and shell beans are more merciful and may be harvested at different stages for different uses. The cranberry bean and the tongue of fire bean may be snapped and eaten whole when young, shelled in middle age and left on the vine to dry and keep over winter when they have passed the first two stages. This is also true of flageolets, great northerns, limas and, I suppose, any other snap bean. Since we can't consume all the beans we've planted while they are still young, I ignore those that dry well, such as Mexican reds, pintos, blacks and great northerns, let them dry on the vine and shell them in the fall for winter use. We try to eat the haricots verts when they are young, small and tender, pickling some with dill to keep into the cold season. Yellow wax beans are also eaten young, fresh and whole, so there is little incentive to shell fresh beans.

The Christmas limas, theatrical with their gaudy magenta pattern, are slow to develop and have never produced more than a few cups of mature beans. Their leafage is magnificent, but even at the end of August there are often more blossoms than developing beans. They are such a slow-growing variety that I probably shouldn't continue to plant them in this climate of early frost, but they are so delicious and beautiful that each year I hope for a miracle and a better harvest.

Our sweet peppers have produced bushes laden with large, heavy, succulent fruit this year. The cool weather and rain have given us green fruit, not yet turned to the red and brown hues they are purported to exhibit. Only the yellow peppers are born to that color. All the others turn from green to red or brown, and this year they are turning ever so slowly.

Eggplants and melons are also slow to ripen. It seems odd that these—the juiciest of fruits—do better in hot and often dry weather than they do during rainy times. A neighboring farmer is giving his melons away, saying he would be embarrassed to sell them. His explanation for their taste-lessness is the extra acid in the rain. Whatever their problem, they are not a gift of value.

The object of almost everyone's greatest anticipation in August is the ripening of corn and tomatoes. They have both matured late, but by mid-August there are enough of both to begin the annual orgy to celebrate what must be many people's favorite vegetables. No store-bought example can ever come close to the taste of the ripe tomato right off the vine and the ear of corn boiled just minutes after picking it. There are dinners in August when there is very little else we care to eat, perhaps a fresh lettuce salad or a dish of cold pickled beets, but the corn is the main thing, barely cooked, coated with sweet butter, salt and freshly ground pepper and accompanied by juicy slices of tomato with a sprig of basil. This and a glass of light red wine are heaven!

It is hard to imagine Italy without the tomato; yet, as a New World fruit, it was unknown in Europe until the sixteenth century. Even then it was raised mainly as an ornamental for over a century, until some brave souls convinced the gastronomic world that it was not poisonous. Today tomatoes are so widely used that people are even willing to buy those hard, mealy, pallid and sometimes square substitutes that supermarkets actually call tomatoes. They are not. Anyone who has raised his or her own knows that the red, juicy, luscious fruit picked from the vine in the noonday sun is a tomato. There is no other.

Although tomatoes have always been a part of our garden's produce, we gave up corn for several years after losing it to our local raccoon adversaries and their superior ability to judge the sweetest and ripest and eat it a day ahead of us. I think I wouldn't hate raccoons so much if they merely ate a few ears of corn here and there, but they don't leave it at that. They pull down stalks, precluding a second ear's ripening, and worse, they are samplers. They finish no more than a third of each ear they find, leaving a corn patch littered with mutilated stalks and unconsumed food.

When we first began raising corn, we tried every method we knew to discourage these clever beasts. We left a radio playing, but they seemed to enjoy the dinner music. We interplanted with scratchy, uncomfortable-to-traverse squash vines, but they laughed at our naiveté. I even enlisted my three sons to pee around the patch and define the territory as wolves do. The raccoons were not fooled. It is only with electric fencing that we have finally thwarted their annual invasion, with a bow to superior weaponry rather than superior intelligence.

At the height of the vegetable season, I suppose it seems odd to continue to plant even more of the same things that are flourishing, but I am still at it. Though the New England summer is short, there are still varieties that can stand up to the early Connecticut frost and sometimes produce a second crop better than the first one. Sometimes. A dry, hot August can stunt baby seedlings. An early spate of cold can retard them. But for the price of a few seeds and a few moments of contented toil, the chance is worth taking.

As spring lettuce bolts and the Bok choi and Chinese cabbage are used up, the taste for more exceeds the pragmatism of simply using the existing abundance of vegetables already ripe in the garden. A bed of onions is harvested and gives way to three rows of lettuce. Browning pea vines are pulled up to provide space for more lettuce two weeks later and four rows of Chinese greens are planted in a space where early lettuce has bolted. Several weeks later, these are thinned and transplanted in the space of the newly harvested winter onions and shallots. Gardening now becomes an undulating patchwork of increase and decrease, a hasty triumvirate of planting, weeding and harvesting, and all the while attending.

The Kitchen

August is the ideal time for our reunion of gourmands, for the garden is replete with ingredients basking in the radiance of their prime. As the patch quietly confirms its cornucopial capacities, the family invades, pulling and picking, with an enthusiasm heedless of the dirty pots and pans to follow. Decisions must be made. "Shall it be corn or new potatoes? Both? Why not?" "Green beans getting too big? Let's pickle some." "Beets or zucchini?" "I know there's a lot of zucchini, but I love beets." "Just don't cook them together." "Don't even let them touch each other." "I want blueberries." "Not before dinner, dear."

In our zeal, our favorite meals turn out to be those that offer nothing store-bought except salt, pepper, sugar and the like. We are now eating our broiler chickens and an organic half hog we bought from a neighbor. Both meats are tender and juicy and of a flavor more delicate and more savory than that of their commercial equivalents. The half hog was a first for us, and such a success that I wish we had purchased a whole one. However, it is vegetable food that is the mainstay of the table. Without making vows, we have become more and more vegetarian in our tastes, and the thought of a rare, juicy steak brings no greater salivation than the thought of a tender tomato or a husky ear of corn.

One of nature's late-summer favors is the affinity of the available food to the balmy weather. This month's fruits and vegetables need little cooking, no lengthy preparation in a steamy kitchen to reach the height of their potential. They are stars in their own right and need little makeup to shine.

There is a saying about having the water boiling before you pick the corn, and if that is possible, it is a good idea. Corn begins to lose its sugars when it is picked, but an hour or two between garden and pot is acceptable, especially with the new supersweet corns.

Perfectly ripened corn is hard to ruin. Even if you overcook it, it is still sweet and tender, just a little mushy. I put very fresh, just-husked corn into a pot of fully boiling water, leave it until the water just begins to boil again and take it out and serve it. This is the way we eat most of our corn.

Corn Chowder

If there is leftover corn, I cut it off the husks and freeze it. Sometimes I even make this corn chowder. The key ingredient in this recipe is the fresh cilantro. Don't even bother to try it without this pungent flavor.

Or, if you haven't acquired a taste for cilantro, substitute a more favored herb to add that necessary tang. This recipe is an adaptation of one taught to me by Virginia Lee, a superb Chinese cook and teacher. When I first ate the cilantro, I was repulsed. Now it is my favorite herb. Try it, you'll see.

INGREDIENTS:

2 chicken breasts
2 egg whites
1/2 pound fresh shrimp, shelled
Vegetable cooking oil
4 cups chicken stock
1 pound fresh corn, cut from the cob
1 tablespoon sherry or rice wine
1/2 cup cream
Salt
2 tablespoons cornstarch
1/4 cup prosciutto, finely diced
Fresh cilantro to taste

PROCEDURE:

1. Debone and skin the chicken. Cut it in pieces and puree it in a blender, adding a little water if necessary to make it smooth.
2. Remove the chicken from the blender and combine it with the egg whites and about 1 teaspoon of the cornstarch. Set aside.
3. Mix the shrimp with another teaspoon of the cornstarch.
4. Heat the oil in a wok or skillet. Stir-fry the shrimp for 1 minute until they just turn pink. Remove and drain them.
5. Heat the chicken stock in a pot. Add the corn, salt and sherry. Add the shrimp and then slowly stir in the pureed chicken. Mix the rest of the cornstarch with a little cold water and add it a little at a time until the soup has the thickness you desire. Add the cream.
6. Garnish each bowl with the prosciutto and cilantro. Serve.

Succotash

If you have ever struggled through a helping of canned succotash, remember that the fresh form is not the same.

INGREDIENTS:

2 cups shelled fresh beans, cooked until tender but not mushy
2 cups fresh corn, cooked and cut from cob
   (Put 4 ears of fresh corn in boiling water. When the water returns to
   a boil remove and cool, then remove the corn from the cob.)
2 large sweet red peppers, or 1 red and 1 green sweet pepper, chopped
2 chili peppers
1 large onion, chopped
1 to 2 tablespoons cooking oil
Salt
Pepper

PROCEDURE:

1. The corn and beans must be cooked separately, since they require very different amounts of time. When they are ready, sauté the chopped onion in a skillet.
2. Add the sweet and chili peppers to the onions. Stir.
3. Add the beans. Continue to stir.
4. Add the corn. Mix thoroughly. Season with salt and pepper. Serve warm.

Garden Pizza

Sometimes after a few weeks of eating off of the garden's produce, everyone is ready to send out for pizza, an easy thing in New York where pizza parlors are everywhere. In the country, however, the nearest takeout pizza is a twelve-mile drive away, a long time for a pizza to be kept hot and crisp. The answer is homemade pizza, but in a family of folks who think they are expert in the evaluation of pizza, this is not an easy task. What appears below is the result of experiments gone awry and more experiments that have worked. The trick is the dough. Good luck.

INGREDIENTS FOR DOUGH:

(This is enough for 2 14-inch pizza shells.)
1 package dry yeast
1 cup warm water (about 110˚)
1 teaspoon salt
3-1/2 cups unbleached flour
2 tablespoons olive oil, plus olive oil for greasing bowl and dough
Cornmeal

PROCEDURE FOR DOUGH:

1. Dissolve the yeast in warm water. Let stand for about 10 minutes to proof. It should be bubbly.

2. Place the flour and salt in a large mixing bowl. Add the yeast mixture and olive oil. Knead by hand for about 10 minutes until the dough is smooth and elastic and doesn't stick to your fingers. If it is too sticky, add a bit more flour. If is seems too dry and hard, add more water.

3. Place the dough in a bowl greased with olive oil. Cover it with a damp cloth or dish towel and put it in a warm place until the dough has doubled in bulk. This should take between 1 and 2 hours.

4. Preheat the oven to 450°.

5. Punch down the dough and divide it into 2 equal pieces. Roll it out on a lightly floured surface. Fit the dough into a 12- to 14-inch pizza or pie pan, or place it on a paddle used to transfer pizza onto an oven stone (see below). If a paddle is used, sprinkle it liberally with cornmeal to facilitate slipping the pizza onto the stone.

6. Sprinkle a small amount of olive oil on the dough. Put on the topping. Bake for 20 to 25 minutes until the crust is crisp and browned.

TOPPINGS:

Plum tomatoes, chopped
Onions, sliced
Sweet peppers, zucchini or mushrooms, sliced
Fresh oregano or basil, minced
Anchovies, drained (optional)
Faux capers (see the July chapter)
Mozzarella cheese, sliced and chopped
Parmesan cheese, grated
Salt to taste
Olive oil

PROCEDURE FOR TOPPINGS:

1. Skin and chop enough tomatoes to cover the pizza dough. Sprinkle them with a little salt (about 1/2 teaspoon) and place them in a sieve or colander to drain away extra juices. Set aside for 30 minutes.

2. If possible, place several bricks or a large tile on the oven shelf. Preheat the oven to 450°.

3. Prepare all the other topping ingredients.

4. Rub the pan or pans with the olive oil. Flatten the pizza dough and press it into large pie pans or a pizza pan.

5. Cover the dough with tomatoes, then onions, peppers, anchovies, faux capers and herbs. Sprinkle mozzarella and then Parmesan cheese over everything.

6. Place the pizza in the oven on the bricks. This heats the pan bottom and prevents a soggy crust. Bake it for about 20 minutes. Remove when the crust is lightly browned and the tomatoes are bubbly.

If you make pizza often enough, it might be worth the expense to buy a pizza stone, a large, flat stone designed to be placed in the oven and preheated, on which to bake pizza. The even heat of the stone seems to make a crispier undercrust and gives the pizza that "stony" flavor that speaks of ancient cooks, adobe ovens and the fragrance of clay.

Do not use an unclassified piece of stone or ceramic to put food on directly. It might be contaminated.

Pasta Salvia with Broccoli Romanesca

INGREDIENTS:
2 large bunches Romanesca broccoli (or regular broccoli)
1-1/2 cups shallots, peeled
1/4 pound sweet butter or 1/2 cup good olive oil
1/2 cup chopped fresh sage or salvia
Freshly ground pepper
Salt
1 pound pasta, preferably 1 of the round shapes like rigate or gnocchi

PROCEDURE:
1. Divide the broccoli into individual florets by cutting at the bottom of each flower stem. Each floret should be carefully cut so it looks attractive.
2. Pick over the shallots, cutting in two those too large to eat easily. Heat the butter or oil in a skillet or saucepan and add the shallots. Stir until they are softened. Add the chopped sage and continue to stir until it is softened. Set the pan aside.
3. Steam the broccoli until it is bright green and still a little crisp. Set it aside.
4. Cook the pasta. Toss all the ingredients in a wok or large skillet, heating as you toss.
5. Serve with grated Parmesan cheese if you wish.

One-Dish Garden Dinner

This is a meal of numerous variations. My daughter-in-law executed the original version, a quick supper often made during the busy harvest season on the farm in Ohio. It can be expanded or contracted easily. It may be modified by what is available in the garden. The only constants for me are the potatoes and the onions. The other vegetables listed are suggestions only. The herbs may be used singly or in combinations. Some vegetable combinations work much better than others, but that is a matter of personal preference. This is a good recipe to experiment with, for it can never go completely wrong.

INGREDIENTS:

New potatoes, scrubbed but unpeeled
New onions, sliced with their green leaves, if available
Sweet peppers, sliced
Celery, sliced
Zucchini, sliced
Green beans, cut in 1- to 2-inch lengths
Cabbage, chopped
Brussels sprouts
Corn, removed from the cob
Broccoli, with florets separated
Carrots, sliced (optional)
Tomatoes, sliced (optional)
Corn oil
Chicken stock
Fresh herbs (basil, thyme, summer savory, parsley or sage)
Salt
Pepper

PROCEDURE:

1. Sauté the potatoes and onions in a wok or large skillet, stirring frequently. If carrots are used, add them at the beginning.

2. When the onions are translucent and the potatoes are beginning to soften, add the peppers, celery, zucchini, corn, green beans and whatever vegetables you wish to use. Continue to stir-fry, adding a bit of chicken stock if the mixture is too dry.

3. Add the herbs, salt and pepper. Add the tomatoes, if you wish. Cook until the potatoes and carrots are just done. Serve.

September

While not a leaf seems faded; while the fields,
With ripening harvest prodigally fair,
In brightest sunshine bask; this nipping air,
Sent from some distant clime where Winter wields
His icy scimitar, a foretaste yields
Of bitter change, and bids the flowers beware ...

—William Wordsworth
"September, 1815"

The Land

For most of my life, each calendar year has defined itself around the boundaries of schooltime. Either as student, mother of students or teacher, I have looked upon the summer months as vacation—no matter how hard the garden work—the weeks around Christmas, Easter and the February presidents' birthdays as special retreats and the beginning of September as the turning point of the year. It seems like the New Year, the time to make resolutions, put commitments into effect, begin new projects or jobs. In September vacation ends, and August sloth is exchanged for autumnal industry.

It is only since becoming a gardener that I have appreciated that schooltime in North America has historically defined itself around the outmoded demands of the family-based agricultural system. Our lengthy summer vacation may have been a time of idleness for me as a child, but it was clearly no vacation for the farm children of the eighteeenth and nineteenth centuries. They were indispensable laborers during the toilsome months between plowing and harvest.

The family farm, so rare today, was home for much of the American population a hundred years ago, and most farm employees were family members. There was no worry about a population explosion then. A farmer's main concern was to have enough hands to cultivate the fields, sow the grains and bring in the sheaves. Large nuclear families made up the production base.

My forebears, on a long-ago western Pennsylvania farm, were such a family. My father was one of ten well-employed children, nine of whom lived to adulthood, an average better than most back then. They were a production force, awake each day before dawn to haul water from the well, milk cows, distribute food to pigs and chickens and bring hay and oats to workhorses. In the summer their workday extended until sunset.

Male family members took charge of plowing, planting and harvesting operations. They also herded sheep and cows; sheared the sheep; mended fences, barns and tools; slaughtered what they needed for home use or for sale; baled and stored hay; and occasionally took the horse and buggy to town for sugar or nails.

Females cooked, cleaned, washed, carded and spun wool from which they wove cloth and made yarn; knitted socks and sweaters; sewed; churned butter and preserved the incoming harvest for winter use. For the children, the September return to the one-room school with its wood stove and stern schoolmaster might well have seemed a comfortable respite from the toil of summer, even though it was a five-mile walk from home.

Today, in many parts of the world, the mobilization of family labor is still the most common method of farming. In China in 1979, schools were closed for the late-fall cabbage harvest, and every student went to the fields to help in collecting. Mountains of cabbages were carted to the villages and towns, where they were piled six feet high in the streets and distributed to every resident. Only after the last cabbage was picked did school resume.

In our country on the modern family farm, mechanization has supplanted much of the human energy. On the farm next to us, only one of the grown children and his small family remain to manage the land, and they purchase most of their food at a supermarket. Other family members have left to become mechanics, teachers or carpenters. A farm can no longer support the large numbers it once did. However, the agglomeration of state-of-the-art equipment it amasses boggles the mind.

The American farmer who cultivates hundreds of acres singlehandedly from the cabin of a mammoth tractor is an anomaly to the Chinese peasant of Pearl Buck vintage, laboriously trying to pull a year's worth of food out of one li of land. Yet both must share similar feelings in September, satisfaction at a mounting accumulation or apprehension if the harvest is poor. In their own ways they both prepare for the change to come.

Harvest time or schooltime, September is a time of transformation, an inevitable move from one condition to another. A New Year? Why not?

Few cultures, save ours and those of our northern European ancestors, celebrate the official New Year as we do, just after the winter solstice, the beginning of lengthening hours of sunlight in each day. Although for northern Europeans the gradual turning from those short, bleak days of December seems as good a reason as any for celebrating the New Year, many cultures that have delineated the New Year as a pivotal time of change and growth have equated such a time with harvest, the preparation and storage of food for winter, the culmination of the activities of survival.

Using the short calendar, the Mayans celebrated the New Year in July, when the maize ripened, a logical time, the ending of one process and the beginning of the next.

The ancient Egyptians, who gave the world its earliest solar calendar, also celebrated the New Year at the end of an agricultural cycle. In what would be late June to us, the annual inundation of the Nile began. Spring plantings had to be gathered before the waters rose to submerge them. Then there was a waiting period while the silt-rich waters covered the Nile valley and slowly receded, leaving a natural fertilization over the land. This annual flooding was awaited with high expectation, for it contained the lifeblood of the agricultural system. Priests—the inventors and holders of the calendar—could predict the flooding time, thereby impressing the populace and reinforcing their own power. The religious rites that celebrated the New Year were thought to have been influential in bringing forth this fundamental ingredient—the flooding and subsequent fertilization of the land—that sustained Egyptian culture.

Following an ancient tradition, the Jews still celebrate Rosh Hashanah, their New Year, in the fall, when I instinctively celebrate my own. They believe that the world began in the autumn. Here again the New Year is associated with the harvest and its grand accumulations.

Today the importance of the harvest is of minor interest to most of us who live in an industrial world, for it happens out there, somewhere far from our lives or our control. But to our agrarian predecessors it was a preeminent event.

Their harvesttime wasn't merely a time for extravagant consumption of the season's riches, although that happened too. At feasts and rituals the gods were thanked for the bounty given, but behind the scenes the real work of stockpiling and preserving enough to live on through the seasons ahead was taking place. Work forces, in a series of labor-intensive tasks, invented ingenious methods of drying, pickling, smoking, salting and even burying the fruits of the autumn harvest. These tasks, often within the woman's domain and viewed by some as the tyranny of the kitchen, have kept the wolf from the door throughout human time.

The tyranny of the kitchen in September really was a tyranny of necessity. For those of us who are amateur gardeners and preservers, the pleasure of canning a dozen jars of tomatoes, freezing the extra broccoli or shelling dried beans in no way simulates the labor of our foremothers and forefathers or many people in other parts of the world today. My shelf of winter stores would not go far in keeping our family from the threshold of starvation, nor would the packages in the freezer. The incentives for our own efforts are high-quality, nontoxic food and the pleasure of growing it—no more.

My daughter-in-law, who grew up on a farm in Ohio, talks with little enthusiasm of the hundreds of jars of vegetables that her large immediate and extended family mobilized themselves to prepare each fall. She describes picking, peeling, shelling, boiling, sterilizing and storing. It is a picture of drugery she paints: a room steamed by hours of uninterrupted cooking, children confined to the mundane tasks of peeling tomatoes or stringing beans, cross adults sweating from the heat and steam, the requirement of sterility and the pressure to finish the processing of a mountain of food.

She also speaks of the partial escape from autumnal servility granted by the first large freezer. I wonder if the wives and children of earlier farms and farmers felt relieved when the technique of canning—an invention of the nineteenth century—became available and could be added to the other means of food preservation—drying and curing. And I wonder if they would have laughed if they'd known that within a hundred years, few people would preserve food at all, that Chilean asparagus would be available in October, Jamaican mangoes in January, freeze-dried dinners ubiquitously and that all manner of exotica would be transported around the world daily in aircraft.

I remember well a story my father told of his delight upon receiving a fresh orange in his stocking one long-ago Christmas during his childhood. No one in his large family received more than a stocking's worth of yuletide cheer, and an orange was a special treat. This he pointedly let me know when I seemed dissatisfied that my stack of Christmas gifts was smaller and less grand than that of my friends. I still recall my astonishment that anything as ordinary as an orange could bring such delight. I still do not know if its uncommonness in the Adams household was due to poverty or inaccessibility. I now even doubt the veracity of my father's story, which filled me with such guilt at my own acquisitiveness. Would the larger towns of western Pennsylvania have had citrus fruit in the 1890s? Would it have been rare and expensive in a small farm community? Did people relish oranges in winter? And how my father did love to tell stories.

Most of his tales described an idealized life on that farm, a life of warmth, love and connectedness, a time of joy in bringing in the cattle or hiding in the hayloft or climbing the apple trees to gather the highest fruits. To me it never seemed a life of privation. The labor involved in accumulating enough to live on was never stressed, never presented as a negative. He always spoke of the farm with such sweet nostalgia that I couldn't imagine why he gave it up for a dry prairie and drilling wildcatters. My father, a younger son, left the farm and its cycles, and in the 1930s his older brother lost it, participating in another sort of transformation.

The Garden

September gardening activity is perhaps a stepped-up version of that of August. Planting continues, but now it is annual rye that replaces the emptying rows of harvested vegetables. Reaping continues, but now the accumulation is too great merely to consume or give away, and the impetus of impending frost forces us to switch from baskets to wheelbarrows as collecting gear. There is a new urgency in the air. We must stay a few steps ahead of winter.

As a vegetable gardener, one learns early on the difference between those plants that can weather a freezing frost and those that cannot. The cabbages, lettuces and most root vegetables are survivors and can remain in the earth almost until the ground begins to freeze, but for tomatoes, peppers, eggplants and squash, even the first light frost can be a killer, so they must be protected or picked. Other vegetables must be harvested because they are ready, regardless of the weather.

Onions, though frost-tolerant, are mature when the tops die back and they cease to grow. This happens anytime from mid-August to October, depending upon when they were planted and whether they were started from seeds or onion sets. We have picked a bushel or two, which now lie drying on the garage floor. I will eventually braid them and hang the long garlands in the pantry.

Potatoes are also ready to dig when the tops brown and wither. I dig them carefully with a pitchfork, starting well away from the center of each plant and digging down and under, hoping to lift out the potatoes without puncturing them. They must never be left in the sun for any length of time, for the sun greens potato skins, and green skins are bitter and apparently toxic. Our potato crop also goes quickly to the garage floor to dry, and then into barrels that are kept in a cool corner of the pantry. I never wash them until they are ready to be used. Dirt falls off as they dry and what remains can be easily rinsed away later on.

Our largest garden crop in terms of cubic footage is our batch of winter squash and pumpkins. Although their vines and leaves go limp at the first hint of a freeze, the tough hides of the acorns, butternuts and hubbards protect them, and they can stay on the ground until the last moment before the first frost (or sometimes a few moments after) and then be gathered. There are usually enough to heap high in a very large wheelbarrow. They also go into the garage until the weather threatens to freeze and then are brought into the pantry. All of the above have good keeping properties and, if checked periodically to remove the odd rotter from the barrel, can last the winter.

Dried beans are also good keepers. A hard frost will kill their leaves, but the beans themselves can be salvaged and preserved. I let them dry on the vine, then pick and shell as I find the time. After they are shelled, I leave them in open baskets for a few weeks until they are thoroughly dried; then they are stored loosely sealed in glass canning jars. Only twice in many years have I had beans go bad, and in these cases they were probably packed in airless jars before they were thoroughly dried out. Once dry, they could probably last forever. In fact, I have some kidney beans glued to a piece of cardboard that my twenty-seven-year-old son made when he was in nursery school. They look fine.

First frost ... It is always on the gardener's mind in September. Will there be a forewarning, or will it come stealthily, leaving destruction under a glittering carpet of icy prisms? It almost always comes in late September, sometimes covering everything, sometimes selecting only the hollows, sometimes limiting itself to a freckling across the landscape.

The first frost came on the twenty-fifth of September this year. It was expected and reported on the local weather stations, so on Sunday the twenty-fourth we spent the morning picking several bushels of red, pink and green tomatoes; two wheelbarrows full of squash, pumpkins, melons and eggplants; bunches of basil; almost a bushel of green, brown, yellow and red sweet peppers a small basket of jalapeños. The frost arrived in early morning, not as "killing" as was expected, but nevertheless enough to coat its victims with a thin layer of ice, leaving many of them limp and lifeless as the sun hit them later in the morning. They can be left where they are and turned into the earth or piled on the compost heap.

In other years we have covered bushes loaded with green tomatoes or small peppers with old sheets to fend off the freezing, for often a spate of warm weather will lengthen summer by several weeks after frost has killed a tender group of plants. Whether one is gathering or safeguarding, there always seems to be a need to save, to accumulate as much as can be handled. An instinct handed down from our ancestors? Who knows.

I do know that I am able to buy apples and pears the whole winter through, but I am still frustrated by the waste when an overwhelming crop of these fruits arrives from time to time and I have no means to preserve it all. On our hilly, northern slope, spring fruiting is always problematic, and too often the whole orchard will be nipped in the bud by a late cold spell.

This year was a happy exception. Whether it was the lack of frost after blossom time, the organic spray program (which became basically pheromone lures and Imidan spray), perfect summer conditions or the fruit-tree gods, our trees are now laden with fruit. On the hill, even some old "escape" trees (wild trees grown from seeds dropped by birds or deer) have brought forth bounties of delicious, unclassifiable apples and pears, with no help from lures or sprays of any kind.

We have five bearing pear trees and more than a dozen apples that have been producing mature fruit since Labor Day. We store what we can, make apple pies, pickled pears, religiously eat an apple a day, and yet last weekend, we picked three bushels of windfalls from which we made six gallons of apple and pear cider, and still have heavily laden branches. It is a bonanza that can't be counted on, but it is surely savored when it happens.

In the frenzy of harvest it is too easy to forget about, or put off, the preparation of the garden for winter, but prepare one must. The entire process may be spread over the next two months until the ground freezes, but one must not delay in the seeding of green manures as beds are emptied and bare ground is exposed to the harshness of wind and rain.

Green manures secure the earth and prevent winter erosion. They fertilize the soil by capturing nutrients that might otherwise leach away during the rains and snows of the months ahead. They help develop the good tilth that plants like to grow in. And in the spring, when these cover crops are tilled under, they add humus, loosen hard soils and bring up, by way of their roots, more soil nutrients.

Whether they're called cover crops or green manures, these magical plants are indispensable to us on our north hill, which tends to wash away during the winter. Rye, oats, alfalfa, vetch, white clover, buckwheat, soybeans, mustard and kale are all used as green manures. Each has its own advantages and disadvantages, and one may fit a specific soil-climate situation better than another. After experimenting with clover and rye, we have settled on annual rye. It germinates in the blink of an eye, continues to grow until the ground freezes, is easy to till under in the spring and its roots hold down the earth. It is foolproof. I order ten pounds of unsprayed rye seed with my spring seeds and use it as needed to bind the earth and enrich the soil.

We rake the remaining rubble and then sprinkle seed over each garden area as it is emptied. It is an easy job, this planting, for all one must do is broadcast the seed with a swing of the arm, truly a "broad cast." Another sweep of the rake over the seeded area will partially cover the seeds and help to hide them from greedy birds, but it isn't absolutely necessary. A scattering of hay over the area will also hold the seeds and earth in place until they germinate, but rye seeds are a hardy lot. If time is short, a simple watering will get them started. Even abrupt temperature changes will not daunt this vigorous grain. The garden becomes a checkerboard of grassy green at varying stages of development.

To replenish and sustain with such ease reminds me of Ladakhi farmers and their difficulty with winter erosion. Because there is no rainfall and little runoff from the mountains then, and because of high winter winds, the farmers of that Himalayan hinterland spade their topsoil a shovelful at a time into carts and store it in outbuildings until planting time, when it is returned to the fields. Soil is that precious.

The Kitchen

September in the country is a time when the human tendency to accumulation seems even more apparent. Nothing gets thrown away. Everything needs special care and attention. Tomatoes must be canned, frozen or dried. Beans must be frozen or dried. Apples and pears must be made into cider, pie, chutney—or something. The adage "Waste not want not," comes to mind and makes one feel twinges of guilt at the exclusion of any potentially edible product from the salvaging process. So with summer garden chores at a low point, September is indeed the time for devotion to putting by, incorporating both the technologies of our ancestors and those of the twentieth century.

Our modern inventory of methods for saving our produce hold no threat of starvation if they fail, but they do give us a certain satisfaction, not to be confused with vanity, for our yield is modest. We have experimented with numerous methods of preserving our summer stores, and although a canned tomato is definitely not a fresh ripe one, nor a frozen green bean like one newly picked, home preserving methods can give results far better than commercial ones, and on occasion even create quite wonderful foods, delicious in their own right and with lingering memories of summer past.

Dehydrating, probably the oldest and simplest of preserving forms, gives us tomatoes, beans and cornmeal for winter use. Corn and beans may be simply laid out or hung to dry, but the juicier tomato cannot endure the New England humidity without growing an exterior of fluffy, white mold. Our "sun-dried" tomatoes are really oven-dried. Smoking is reserved for meats and only used on occasion for hams and bacon. Brine-cured cucumbers are a continuous summer project, as is the making of cornichons. Things pickled in vinegar are canned. Those pickled in salt are refrigerated and eaten without delay. Unpretentious parboiled vegetables are frozen.

Shelves, refrigerator and freezer fill with the results of ordered activity, leisurely gathering and, on occasion, a trip straight from the garden to the chicken yard, where a load of overripe or overgrown vegetables will add nutrients to our forthcoming eggs.

In a climate of "first things first," it is the surfeit that cannot grow on, that cannot withstand first frost and must be attended. Carrots and cabbages are hardy lots and can stay in the ground until November, but tomatoes, peppers and cucumbers turn into wet and slimy has-beens on the first frigid night, so they must be gathered, stored and then converted into something that will last the winter.

Each year quarts of canned tomatoes line the shelves, "sun-drieds" soak up olive oil and jars of tomato soup sit in the freezer along with a few plastic bags of pure and simple tomatoes.

Peppers, in lesser abundance, are also frozen, dried and roasted, then packed in olive oil. Many things, from cabbage to zucchini, are pickled. In a few months, these flavors will be, if not as perfect as they are now, agreeable enough.

Canned Tomatoes

Over the years I have made various tomato sauces that I canned with miscellaneous spices and herbs. Now I do nothing more than preserve plain tomatoes with a touch of salt and sometimes a few sprigs of basil. I then use this as a base for whatever tomato-based dish I wish to make.

These tomatoes may also be frozen without the fuss of sterilizing. One's choice depends upon the amount of freezer space available.

INGREDIENTS:
> *Fresh tomatoes, preferably the Italian plum variety*
> *Boiling water*
> *Salt*
> *Fresh basil*

IMPLEMENTS:
> *Canning jars, sterilized*
> *Large pot for water bath (see below)*

PROCEDURE:
1. Dip the tomatoes in the boiling water, which facilitates peeling them easily. Peel them, slice them in two and cut out the hard part at the stem and any bad spots. Put the tomatoes and about 1/2 teaspoon salt for each quart of fruit in a large kettle and bring it to a boil. Reduce the heat to medium and continue to boil until the tomatoes are thoroughly softened and as thick as you desire.

2. At this point, you may plop them directly into sterilized Mason jars, send them through a food processor to turn them into a smooth sauce or put them through an old-fashioned puree machine that takes out the seeds and purees them. (I have used all three, but I prefer the simple puree gadget to the food processor. It takes longer but washing it is simpler.)

3. Reheat the sauce for a few minutes and then ladle it into the sterilized jars, cap them and put them into a water bath for 10 to 15 minutes.

4. Remove the jars from the water bath. Let cool for several hours. Test the seals. Label with year and month and store.

Water Bath

Most hardware stores carry very large, enamel water bath pots with racks that hold seven glass canning jars. They are a good investment because they double as lobster pots or dyeing pots (but not both). A water bath is good way to sterilize any acidic or pickled fruit or vegetable. It is not good enough for straight nonacidulated fare.

When I am canning, I start water to boil in the pot, sterilize clean jars in a 300° oven and simmer the lids in another pot of water.

After filling the jars, I seal them tightly, making sure there is no food spilled on the rim, which will break the seal.

The jars (which will be hot from the food) are carefully placed in the rack and lowered into the boiling water. Never put very cold jars into boiling water or they will crack.

The boiling will stop. Watch for the water to return to a boil and time the sterilization process from then. Usually 10 to 15 minutes is adequate.

You will notice air bubbles rising out of the jars. This action is necessary to form a seal on the jars.

At the appropriate time, carefully raise the rack and remove the jars carefully. Use sturdy tongs or a good hot pad. Don't put the jars down on a wet surface or they may crack.

Let the jars cool. If you are using Mason jars with aluminum lids you will hear a ping or pop as they cool and a vacuum is formed by the decreasing steam. When the jars are cool, test to make sure a seal has formed. If you are using the aluminum tops, unscrew the ring, test for a seal and leave the ring loose around the jar. That will make it easier to open in the future.

All of this may seem complicated, but it isn't. After you've gone through the process once, it will fall into place and be what it is—easy.

"Sun-dried" Tomatoes

The first time I attempted to make sun-dried tomatoes I put them on drying racks in the backyard sun. But I was in New England, not Italy or Arizona, and within a few hours they were covered with white, snowy mold. Now I find my oven pilot light more reliable. I check the tomatoes often and turn the oven up to "low" if I think they aren't drying fast enough.

INGREDIENTS:
> *Plum tomatoes*
> *Salt*
> *Good olive oil*
> *Garlic cloves (optional)*

IMPLEMENTS:
> *Oven with pilot light or electric drying rack*
> *Screen, trays or cake rack*
> *Canning jars, sterilized*

PROCEDURE:
1. Slice the plum tomatoes in half lengthwise. Put them in a large bowl. When the bowl is filled or the tomatoes are used up, sprinkle salt over all of them. Leave for several hours or overnight.
2. The salt will have softened the tomatoes and taken out some of their moisture. Take them out of the brine and remove the seeds. Rinse thoroughly.
3. Place each tomato half on a screened tray or cake rack skin side up. Put them in an oven with only the pilot light for heat. Leave for 6 to 8 hours, perhaps more. Check them every few hours. When they are dry, but not too dry and similar in texture to a dried apricot or peach, remove them from the oven. Pack them into the jars and cover with a good olive oil. Add a garlic clove to each jar if you like. Eat only after several days of marinating.

Green Tomato Chutney

When frost is threatening and the tomato vines are heavy with green to pink fruit, this is a good recipe to use. It will help rid you of the extra tomatoes—those that won't fit on the window sill—to ripen. It also tastes of the bazaars of Delhi and turns a modest lamb chop into an exotic event. Green, pink and red tomatoes may be used, but if at least half of them are the more solid greens, the chutney will be less soupy and have more substance.

INGREDIENTS:

5 to 6 pounds green and pink tomatoes, peeled
1 pound onions, sliced
1 head garlic
2 teaspoons fenugreek
3 to 4 tablespoons coriander seeds
1 teaspoon grated nutmeg
1 teaspoon cardamom seeds
2 tablespoons fresh basil, chopped
1 quart cider vinegar
2 cups raisins
2 to 2-1/2 cups light brown sugar
Dried hot peppers to taste
Salt to taste
(All of these ingredients may vary according to individual taste.)

IMPLEMENTS:

6 to 8 pint canning jars, sterilized
Large pot for water bath

PROCEDURE:

1. Chop the tomatoes coarsely. Place them in a large pot. Add half the vinegar and bring it to a boil. Simmer until the mixture is reduced to a thick consistency. Stir frequently to prevent the bottom from burning.

2. Chop the onions and garlic. Grind the fenugreek and coriander seeds (a few minutes in the oven will render them easier to grind). Combine all the other ingredients except the tomatoes and simmer. (This cooking will take less time than reducing the tomatoes.)

3. When the tomatoes are reduced, combine both mixtures. Adjust the seasonings. Cook for a few more minutes.

4. Ladle the chutney into the pint jars, cap them and process in a water bath for 10 minutes.

5. Set out the jars to cool. After they are thoroughly cool, test to make sure the seals are tight. Label and store.

Salsa

Frozen and canned tomatoes taste quite different from one another, and the fresher flavor of the frozen makes a better salsa, with a more Mexican quality. Salsa is another way of dealing with the plethora of green tomatoes. It may be used in many ways: a dip for taco chips, a sauce for broiled chops or a topping for scrambled eggs. It freezes well and thaws quickly if stored in small plastic containers.

INGREDIENTS:
> *4 parts red and/or green tomatoes*
> *2 parts red and/or green peppers*
> *1 part onions*
> *Several garlic cloves*
> *Several dried hot peppers*
> *Vinegar*
> *Powdered mustard*
> *Coriander seed, freshly ground if possible*
> *Salt*
> *Pepper*

PROCEDURE:
1. Peel and chop the tomatoes. Chop the peppers, onions and garlic. Put them in a pot with the other ingredients and slowly reduce to sauce thickness. Adjust the seasonings to please your palate.
2. Either serve fresh or store in the freezer until needed.

Tomato Ketchup

Another recipe for an overabundance of tomatoes, ketchup is an excellent way to use frostbitten or otherwise imperfect ripe tomatoes. The reduction process really can put "eight great tomatoes into a little bitty can." However, don't expect this to taste like any commercial ketchup you've had.

INGREDIENTS:
> *10 to 12 pounds tomatoes, peeled and chopped, with blemishes removed*
> *2 cups sugar*
> *2 cups cider or white vinegar*
> *1 tablespoon salt*
> *2 tablespoons finely chopped gingerroot*
> *1 to 2 tablespoons whole cloves*
> *1 tablespoon grated nutmeg*
> *1 teaspoon allspice*
> *1 tablespoon five-spice powder*
> *1 or 2 garlic cloves*
> *1 piece licorice root (optional)*
> *Paprika to taste*
> *Cayenne to taste*

IMPLEMENTS:
> *6 to 8 pint canning jars, sterilized*
> *Large pot for water bath*

PROCEDURE:

1. Chop the tomatoes and put them into a large pot. Bring them to a boil and then simmer with all the other ingredients until the mixture has thickened somewhat.
2. Put the mixture through a sieve or puree machine to remove the seeds and the clove, licorice and ginger bits. Return it to the pot and continue to simmer until the mixture is reduced to the desired thickness. Remember that it will be thicker when cool. Adjust the seasonings to taste.
3. Ladle the mixture into the pint jars and seal. Water-process for 10 minutes.
4. Set the jars out to cool. After they are cool, check the seals. Label and store.

Roasted Sweet Peppers

When I have a large amount of peppers, I put masses of raw ones in the freezer after splitting them in half and removing the seeds. They can then be pulled out and used in any recipe that calls for cooked peppers. Simply take what you need from its freezer container (a bag is easy to fill and extract from), place it on a cutting board and smash with a cleaver. Each one is automatically segmented and ready for the pot.

My favorite way of packing away peppers is the method below. They must be refrigerated and they only last for a few weeks, but they are so delicious that I doubt they would last much longer anyway.

INGREDIENTS:

Sweet peppers of varying colors (the more red ones you use the prettier and sweeter)
Salt
Pepper
Olive oil
Capers

PROCEDURE:

1. Preheat the oven at 450°. Slice the peppers in half lengthwise, remove the seeds and place them skin side up on a baking sheet or in a large roasting pan. Sprinkle them with salt and pepper. Dribble olive oil over them.
2. Place them in the oven for about 20 minutes. Turn them several times with a spatula so they don't burn. When they begin to deflate and soften, sprinkle the capers over them. Remove the peppers from the oven when much of the water has cooked away and they are soft and slightly browned in spots.

3. Pack the peppers into a sterilized jar. Pour olive oil from the pan over them. They can be eaten immediately or stored in the refrigerator. They are wonderful hot, as well as cold. If there are a few burned spots on them, they are even better.

Corn Relish

This is a way to combine the fresh flavors of the corn, tomatoes and peppers that ripen in August and renew your acquaintance with them in winter. There are any number of relish combinations that work very well. Just remember to use about twice as much corn as the other vegetable ingredients. Otherwise, the blander corn may be overwhelmed by the stronger flavors.

INGREDIENTS:
4 to 5 cups corn kernels
1 cup chopped green peppers
1 cup chopped sweet red peppers and/or tomatoes
1/2 cup chopped lovage leaves and tender top stalks
1/2 cup chopped onions
1-1/2 cups cider vinegar
1/3 cup sugar
2 teaspoons salt
2 teaspoons dry mustard
2 teaspoons turmeric
1 dried hot pepper for each jar

IMPLEMENTS:
4 pint canning jars, sterilized
Large pot for water bath

PROCEDURE:
1. Boil salted water in a large pot. Add about 10 ears of corn to the pot. Turn off the heat and let stand for 10 minutes. Remove the corn and let it cool. When it is cool, cut the corn from the cob with a very sharp knife. Place it in a large mixing bowl.
2. Add the chopped vegetables to the corn.
3. Put the vinegar, sugar, salt, dry mustard and turmeric in a saucepan and bring it to a boil. Pour the mixture over the vegetables. Stir. Adjust the seasonings to taste.
4. Fill the canning jars to within 1/2 inch of the top. Add a dried hot pepper to each jar. Add more vinegar if there isn't enough to cover the relish. Seal the jars and water-process them for 20 minutes.

5. Allow the jars to cool. Check the seals. Label. Store them in a cool place that will not reach freezing temperatures during the winter.

Gingered Pears

Unlike peaches, pears are better if picked when still hard and allowed to ripen in the cool and dark of the pantry. Tree life makes a ripe pear a bit mealy, and it goes from ripe to rotten rapidly.

INGREDIENTS:
Pears (not quite ripe), pealed, cored and halved
Sugar, half white, half light brown
Water, twice as much as sugar
Cinnamon stick
Whole cloves
Gingerroot, sliced
Juice of 1 lemon for every 8 cups water
Lemon peel, 4- to 5-inch slice

IMPLEMENTS:
Quart canning jars, sterilized
Large pot for water bath

PROCEDURE:
1. In a large pot heat enough water to cover the pears. Add the sugars, lemon juice and lemon peel and spices. Stir until the sugars are dissolved. Turn off the heat.
2. Put the pears into the syrup quickly to prevent them from discoloring.
3. Simmer the pears until they are soft but not mushy. Test them with a fork and remember that they will cook a little more in the water bath.
4. Transfer the pears to the jars, adding gingerroot, a bit of cinnamon stick and cloves to each jar. Discard the lemon peel. Reduce the syrup a bit and cover the pears in each jar with the syrup. Remember to leave 1 inch of air space at the top of each jar.
5. Seal the jars and put them through a water bath. Label and store.

Bread and Butter Pickles

When I was a child, there were always bread and butter pickles in the icebox. I could never figure out why they were called "bread and butter" since they contained neither, but I loved them and still do. Mother's pickle recipe called for cucumbers, and she never deviated from tradition. Admittedly her daughter has strayed, and the pickles in the following recipe are often made with cucumbers, zucchini, eggplant or sweet peppers, or a combination of the four. Use whatever is available.

INGREDIENTS:
> *1 gallon cucumbers, zucchini, eggplant (preferably the small Oriental variety) and/or sweet peppers*
> *2 to 3 cups chopped onions*
> *1 hot pepper for each jar*
> *1/2 cup pickling salt*
> *5 cups cider vinegar*
> *5 cups white or brown sugar*
> *2 teaspoons turmeric*
> *2 teaspoons whole allspice*
> *2 tablespoons celery seed*
> *2 tablespoons mustard seed*
> *2 or 3 whole cloves for each jar*

IMPLEMENTS:
> *4 quart canning jars or 8 pint jars, sterilized*
> *Large pot for water bath*

PROCEDURE:

1. Cut the vegetables into 1/4-inch slices. Remove the seeds from the peppers. Place all in a large bowl and pour the salt over them. Set aside for at least 3 hours. Stir occasionally to distribute the salt.

2. Rinse the vegetables thoroughly with cold water and drain.

3. Place the sugar and vinegar in a pan and bring it to a boil. Turn off the heat.

4. Carefully pack the vegetables into the jars, leaving 1 to 1-1/2 inches of space at the top of each jar. Add equal amounts of the spices and a hot pepper to each jar.

5. Carefully ladle the sugar-vinegar mixture into each jar, covering the vegetables but leaving a 1-inch air space at the top. Make sure the rims of the jars are clean. Seal the jars tightly.

6. Place the jars in the water bath. Bring to a boil and leave for 10 to 12 minutes. The water bath will cook the vegetables but not make them soggy as precooking often does.

7. Remove the jars from the water bath. Let them cool. Test the seals. Store for a few weeks before using.

OCTOBER

I want to tell you what hills are like in October
when colors gush down mountainsides
and little streams are freighted with a caravan of leaves.
I want to tell you how they blush and turn in fiery shame and
     joy,
how their love burns with flames consuming and terrible
until we wake one morning and woods are like a smoldering
     plain—

                              —Margaret Walker
                              "October Journey"

The Land

People from all over the United States—probably from all over the world—know of the flaming miracle of New England in October. They come from all over, in buses and cars and under backpacks, to observe for themselves the colorful foliage they have seen on calendars and in travel magazines, the reds, oranges, purples and golds that paint the hills and valleys and fill the crevices of ancient moraines.

Autumn color. It is always a subject of conversation and interest. We stay in the city for an October wedding one weekend, and Monday morning I get reports from the country: "It was perfect. I think you missed the peak." "You're okay. The height will probably be next week." "If we don't have a windstorm they should last." "This year's the best ever." "This year's not so fine. Must be the wet August."

No matter how often I see the autumn array—the bracing morning air, the azure sky, the honking of south-flying geese, the Indian summer afternoons, the earthy smell of drying leaves, the kaleidoscope of colors— it is always different yet always the same, and worth the detour from wherever you are.

The chemical changes that generate nature's yearly arboreal exuberance are admittedly less romantic than their splendor would have you believe, yet they embody a process as basic as what they make—food. It is a story of the life and death (and ultimate resurrection) of a simple molecule that, when you think about it, feeds us all. I'm not sure anyone fully understands what causes the fall color of the forests of the northeastern United States and eastern Asia, but it begins with the story of chlorophyll.

As we learned in school, the green of all living plants is caused by chlorophyll, a light-absorbing molecule that directs photosynthesis, the process by which green plants manufacture food out of sunlight and a few lifeless elements. All summer long, green leaves are everywhere making food: the sugars and starches and proteins that make up the lettuces in our salads, the tubers in our stews and the oak and maple trees of our forests. Then, as the days of sunlight shorten, and the atmosphere modifies into bright, temperate days and cool nights, another process begins. Each plant in its own way begins to prepare for freezing weather. This is the time that deciduous trees native to eastern coastal areas are genetically programmed to turn.

It begins when a layer of cells forms around each leaf stalk, choking the flow of fluid in and out of the leaf and eventually causing the leaf to drop. In the meantime, the production of chlorophyll slows down and ceases, allowing other pigments to have their "day in the sun." This doesn't happen to all leaves. It doesn't even happen to all leaves in New England. Our apple trees become a boring brown and our linden simply drops its leaves. But for some, the presence of such pigments as carotenoid (yellow and orange) and anthocyanin (red and purple) in the leaves creates an aura that makes October shine.

This all represents a tree's practical, inherited, evolutionary way of preparing for a frozen, foodless season. By taking nourishment from its leaf molecules and storing it, broken down into sugars and proteins, in its roots, the deciduous tree makes ready for a winter hibernation. And in the process of preparing for a long sleep, nature is having a last, lively fling by creating a landscape of multicolored intensity. This is what tourists come to see, the last hurrah, the final grand opulence of the October woods.

The maples begin to turn first. Sometimes as early as the end of August one catches a flash of gold or scarlet at the top of an old maple tree. The ashes come later, restricting their color code to gold and brown, and Virginia creeper, which winds its way so virulently up the trunks of trees and through their branches, redeems itself in a vermilion glow. Burning bush seems to suddenly come ablaze, generating such a bright magenta that its name seems understated, but barberry turns slowly, its tiny leaves mingling with red berries and hidden thorns in subtle shades of gold, orange, red and almost purple. The oak trees take their time about the whole event, changing first this part of a single leaf and then that, making a dapple of green and brown and red before they finally turn a rich terra-cotta. The beech leaves wait until last of all, drying to a parchment of pale yellow and then hanging tenaciously from their branches sometimes the whole winter through. Blueberries and briars of wild raspberry and blackberry redden in imitation of their taller neighbors. The Russian olive leaves become a shimmering silver that enhances the ruby luster of their berries. Even the pines give out a golden portion of their needles, which weave a pavement of sweet-smelling softness underfoot. These silent endeavors are not for the eyes of those restrained in their tastes, for here is gaudiness and pretension making an effort to mock the meek and proclaim that death can indeed be proud.

The flora of October do make a glorious last-ditch splash, but they are not simply scoffing in the face of inevitable destruction. They are also planning for the future generation and planning well, as only those who have experienced the trials and errors of evolution can. While leaves are waving red flags, brilliant berries are decorating a bush, enticing birds and deer, who eat and then excrete them, carrying seeds to new destinations and new lives. Inedible seeds have evolved in a multitude of ways to transport themselves to spots where they can germinate and grow. From the delicate wings of the milkweed to the clawlike burrs of the burdock, they fly or slog in the quest for an inviting, nurturing environment. Some plant seeds, like frogs' eggs, reproduce by the thousands, even the hundreds of thousands, in hopes of a few hardy survivors. Others, like the acorn or the walnut—representing the few but strong—are aided by squirrels or chipmunks who bury them in caches that are forgotten often enough that occasionally the contents take root and grow.

In these different ways the natural order celebrates the life-and-death cycle of all organic beings with insouciance, and many human cultures have either wittingly or unwittingly emulated this yearly process. Dull though we may be, we have noticed that the height of abundance and wealth comes directly before the death of the creative elements of the earth. In disparate cultures all over the world, people have felt the need to ritualize this dichotomy.

In New England, as in many areas in the Northern Hemisphere, October's end represents the end of a cycle, and its symbols and activities mingle bitter and sweet, life and death, abundance and decay. This is the time of richness from the earth and the abiding prophecy that it will soon end. The house and garage fill with baskets of potatoes, squash, onions, beets and carrots; the rafters hang with drying flowers and herbs; the pantry shelves creak with the weight of jars of pickles, tomatoes and dried beans and the freezer fills again with broccoli, cabbage and cauliflower. In the sky looms the possibility of a deadly cold that will turn the thin-skinned annuals to wretched black slime and warn the hardier perennial vegetation to slow down, toughen or drop their leaves and store their energies in their roots for next spring. The first frost in late September is the sky's signal that autumn has arrived. But the increasingly frequent frosts of October send a message that growth must stop, that death is on its way and the soon-to-die must prepare their heirs for the rebirth to come.

If harvesttime can be symbolized in some cultures by a New Year's celebration, the end of October can signify another sort of transition in our northern climate: the beginning of dying.

Consider our own twentieth-century Halloween, or All Hallow's Eve. Originally a synthesis of pagan and early Christian beliefs in northern Europe, it is now a pallid facsimile of such festivals as Druidic Samhain, or summer's end. The early Celts must have felt a closeness to the dead that has been taken away from us, for their October ghosts, hobgoblins, witches and elves were spirits of familial import and reality, not simply cardboard dolls in store windows, and they were honored during their mystical rituals. To the ancient peoples the spirits of the dead were real and significant, probably at least partly because the living would sooner or later be spirits themselves and hoped to enjoy attentions similar to those they were dispensing.

According to Druidic belief, on Samhain the spirits of the dead returned to earth to the homes of their living kin. These kin, anxious to please their forebears, lit great fires to guide the kindred spirits and to ward off the evil ones that roamed the countryside. Why one group would be attracted to such fires and another repelled is a mystery to me. The abundance of the harvest was proffered in ritual appeasement that the dead be content, that the living might abide unmolested by haunting ancestors for another year.

Even in the twentieth century, our cousins south of the border celebrate the Day of the Dead on November 1 with a vigor we might imagine was present at Druidic rituals. Mexico's El Dia de los Muertos, a blend of Christian and pre-Columbian beliefs, honors dead kin with that special Mesoamerican blend of festivity and solemnity.

Like the Celts, Mexicans light fires to guide their spirit relations to earth and to a festival in their honor. In modern Mexico, skeleton dolls, toys and candies are sold on every corner. These skeletons take on a jaunty air, often dressed in cowboy hats and boots, slinky red dresses or rock-and-roll apparel. As symbols of death they embody less a Western specter than that of a carefree, satirical rogue, skinless to be sure but cheerfully involved in activities of the earth. These folk figures are plucky reminders of the reality of death, its inevitability and its necessity to the cycle of all life.

In preparation for El Dia de los Muertos, Mexican villagers clean cemeteries, freshly paint tombs and decorate each family plot with candles and golden flowers, the Aztec symbol for the dead. A feast of the season's abundant foods and liquors is carried to the family burial place to be offered and enjoyed by both living and dead. Since the dead cannot actually eat, aromas are an important part of the menu planning. The dead may take pleasure in the scent of tacos and tequila. The living do not waste the substance. El Dia de los Muertos is not a solemn time.

This sort of ritual might seem macabre to those of us who are less connected with death here in our modern compartments. For us, hospitals are allocated for the dying, and funeral rituals hurry us into a period of mourning but seldom of celebration. To many native peoples, death and life are not antithetical but simply two aspects of a single process, which is the way all of us see death in the plant world. Perhaps we are not so different after all.

The Garden

For the gardener in October, the damp and buggy discomforts of summer abate, the trees offer technicolor, the chillier winds cool the vigorous toiler and the continued production of carefully fostered autumn plants gives satisfaction at beating the odds—but only a little, for there is still work to be done, and hubris does not inspire diligence.

Vegetable garden labor now falls essentially into three categories: fall cleanup, spring garden preparation and the continued reaping and processing of the fruits of the harvest. Doing cleanup and the groundwork for spring go hand in hand and follow, as in September, the last picking of any particular vegetable. Although rototilling a newly emptied bed is still a common practice among some gardeners, we no longer do it, for we found in our early years of gardening that the loosened piles of turned soil washed down our hill with greater ease during the barren months. Now a simple raking and the planting of annual rye have become our standard strategy. Rye germinates so quickly that its interlocking network of roots almost immediately secures and holds the soil intact until we turn it under in the spring.

After sufficient frosts have assured us that no spate of warm weather will send our perennials the message to grow again, we enrich them with compost, manure, lime and bonemeal, and mulch them with fallen leaves or salt hay. This is a late autumn job, designed to protect and nourish but not smother or encourage growth at the wrong time of year.

After the dry and yellowed fronds of the asparagus patch have been cut down and removed, we cover the bed with compost, manure and a blanket of leaves. The raspberries and blackberries are cut back to within two or three feet of the ground, then fertilized and mulched with leaves. Blueberries are fertilized and mulched with pine needles from a nearby grove, for they have an affinity for the acidic. To strawberries, however, we usually provide the luxury of a salt-hay covering, for their leaves and tendrils never completely die back, and the heaviness of a leaf cover could crush and asphyxiate them. Rhubarb is left to its own devices, for nothing seems to discourage it.

Raking leaves, a major late fall endeavor, is our primary source of mulch for both winter and next year's garden. We pile a mountain of willow, maple, linden, birch and ash leaves in a corner of the garden to remain until they are pulled into service next summer. We use the rest to mulch not only the vegetable perennials but such treasures as tree peonies and deciduous azaleas. In the days before the town dump stopped taking residents' leaf refuse, we even borrowed a few bags from there now and then. Next to compost, leaves are the freest, richest source of aid to the gardener, and, in the end, they become compost too.

After the early mild frost this year, we had a stretch of warm weather, warmer than usual, that kept straggly tomatoes still ripening into October, green peppers still producing, eggplants still alive but not producing fruit and pole beans still growing. Now at the end of the month we are still gathering lettuces, Chinese and European cabbages, carrots, beets, leeks, parsnips, kale, chard, broccoli and Brussels sprouts.

Our cabbage crop is noteworthy this season for its quality and size. We have one red cabbage that weighs almost twelve pounds, a record for us, and many more that demand a search for new ways to use cabbage. The red cabbages have always been good keepers, often maintaining themselves for several months in the refrigerator. Savoy types are less robust but delicate to taste and beautiful to behold. This year two crows, enamored of their frilly leaves, ravaged them and nothing else in the garden, returning every day to pick further into the aromatic interiors of two huge heads.

Our branching broccolis have filled our freezer with small, tasty buds. They grow so quickly that they can be picked daily, and a week in the city will leave the gardener with florets blossomed into yellow posies by the weekend. Kale, chard and Brussels sprouts continue to grow slowly, adding more sugar to their leaves with each frost. I have recently learned that the apical tip of the Brussels sprout plant secretes a hormone that inhibits growth in the sprouts that form along each stem. This is why the lower sprouts are always bigger than the upper ones—they are farther away from the hormone. I have now lopped off the offending apical tip and await the outcome. Will our upper sprouts grow larger? Did I lop too late? Next month will tell the tale.

Herb gathering is another October chore, although ideally it should have been going on all summer when herb leaves are freshest. This is a last-ditch effort to dry enough thyme, sage, basil, oregano, marjoram and savory to last the winter. We tie small bunches by the stems and hang them from the beams in the ceiling. When they are thoroughly dry, the leaves are crushed and put in a tightly closed glass container. They are aromatic and tasty for at least a year, and when the next crop surfaces next summer, I can toss them to the chickens with less remorse than I would feel flinging away a three-dollar jar from the grocery store.

There are other herbs—mint, chervil, tarragon—that I feel lose much of their fresh flavor in the drying process, so I freeze them in small plastic bags. Plastic is not my favorite container material, for I am convinced that I can taste the plastic in something that has been stored too long. Therefore, I try to use these herbs within a few months. Nothing, of course, is as tasty and aromatic as a leafy bunch fresh from the garden.

Another October treat is the produce from the second lettuce and Chinese cabbage sowings. Both these crops taste different in the fall. The cabbages seem sweeter, crisper and bigger, and they don't go to seed. The lettuce is sweet, but as the nights cool it develops a thicker, slightly harder skin. These are not the melt-in-your-mouth spring lettuces but hearty, vigorous greens full of vitamins and flavor.

Serendipitously we've discovered a new mesclum that we've enjoyed for weeks. Taisai greens, arugula, mache and cilantro that I had planted close to each other in the spring reseeded themselves when they went to seed in early August, and now appear in a mature leafy mélange that can be snipped right into the salad bowl, a perfect harmony of flavors.

Another newly surfaced addition to the fall table is the shiitake mushroom. These we have "planted" and left to grow as they will. No soil preparation can encourage them, but when they emerge they are a special treat.

Shiitakes may be started either in the fall or the early spring. Their growing requirements are few but explicit: dampness and relative cool. They sprout—at least my variety do—twice a year in October and May, sometimes sporadically, but always after a rain. Preparing them for future growth is a bit of a job, but once it is done, waiting for the delicious outcome is the only labor they require of us.

Shiitake spore may be ordered from a number of mushroom farms these days. It usually comes in the form of wooden plugs that have been saturated with the spore. The gardener's job is to situate them in the correct environment: inside a fresh red oak log, preferably under the branches of a pine tree. Requirements for the job include a good drill, a hammer, a container of melted canning wax (the sort one uses to cover homemade jelly), a small brush for spreading the hot wax and, of course, the spore plugs and logs.

The procedure begins with drilling holes about six inches apart on three sides of each log, tapping in the spore plugs and then sealing each plug with wax. The purpose of the wax is to keep contaminants out and moisture in. The hole-free side is for laying against the ground. If logs are stacked in a square, open arrangement, holes may be drilled all around.

Since we have few logs and much space, we simply lay our logs out on a thick layer of pine needles in a grove on the back slope. The higher end of each log rests on the ground and the other end is raised up a bit by placing it on another log that has not been injected. The logs should be kept damp but not so wet that they will rot quickly. My simple placement theory holds that the earth embedded log end will absorb moisture while leaving the rest of the log open for air circulation and, one hopes, long life. The trick to mushroom growing is constant dampness, so during dry spells a pine-needle mulch and an occasional watering will keep the environment correct.

Mushrooms emerge and grow rapidly after a rain, but languish in dry weather. A newly planted batch takes about a year to really get going, but a few mushrooms begin to appear in six months if conditions are favorable. Our logs have produced for two years and are said to last from three to five. A fine reward for a couple of hours' work.

Snails or slugs seem to love shiitakes, for I often find evidence of their presence, as I do on wild mushrooms. A partially munched but unknown woodland mushroom tells me that it is not poisonous, yet I have never dared to trust such evidence. I assume most wild creatures know what is good for them or they would never have endured. However, I'm not so sure they know what is good for us.

Woodland mushrooms that are good for us in the fall are puffballs and oyster mushrooms, both easily identifiable (remember that mushroom guide), delicious and easily detectable. A puffball grows in meadow grass and from a distance looks like a lost golf ball—that is, except for a variety that grows to gigantic proportions, which, if found while still young and fresh, can supplant a rib roast in both amplitude and flavor. We have found only one in all our years in the country. Unfortunately, it was over-the-hill, its interior turned yellow and sulphurous, but it was a magnificent sight to see.

Oyster mushrooms grow on old wood in beautiful white, beige or purple, fan-shaped clusters. Their flavor is delicate, their texture firm. Like shiitakes, they are easily dried and even more easily reconstituted with a bit of hot water to be used through the winter months. Oysters also freeze well and, since they are often found in large clusters, it is useful to remember that a plenteous batch may be eaten fresh, hung to dry or frozen.

As gathering continues, we move outside the garden to the orchard, where apples and pears continue to pile up in baskets and wheelbarrows, hardening into cider when we assist them, softening into an aromatic pablum when left too long.

Several years ago, I individually wrapped each of a bushel of pears in newspaper, having read that the paper retarded overripening. With no room left in the refrigerator, I sent them off to the cellar, asking a family member to put them in a cool corner. Two or three weeks later, we arrived for the weekend to find the house redolent with the scent of fermenting pear. The baskets in the cellar held masses of soupy pear and newspaper, all rapidly turning into a doubtful form of alcohol. The chosen location for this mix was next to the furnace.

In our last-but-not-least category, we gather fall raspberries and wild grapes for jam and plant garlic cloves and tulip and daffodil bulbs, reflecting all the while on winter and the remoteness of April. We've slaughtered a few of June's broiler chickens, now seven or eight pounds in weight and perfect for roasting. We are raising our annual veal and we've ordered a lamb from our neighbor. Our cornucopia overflows. Our backs ache, but our hearts are mellow. Again our land has served us well.

The Kitchen

In my Texas home there were only two cookbooks, *Fannie Farmer* and *The Joy of Cooking*, but there was a large recipe box full of handed-down recipes and a code of laws embodying virtually everything that was eaten or cooked. Little flexibility was allowed, and since flavors were mixed in tried-and-true ways, a certain sameness dulled the daily fare.

Potatoes were never served with chicken, only with beef. Rice, plainly boiled, was always the chicken accompaniment, as were sweet vegetables like carrots, winter squash or sweet potatoes, which were always cooked with a little sugar and butter. Lamb, not eaten at all by many Texans, was cooked "until it fell off the bone" and was also always eaten with rice, this time brown. Pork chops went with apple sauce, salad greens with steak. Garlic was reserved for the chili recipe acquired (and toned down) from a Mexican cook, and one head lasted for years. I remember what it looked like: small and wizened, sometimes powdery. What would you expect of an undervalued garlic?

These culinary rules and dozens of others were writ in stone and never violated. To find out later in life that wholly different approaches to combining and cooking foods existed and often surpassed those I knew was as enlightening to me as learning that everyone didn't have to be a Protestant.

Years ago in Brooklyn, I remember watching in surprise as a Haitian friend took sizable slices of fresh garlic and placed them under the skin of a roasting chicken. It was delectable, of course, but contrary to the Adams family edict of only sweet flavors with fowl, and garlic only—and sparingly—with chili. I was beginning to learn.

I remember vividly my first cooking class with Virginia Lee not only because she introduced us to cilantro, but because she sprinkled ground pork over a steamed fish, combining a taste and a cooking method I had never dreamed could be. I became an adventurer in the world of flavors.

In the following years I have never wavered in experimenting with new combinations of foods and seasonings. I've even come back to some of those of my childhood, such as greens cooked with salt pork (now sausage) and watermelon dusted with salt. But it is the cooking methodology of the faraway that intrigues me most.

Both Chinese and Indian cuisines have for centuries succeeded in creating innumerable tastes from both abundant and limited resources. I often turn to them and the condiments they use. When I am faced with a vegetable surplus, as happens in the fall, the knowledge that a cabbage may be stir-fried, steamed or boiled with a hundred different spice combinations adds immeasurably to dinner diversity and to the willingness of a family to eat cabbage (or whatever is abundant) yet again.

Although Bok choi and Chinese cabbage have been part of our menus for the last three months, I still think of autumn as cabbage season. While tomatoes and cucumbers demand our attention all summer long, the beds of cabbages grow evenly and slowly, finding what they need in the earth, fending off cabbage loopers and opening into the mammoths of October.

This year we have a frilly-leafed and a regular Chinese cabbage, Bok choi and the smaller, green-stemmed Mei Ching choi for Asian cooking. This is the second crop of each, all planted in late July. There are red and savoy cabbages for Western foods, and the broccolis and Brussels sprouts, first cousins to the cabbage family. These slow-growing Western vegetables were started indoors last spring.

Cabbages are good keepers, a major reason for their development as a staple peasant food throughout large areas of the world. Although they need a cool atmosphere, it need not be a refrigerator. Rural Chinese bury a winter's allotment of cabbage in earthen pits. Urban Chinese keep them in the unheated hallways of their apartment buildings, stacked in high mounds and turned periodically. A winter visitor to China might well find cabbage in some form at every meal.

The stronger-flavored Western cabbages are equally long-lived after harvest, but our centrally heated houses are no match for a Chinese pit or hallway, so we must refrigerate or cook and freeze them. The recipes below are only slightly less desirable thawed from the freezer. Sometimes when cooking a cabbage dish, doubling a recipe and freezing half of it is an easy way to process the stuff.

Kimchi (Korean Pickled Cabbage)

My Korean friend tells me that in the old days in Korea—that is, before mass use of refrigeration—this was made in enormous crocks ("Almost as big as I am," she claimed) and buried in pits in the yard. In that way it would last for several months. When pulled up, ice crystals would have formed around the cabbage, keeping it near freezing. Kimchi was always made in November when the fall cabbages were hardened by autumn cold. In the crock-and-pit version, the cabbages were simply split in two, not chopped. The dish was served throughout the winter months and was especially good with hot noodles.

My friend adds that nowadays people have refrigerators, so the practice of making a mountain of kimchi has disappeared. This refrigerator rendering she finds woefully inferior. It begins to soften after a few weeks, so it does not have the staying power of its illustrious ancestor. Still, to the uninitiated it is quite delicious.

INGREDIENTS:
1 large head Chinese cabbage
6 heaping tablespoons pickling salt
1 ground hot pepper, or to taste
2 or 3 garlic cloves, chopped
1-inch slice gingerroot, chopped
2 scallions with tops, chopped
1 teaspoon sugar

PROCEDURE:
1. Wash and roughly chop the cabbage. Place it in a bowl and sprinkle it with the salt. Stir so that the salt contacts all the cabbage.

2. Put the cabbage aside for about 2 hours.

3. Rinse and drain the cabbage. Combine it with the other ingredients. Store in glass jars in the refrigerator for several days before using.

Pickled Red Cabbage

INGREDIENTS:

1 large head red cabbage

1 to 2 tablespoons sweet butter

2 or 3 large, tart apples (such as Cortland, Northern Spy, Winesap or Granny Smith)

4 to 6 tablespoons good red wine vinegar, balsamic if possible

8 to 10 whole cardamom seeds

Salt

Pepper

PROCEDURE:

1. Peel away the rough outer leaves of the cabbage and discard them.

2. Cut the cabbage in two and remove the hard core. Slice it as thinly as possible and wash it carefully.

3. Melt the butter in a large pot and put in the moist cabbage. Cover the pot tightly and simmer the cabbage for about 10 minutes.

4. In the meantime, peel and core the apples, slice them rather thinly and mix them with the cabbage. Continue to simmer. Stir occasionally throughout the cooking process and make sure the mixture does not dry out. If it does, add a little water to the pot to prevent the cabbage from burning. (You shouldn't have to do this if the lid of your pot is tight and your flame is low.)

5. Shell the cardamom seeds and mash the small inner seeds with a mortar and pestle. Add the cardamom seeds, vinegar, salt and pepper to the cabbage. Stir the mixture. Adjust the seasonings to taste. If you feel there is too much vinegar, add a little salt, or sugar. (I once put sugar regularly in this dish, but now that I am raising my own cabbage and picking it after a fall frost or two, I prefer it without. I believe the frost sweetens cabbage as it does Brussels sprouts, so that it no longer needs sugar.)

6. When the cabbage is soft (which may take 1 hour or more), remove it from the heat. This is a dish that tastes better when the flavors have married.

Cabbage Soup

This soup can make a whole dinner. Try adding rounds of a good dry sausage and homemade croutons at the end. All you need is a loaf of fresh bread and a bottle of wine to complete this meal.

INGREDIENTS:

3 onions, chopped
4 leeks, thinly sliced
5 or 6 garlic cloves, crushed
1 head savoy cabbage, cut into bite-sized chunks
1 quart canned pureed tomatoes
2 to 3 tablespoons good olive oil
1 tablespoon fresh thyme
1 tablespoon fresh sage
2 bay leaves
Salt
Freshly ground pepper
1 to 2 quarts veal, chicken or beef stock

PROCEDURE:

1. Saute the onions, leeks and garlic in the olive oil. Add the cabbage.
2. Add the tomatoes, herbs, salt and pepper.
3. Add enough stock to cover the vegetables. Bring it to a boil, then reduce to a simmer. Skim occasionally, if necessary. Serve when the cabbage is soft.

Lamb and Squash Curry

Even with my array of squash and pumpkin recipes, the arrival of too many squash and pumpkins to count sends me looking for some new techniques. There are many.

The pumpkin/squash/yam cooking notion in the Southwest was that sweet vegetables must be cooked with sugar and butter and served with chicken or pork—sweet meats. In other times and places, squash has been combined with lamb, with mushrooms, with squash tomatoes and with beans and corn.

Indian spices in particular lend themselves to the rich, sweet flavor of squash, giving it a new character that works well both in vegetarian cooking and in combination with the heartier meats. Here is a recipe that took care of a pile of lamb spareribs and a large squash.

The recipe works equally well with chunks of stewing lamb, but those of us who raise our own are always looking for ways to use the odd assortments given to us in brown paper wrap in exchange for an animal on the hoof.

INGREDIENTS:

Spareribs from 1 lamb, about 2 pounds (or an equal amount of stew meat)
Sesame oil
3 or 4 small onions
2 or 3 garlic cloves
Squash, approximately equal in weight to the meat peeled and cut into chunks
Equal amount of potatoes (if you wish to stretch the meal even further), peeled and cut into chunks.
Liquid for cooking (meat or vegetable stock or fruit juice; tamarind juice adds an exotic flavor)
3 or 4 dried hot peppers
3 tablespoons ground coriander
Dash of turmeric
Several bay leaves
2 to 3 tablespoons chopped gingerroot
Good curry paste to taste
Salt
Pepper

PROCEDURE:

1. Heat the sesame oil in a heavy metal casserole. Add the ribs and toss them until they brown.

2. Add the onions and garlic. Stir so they will not burn. Reduce the heat. Add the potatoes to the pot first, since they require slightly longer cooking. Add the squash about 10 minutes later and stir again. Add the cooking liquid. Do not cover the stew with liquid, but add only enough to create a tasty sauce and prevent the bottom of the pot from burning. The liquid should be about 3 to 4 inches deep in the pan.

3. Add the spices. Stir.

4. Cook the stew until the potatoes and squash are soft but not mushy. Do not overcook or the vegetables will disintegrate and you will have a thick soup instead of stew.

5. Serve over a bed of rice.

Baked Squash

INGREDIENTS:

1 sweet dumpling squash or 1/2 acorn squash for each person
1/2 to 1 tablespoon butter for each squash helping
Dash of nutmeg for each squash helping
Dash of brown sugar for each squash helping
(Honey, cinnamon, allspice and ginger are also fine additions. Cranberries
can also be used to stuff the cavities, but then you need more sugar to
counteract their tartness.)

PROCEDURE:

1. Preheat the oven to 350°.
2. Split the acorn squash in half lengthwise, or hollow out the top of the sweet dumpling squash. Remove the seeds and set aside. Use a sharp spoon to remove the remaining fibers.
3. Place the squash, open side down, on a baking pan and pour in about 1/2 inch of water. Bake it for 30 minutes, checking to make sure the water has not evaporated.
4. Just as the squash begin to soften, turn them right side up and put the butter, nutmeg and brown sugar into their cavities.
5. Bake the squash for another 30 minutes or until it is soft and tender. Serve hot.

Squash and Pumpkin Seeds

Squash seeds are high in fiber and protein and tasty. In China and Mexico, they are dried and used year-round as healthy noshes. They may be found packaged in Chinese grocery stores, but they are not as crisp as this homemade snack.

INGREDIENTS:

Squash or pumpkin seeds
Salt
3 to 4 tablespoons cooking oil, preferably sesame
Finely chopped gingerroot (optional)

PROCEDURE:

1. Remove the seeds from the squash and separate them as well as you can from the large batches of surrounding fibers. Don't worry about the small fibers; they will disappear in the cooking process.
2. Pour sesame oil into a heavy iron skillet. Slosh it around to cover the bottom of the pan. Add the seeds and turn the heat to medium-high. Stir the seeds to coat them with the oil. Add the salt. Reduce the heat to as

low possible, and continue to brown and dry the seeds. Stir occasionally. (This is a good project to put on a back burner and keep an eye on while other food preparations are being done.)

3. The seeds will pop and sputter as the liquid evaporates. Sometimes one will fly across the room, so you may wish to cover the pan with a sieve or wire mesh cover, but do not put a lid on the pan or the seeds will become tough and rubbery instead of crisp.

4. Keep stirring occasionally throughout the cooking process. Taste-test the seeds for crispness. Add the gingerroot, if you like, toward the end of the cooking. Depending upon the size and species of squash seed the cooking time may vary from 45 minutes to over 1 hour. (This is no bother if the cook is bustling about in the kitchen and remembers to eye the product from time to time. If this is not possible, simply put the skillet in a low oven to finish cooking.)

5. When the seeds are done, place them on a paper towel to cool and drain. Leave them in a dish on the kitchen counter and wait for them to disappear.

Applesauce

If you haven't tasted applesauce since you fed it to the baby out of those Heinz jars, think about trying it again. It's a cinch to make, especially if you have an old-fashioned food mill to use as a strainer. It freezes well. It is just as good made with misshapen apples as with perfect ones.

INGREDIENTS:
> *Enough apples to fill a large pot*
> *Water*
> *Sugar to taste*
> *Cinnamon to color and flavor*

PROCEDURE:
1. Wash and pick over the apples. Do not core or peel them. Slice them into wedges.
2. Place the apples and cinnamon (which turns the sauce pink) in a large pot with enough water to prevent the bottom apples from burning before they secrete their juices. About 1 inch is probably enough.
3. Cover and cook the apples over moderately low heat until they are soft.
4. Put the apples through a food mill or sieve to remove the skins and seeds. Add the sugar to taste. Stir until it dissolves. Reheat, if necessary.

Applesauce Bread

If applesauce is the solution to too many apples, this cake or bread is the solution to too much applesauce. According to my sister, our mother used to make this recipe with bacon grease in true waste-not-want-not tradition. But that was before cholesterol was discovered.

INGREDIENTS:

1 cup vegetable shortening or oil
1-1/2 cups sugar
3 eggs, room temperature
2 cups homemade applesauce with cinnamon
2-1/2 cups flour
1 teaspoon mace or nutmeg
3 teaspoons baking soda
1 teaspoon salt
2 cups pecans, chopped

PROCEDURE:

1. Grease and flour either 2 loaf pans or 1 ring-type cake pan. Preheat the oven to 375˚.
2. Sift the flour, mace or nutmeg, salt and baking soda together. Set aside.
3. Cream the shortening or oil and sugar. Beat the eggs into this mixture 1 at a time. Fold in the applesauce and the flour mixture, adding first a little applesauce and then a little flour, continuing until all is folded in. Add the pecans.
4. Pour the mixture into the pans. Place them in center of the oven. Bake for 1 hour. Test for doneness with a knife or toothpick. Cool on a rack.

NOVEMBER

The fields of November
Fit like a lion's hide:
Old, dreaming lion,
Cold, sleepy ground

The hollows and the rises,
The boulders, the long swells,
All of them are one there,
Breathing under brown.

But faint breath, and slow beat:
The fields of November
Fit like a warm skin
The dark of the world.

—Mark Van Doren
"The Fields of November"

The Land

When Mark Van Doren speaks of November's brown earth, he speaks of our hill—actually the other side of it—with its sun-facing pastures and woods, for the home of his last years is not a mile from us as the crow flies, over the edge of the south slope and in a hollow. These are fields and hollows the poet made part of my mind long ago, and they stayed rooted there until we moved to our mountain.

It happened one summer in 1951 or 1952 when I was home from college. It may have been that fateful summer when television arrived in west Texas and brought with it the outside world in black and white. We all watched everything obsessively, night after night, and on one of those blistering evenings when you can still see the heat waves rising from the sidewalks, we tuned in to a live interview program where the interviewer travels to the home of a famous person and asks about his or her art, ideas or accomplishments. The program I remember presented Mark Van Doren as he sat in his yard in an unnamed place in New England, an area to which I had never been, but which seemed to resemble the verdant hills my father described in his tales of rural Pennsylvania.

The cameras hazily panned the hills around Van Doren's garden. He talked eloquently of the inspiration those hills provided. I sat spellbound, a naive, romantic girl who loved poetry, watching the poet laureate in a rolling, wooded place, so different from the prairie. I remember saying, "I'd love to live there someday." Everyone laughed, I'm sure, for they too were looking at the snowy television screen, but I never forgot that program or that place. It was many years later and some months after we bought the house in Connecticut that I learned the Van Doren home was across the way.

We have now spent seventeen years in this corner of New England, a mere drop in the bucket compared to the inhabitants who measure their residence in generations. Our house is still referred to as the Smith house, the name of a family who moved away in 1955. Before that the house had always been inhabited by a Sedgwick or a Hurlburt family. The ancestors of these two families moved to our hill around 1748, settled across from each other, intermarried and prospered, wresting the hilly land from nature and charging it with the energy they brought across uncharted forests. The Hurlburt family remains today still stewards of their land. A 240-year-old farm that hasn't self-destructed must be a miracle by today's standards, but there it is beside us, changing little, giving back to the land what it must to sustain a healthy environment. The heifers tread the same pastures; the farmer sows the same fields. The seasons come and go, and the cycle continues.

Winter sends its advance guard now, in frost, rain and winds that blow the last leaves from the trees to form a carpet of crisp, brown stuff that adds music to one's walk. The woods are suddenly opened up, exposing the bare bones of the earth, usually hidden by plant life or snow. They emerge silently to tell us a tale of our planet naked, when it is not dressed in green.

Trees without leafage display diverse sculptural patterns in their trunks, branches and bark, from the swirling singularity of an old apple tree to the towering splendor of the giant black locusts in a neighbor's yard. These two, more than any other of our barren trees, have shapes so distinct that they appear to be nature's boldest artistry against the gray November sky.

The ancient stone walls are also more clearly defined now, reinforcing our respect for the miles and years of labor they represent. Stone outcroppings and boulders emerge as leafy summer curtains drop, reminding the observer of the ancient glacier that laid them down with such indifference. The lowering southern sun, no longer thwarted by a leafy canopy, warms the ledges and feeds their patches of lichen and moss, persistent even in freezing weather.

A few reluctant oak and beech leaves still cling to their branches and combine with the barberry's lingering red berries to color one's path through woods where abandoned bird nests now materialize, secure in a high tree or precarious among the spindly branches of a leafless bush. Wild dogwood branches, bereft of their leaves, are turning a deep wine-red that sets them off against winter snows. Marsh reeds, faded to a soft ecru, have sprouted their fringed topknots, winter hats that nod and quiver in a breeze. November's colors are subtle ones, a thousand shades of brown with touches of green and red. It is the occasional ice storm that adds glitter to the late fall decor.

With most leaves now on the ground, unifying into a homogenous beige, walking is a noisy business, which often makes me think of something I must have read as a child. I was told—and believed—that Amerindians could move silently, setting their toes down first, across any terrain. I tried it and failed for years, frustrated both by my genetic deficiency and the clicking, hard-soled shoes that good mothers used to force their children to wear. Still, I thought it might be possible, if only I had moccasins or sneakers.

Today, with the wisdom of age, I would assure anyone—Amerindian or not—that walking in our autumn woods cannot be done quietly and stealthily. This can be a problem when hiking is charged with the hope of seeing a deer, a flock of wild turkeys, a coyote, a black bear or even a cougar. This year a bear and a cougar have been sighted several times in our neighborhood, as well as an albino deer—magical in the moonlight, I am told.

In our area, such large, feral animals as these have been observed regularly returning to our secondary woodlands for the last ten to twenty years. A hundred years ago, with most of New England's lands cultivated, there wasn't enough forest habitat left to support the foraging needs of large wild animal populations. Probably hunting added to faunal extinctions too. It has taken this last hundred years for the forests to return, if only partially, replacing the fallow farms that were abandoned during the late-nineteenth-century western expansion. Only now are these creatures coming back.

Imagine them, migrating slowly over generations, from some northern wilderness, across highways, around towns, under power lines, through shopping mall parking lots, past factories and over the remaining farmers' fields. Why would they risk coming so close to civilization? Was another habitat impoverished, another environment contaminated? Did their populations explode? How long are they likely to survive here? And how does a territory change and still maintain that fragile balance that allows its various species to endure?

These questions are not easy to answer. The answers are found only in the often unheard, unseen world of the wild, a world we humans rarely confront.

A few winters ago we encountered it briefly. While cross-country skiing, we came upon a heavy layering of hundreds of coyote tracks and, on closer inspection, the almost buried tracks of a deer. The snow was deep, so the heavier deer, with its less adaptive hooves, had sunk down with each step, thus impeding its movements and slowing its gait. The lighter, flat-footed coyotes could run easily on top of the frozen surfaces, and so they did, as the testimony of their tracks revealed, surrounding and hounding their large and increasingly defenseless prey. As we followed this remnant of a recent drama, we found spots of blood still bright against the snow, then more and finally, lying silently as in the aftermath of battle, a buck deer's carcass, cleaned of everything but bone and fur. The coyotes had made it through another day. The deer had not.

Coyotes are not popular animals among farmers and ranchers in any part of the world, for they attack calves and sheep as well as rabbits, woodchucks, wild turkeys and deer. In Texas they were summarily slaughtered as often as possible, as were rattlers and wolves. It is their plight to be carnivorous. I sympathize, but I would hate to meet up with a pack on a cold, dark winter's night.

The Garden

The yard around our house seems gaunt these days, with flower beds bare, the vegetable garden nearly empty and deciduous trees skeletal against the sky. There is one enchanting event though, an autumn phenomenon I look for each year. Behind the perennial garden, a huge, old witch hazel has been covered with blossoms for several weeks. Small, wispy, bright yellow flowers defying the rule of springtime blossoming, they flutter smartly in the frosty breeze, all the more remarkable in their solitude.

Always interested in a nonconformist, I particularly appreciate this rogue whose modest production would be disregarded if it had to compete with May's daffodils and lilacs. It has amended its ways to achieve maximum appreciation from folks like me. I always clip a few branches to bring home, a bit of spring for a shivery fall corner.

For most other plants in our garden, an ill-timed fall blossoming can prove harmful, even ruinous, to the next season's production. In these last few years, patches of unseasonal warmth have sometimes fooled some of our spring-blossoming perennials into swelling their buds and threatening to burst into bloom. With ground not yet frozen, and days of excessive mildness interspersed with seasonally appropriate ones, the earth's messages to roots and leaves are mixed and the results confused. A tulip that uses its limited resources to push up a stalk in November will be unlikely to grow as lustily again in the spring. Trees nipped in the bud have used finite energies to no avail.

I have often wondered about the mentality of the plant, the sensitivities it needs toward water, sun and temperature to survive and prosper. With monumental climate changes at our doorstep, how speedily will the world's vast array of plant life be able to adapt and rearrange its sensibilities to a hotter, drier atmosphere?

Early on in my gardening ventures, when I started growing seedlings indoors to be transplanted outside in warmer weather, I discovered that seeds do not necessarily do one's bidding, however coaxed. Different seeds are awakened at different temperatures, regardless of the earth and water they were planted in. Peas and lettuce germinate in cool, damp weather. Melons need heat and strong sun. The genes of each respond to primeval programming.

One tomato seed, given the proper environment, can produce a massive vine and twenty-five pounds of tomatoes in three months. An Antarctic lichen, given the proper environment, can grow steadily to the size of a dessert plate in five hundred years. Neither could survive in the other's climate and would be lost if required to do so. It's an interesting picture, that of weather change that moves faster than plants are able to adapt, but it could prove a desolate one.

Plant-watching can teach you much about the habits and idiosyncracsies of various species, but it can explain little about the process by which their actions and reactions take place. Wiring up plants to lie detectors—as some have done—and observing their ostensible reactions might discourage the consumer from peeling a carrot, never mind eating it. But knowledge of a plant's particular needs is of advantage to the gardener and the casual plant-tender alike.

Recently I brought a potted rosemary bush from our dining room in the country to a sunny window in Brooklyn. It had been partially killed back the year before, when a careless caretaker forgot to water it while we were away. I had nurtured and loved this plant for so long that I feared another winter in alien hands would surely do it in. I watered it well, sprayed it with mist and found it, within two days, devoid of any live, green leaves—in other words dead. The country house temperature is set at about forty-five degrees when we are absent. The sudden shift to a warmer and drier air must have been the death knell for a fifteen-year-old plant. This time I was the betrayer.

For the gardener, November is a month of tying up the loose ends, minding matters that were forgotten in October, checking the list of fall projects to make sure they are done before the ground is frozen. Two rows of garlic cloves have been planted in a raised bed and mulched with leaves. Many of the parsnips, Egyptian onions, carrots and leeks are also mulched, to be retrieved in springtime. These I pile up heavily with leaves, maybe a foot high. Even so, leftover carrots are usually only strips of orange slime in spring. The others always survive the cold and are a dependable April treat.

Piles of branches and twigs have been burned (always on a damp, windless day and, in our community, with a permit). Pyramids of dried leaves wait for spring, when they will be brought into service. The vegetable garden, still checkered with green rye, is a flat and exposed place, awaiting a blanket of snow and hibernation.

Now that we have donkeys to manufacture manure from grass and clover, we continue to scatter their ovate offerings randomly. By spring they will have transformed into the next stage of their cycle as a home for microorganisms and food for plants. Donkeys tend to have an organized excretion pattern, leaving most of their droppings in the same areas and creating large piles that are easy pickings for the gardener. The sheep spreads her contributions over a wider range, which should make for better pasture next year. We are learning that two donkeys and one sheep have just about the correct appetite for our three-plus-acre pasture. They keep it down, but not overgrazed. Our only problem is the donkeys' habit of girdling trees during the winter months and munching away at barn doors, windowsills, old sheds, scattered lumber and fence posts. We've put chicken wire around as many trees as we can and chopped down the girdled and dead ones, hoping their tops will assuage our voracious beasts, but we have not wholly deterred them. I guess hay, grain, water and an occasional carrot are not enough for our equine epicures.

The Kitchen

The vegetable garden looks empty now, but all is not gone. Still providing pickings are the root vegetables: carrots, beets, parsnips, celeriac, horseradish and leeks. These can be kept in the ground until it freezes, a practice I follow on the premise that the vegetables will remain fresh there and leave room in the refrigerator for other things.

Brussels sprouts are sweeter after a frost, as horseradish is stronger. Arugula also thrives in cool fall air, and other lettuces fare well until a hard frost, which sends them drooping to the ground. Kale and Swiss chard are hardy spirits that hang on, tasting better all the time. And thyme and sage—those staples in the Thanksgiving stuffing—can survive covered with snow.

With the larder full, we have most of the makings of a Thanksgiving dinner right out of our own garden (see menu, page 194). All, that is, save the turkey, for Tom, the lone survivor of our spring turkey-raising project, is protected from our axe. That undertaking has delivered unto us a pet, not a poultry dinner.

Of the three day-old turkey babies we bought in June, one died within two days, and the second lasted until midsummer, when it flew off into the woods and its own destiny. The third, a male, grew in health, size and contentment, but with no models of his own species to emulate he increasingly turned to us for behavioral guidelines. He ate from our outstretched hands, sat in our laps, allowed himself to be petted and hugged and waited in the evening at the barn door to be carried to bed. His size and dignity saved him from harassment by his chicken-coop mates. His blue-headed beauty, throaty gobbles, carefully programmed displays of undulating tailfeathers and elegant manners turned him into an avian Scheherazade, as he used his winning ways to extend his life and make himself beloved.

His gentleness balances his size, and his fans range from three-year-olds to cynical adults and strangers who stop their cars on the road to watch him parade around the yard. Tom has sealed his fate. He will die of old age or obesity, but never at our hands.

Marinated Carrots

Roots are the foods of Thanksgiving, and it is easy to see that the traditional holiday menu evolved out of what was readily available in the New England autumn before the days of widespread food transport, freezers and canned goods.

A hundred-year-old cookbook is likely to have many more recipes for root vegetables than a more modern one. In times before refrigeration, these were the staples of the vegetable diet, and in times before that they were the "meat" of everyday menus for ordinary people. High nutritive value and easy prolonged storage made them the daily fare of many of our ancestors.

This recipe has long been my sister's contribution to holiday meals. With it she turns the ordinary carrot into an epicurean delight.

INGREDIENTS:
1 pound carrots, scraped and cut into 3- by 1/4-inch strips
1 cup white wine
1 cup chicken broth
5 tablespoons olive oil
3 tablespoons white wine vinegar

2 shallots, chopped
1 garlic clove, chopped
1 teaspoon sugar
1 teaspoon salt
Pepper to taste
Bouquet garni (parsley, bay leaf, thyme)
12 walnut halves
Lemons
Parsley

PROCEDURE:

1. Place the wine, chicken broth, olive oil, wine vinegar, shallots, garlic, sugar, salt, pepper and bouquet garni in an enamel saucepan. Bring it to a boil and simmer uncovered for about 5 minutes. Add the carrots and cook, uncovered, for about 5 minutes until they are tender but still have a crispy edge. Let them cool and then chill them in the marinade for 24 hours.

2. Blanch the walnut halves in boiling water for about 2 minutes. Drain them and slip the skins off. Lightly brown them in a little olive oil.

3. Transfer the carrots and some of the marinade to a serving dish. Add the lemon juice to taste. Garnish with the walnuts, thinly sliced bits of lemon and chopped parsley.

Deep-fried Celeriac

Celery root, or celeriac, is the gnarled monster of the garden; an undersized celery plant on top, it hides beneath the ground a brown behemoth of an orb.

Celery root grows at an evolutionary pace, needing to be planted in flats at least six weeks before it is put out in May, where it continues to mosey listlessly toward the sun while the beets and lettuces around it threaten to cover its spindly weak fronds. Even if kept in the ground until November, which is my practice, the bulbous root is not always as large as I would hope. The bulb itself is attached to a Medusa-like conglomeration of subterranean tendrils so massive that one might think they could soak up enough nutrients to grow a celeriac in a matter of weeks. But for all their trouble and acned look, they are well worth the gardener's efforts. They keep well in a refrigerator hydrator, and they have a fresh, earthy flavor that may be savored by itself or in combination with others.

INGREDIENTS:
> *Fresh, crisp celery root bulbs*
> *Salt*
> *Pepper*
> *Vegetable oil*

PROCEDURE:
> 1. Peel the celery roots and slice to make round, flat, very thin pieces. A food processor or a mandoline functions well to create thin, even slices, and the thinner the slices, the crisper the product. Place them on a towel to absorb excess moisture.
> 2. Heat the oil in a wok or deep fryer. Test for readiness by dropping in a small piece of celery root. If it bubbles and rises to the top of the oil, the temperature is right for cooking.
> 3. Put the slices into the boiling oil, making sure they do not stick to one another. They are done when they are lightly browned and crisp, which takes only a few minutes. Salt and pepper them and serve immediately. They taste like celery-flavored potato chips.

Celeriac Rémoulade

Since this classic French use of celeriac is best with raw, crisp slices of the vegetable, use only the freshest, heaviest specimens.

INGREDIENTS:
> *2 or 3 celery roots (about 2 pounds)*
> *1 to 1-1/2 cups homemade mayonnaise (see the March chapter)*
> *Dijon mustard to taste*
> *Lemon juice to taste*
> *Salt*
> *Pepper*
> *Heavy cream*
> *Italian parsley*
> *Lettuce greens*

PROCEDURE:
> 1. Peel the celery root and cut it into thin, even julienne strips, just long enough to fit into one's mouth.
> 2. Mix the mustard, lemon juice, salt and pepper into the mayonnaise. Taste it and adjust the flavors as you like. Add a few tablespoons of cream to thin the mixture to a consistency less solid than the mayonnaise but not soupy.
> 3. Toss the celery root and mayonnaise together. Marinate it in the refrigerator for several hours. Serve on a bed of greens and garnish it with the Italian parsley.

Braised Leeks

By October those frail, green tendrils we planted deep in their compost-lined trough have become robust giants, leaves/stems flirting in the breeze, roots reaching deep into the earth. The trough is filled in now, and a six- to eight-inch, snow-white bulb hides, waiting to be pulled.

I use leeks in many ways this time of year, leaving them in the ground until I need them. They survive until the ground freezes, and even then if they are left behind, will reemerge in spring. Though slimy at first, if left to their own devices they will send up new life. In its second year, a leek produces a stem through the middle of the leaves, and on top of it a large orb of a flowering seed pod, quite beautiful to behold and, with its long stem, a useful element in dried-flower arrangements. I try always to leave a few leeks for their summer flowers.

Now in the fall we concentrate on the flavor and versatility of this symbol of Wales.

INGREDIENTS:

1 large or 2 small leeks per person
Cooking liquid (water, chicken stock or vegetable stock)
About 2 tablespoons butter
Salt
Pepper

PROCEDURE:

1. Peel the leeks back to the first perfect leaves. Cut the green ends down to the point where they are tender. Trim the root end, making sure the leek still holds together. Wash them carefully. Grit can be hiding between the outer and inner leaves.
2. Melt the butter in a pan that will hold all the leeks in a single layer. Place them in the pan.
3. Sauté the leeks over low heat, turning frequently, until they are slightly browned.
4. Add enough cooking liquid to fill the pan, about 1/3 inch. Cover the pan and continue to simmer over low heat until the leeks are tender, about 15 minutes. Serve hot.

Oyster Bisque

INGREDIENTS:

1 quart fresh shucked oysters with oyster liquor
3 or 4 leeks, thinly sliced and chopped
3 carrots, thinly sliced and chopped
2 celery stalks, thinly sliced and chopped
3 tablespoons sweet butter
Fresh thyme
1 bay leaf
1/2 to 3/4 bottle good dry white wine
1/2 pint heavy or light cream
2 egg yolks, beaten
Salt
White pepper
Splash of cognac (optional)

PROCEDURE:

1. Melt the butter in a soup pot.
2. Add the leeks, carrots and celery and stir.
3. Add the oysters and oyster liquor. Cook until the oysters have curled around the edges.
4. Add the wine and a little water, if necessary, to cover the solids with about 4 inches to spare.
5. Add the thyme, bay leaf, salt and pepper.
6. Simmer over low heat until all the vegetables are soft, about 30 minutes.
7. Add the beaten egg yolks and stir.
8. Add the cream and, if you wish, cognac. Serve.

Corn Bread and Biscuit Stuffing

This is more or less the recipe used by my mother, her mother and her grandmother. The Brown women were proud cooks and terrible snobs about their dressing, which they never called "stuffing" and never put inside the bird. It was formed into patties and baked for about half an hour just after the turkey had emerged from the oven. It came out crispy on the outside and juicy on the inside. It never contained sage or, horror of horrors, the powdered stuffing herbs that came premixed in a yellow box with a picture of a turkey on the front. It never contained pecans, oysters, chestnuts or sausage. These women were purists and didn't believe in mixing too many flavors. They also didn't believe in sage. Cooking was a religion to them. Sage was simply bad in dressing. It was a moral issue as well as a culinary one.

Now I have put all of the above in my stuffing, though not at one time, and I put stuffing inside the turkey as well as in the pan in the form of patties. I love sage and use it fresh from the bush. Yet I have clung to the basic recipe, adding and subtracting over the years. Once or twice when the children were young and I felt overworked, I even bought stuffing in a plastic bag at the grocery store. The guilt was overwhelming. I haven't done that in ages.

INGREDIENTS:
Corn bread (1 recipe)
Buttermilk biscuits (1 recipe)
2 to 4 onions
5 or 6 celery stalks
Sweet butter or corn oil
2 teaspoons fresh, chopped sage
2 teaspoons fresh, chopped thyme
2 teaspoons fresh, chopped parsley
Salt
Pepper
Stock made from the neck and giblets of the turkey (not the liver)
Optional (1 of the following): sausage, oysters, 1 to 1-1/2 cups walnuts or
    pecans or whatever you might want to add

PROCEDURE:
1. Make the corn bread and the biscuit dough several days ahead of time to give it time to dry out.
2. Crumble up the two breads with a food processor or your hands. Don't crumble so finely that there are no lumps. Mix them in a large bowl.
3. Simmer the neck and giblets in 3 or 4 cups of salted water.
4. Sauté the onions and celery in the butter or corn oil until they are slightly soft.
5. At this point you may also sauté small bits of sausage, oysters or whatever else you want to add. If the addition is pecans or walnuts, they don't need to be precooked, but anything that requires cooking should be sautéed before it is mixed with the bread crumbs.
6. Add the sautéed ingredients or nuts to the bowl of bread crumbs. Also add the sage, thyme, parsley, salt and pepper. Stir the ingredients thoroughly. Then pour the turkey broth over the mixture and stir again. The right amount of moisture is key to the success of any stuffing, but it all depends on the dryness of the bread and on whether you plan to stuff the turkey or make patties. Stuffing to go in the bird should be drier because it will absorb turkey juices. Patties must be moister because they will dry out in the oven.

7. Stuff both the main cavity of the bird and the neck cavity, securing with skewers and string if necessary.

8. While the turkey is in the oven, make stuffing patties and put them on a cookie sheet. Bake them for 30 minutes after the turkey is removed from the oven. (It will stay warm for at least 1 hour, and the postcooking rest makes it much easier to carve.) Giblets are saved and combined with the liver to be used in gravy.

Corn Bread

Remember that cheating and using a corn bread mix or storebought corn bread is not acceptable. Commercial corn bread almost always contains sugar, which doesn't work well in poultry stuffing. It also usually contains preservatives that change the flavor as well as the nutritive value.

This recipe was sent to me by my great-aunt Jennie when I was first married thirty-five years ago. I wonder if she was thinking of my Bostonian husband when she scribbled after the brief instructions, "Good for those who turn up noses at corn bread."

INGREDIENTS:

> *3/4 cup cornmeal, preferably stone-ground*
> *1-1/4 cups unbleached flour*
> *3 teaspoons baking powder*
> *1 extra large egg, well beaten*
> *1 cup sweet milk*
> *4 tablespoons sweet butter or vegetable shortening*
> *1 teaspoon salt*
> *1/4 cup sugar (optional, but not to be included if corn bread is to be used for stuffing)*

PROCEDURE:

1. Preheat the oven to 375˚.
2. Sift the flour with the baking powder and combine with the cornmeal and salt.
3. Add the egg.
4. Add the milk and stir until well mixed.
5. Add the butter or vegetable shortening.
6. Turn the batter into a buttered baking dish and bake for 30 to 40 minutes.
7. Cool on a cake rack.
8. If it to be used for stuffing, break the cake into several pieces to facilitate drying. Then store it in a dry place so it won't mold.

Buttermilk Biscuits

I love buttermilk biscuits. They are moister and flakier than any other, have a fresh flavor and remind me of breakfast at a ranch we once visited in the Texas hill country when I was a child. There we had them with roast quail, fried pork chops and grits—a delicious memory.

I always use unbleached flour for biscuits and pastry crust because it has more flavor. Shortening is a sacrilege to some cooks, but it has no cholesterol and makes a flakier dough. I like to reserve butter and its richness for dishes that really suffer without it.

Real buttermilk is sometimes hard to find but can be made at home by adding 1 to 2 tablespoons of lemon juice or vinegar to lukewarm sweet milk. After the addition, let the milk stand for a little while before using it.

INGREDIENTS:

2 cups unbleached flour
1 tablespoon baking powder
1/2 to 1 teaspoon salt
1/2 teaspoon baking soda
1/2 cup vegetable shortening
3/4 cup buttermilk

PROCEDURE:

1. Preheat the oven to 450˚.
2. Sift all the dry ingredients into a mixing bowl.
3. Add the vegetable shortening and cut it into the mixture with a pastry cutter or a large pastry fork. Cut for about 1 minute until you have an evenly lumpy mixture. Don't overwork! The leaden biscuits you've had were probably the result of overzealousness in the mixing process. Save your beating arm for egg whites. Biscuits, like pastry, must be lightly handled.
4. Add the buttermilk and mix quickly.
5. Pat the dough together and turn it into a buttered pan.
6. Bake for 12 to 14 minutes, or until the top is lightly browned.

There is no need to cut the dough into individual biscuits if you are using it for stuffing, but the same recipe may be cut into individual rounds with a cookie cutter or a glass or cup turned upside down. In this case, place individual biscuits side by side, touching each other, in the same sort of pan.

As with the corn bread, break up the finished biscuit and store in a dry place.

Roast Turkey

1. Preheat the oven to 450°.
2. Stuff and truss the turkey and place it breast side down in a wire poultry holder in a large roasting pan. This isn't the way the turkey will look on the platter, but it keeps the juices flowing into the breast rather than out of it. If the pan is a bit small, make a collar of aluminum foil around the bird.
3. Baste the bird with butter. Place it in the oven.
4. Roast the turkey for 20 minutes. Baste again, and reduce the heat to 375°.
5. Continue to baste it with butter, and then with pan juices, every 20 to 30 minutes.
6. Turn the turkey right side up and continue to roast until top is nicely browned.

There are all kinds of rules on the amount of time it takes to cook a turkey. I find it never takes as long as it is supposed to. I put a 22-pound turkey in the oven at 11 A.M. and turn it right side up to brown and crisp the top at about 3.30 P.M.. It is always ready between 4:00 and 4:30. (This translates to 12 minutes per pound.) Two ways to check are wiggling a wing (if it is loose, it is done) and piercing the thick section above the thigh with a fork (if juices run clear, it is done).

Once removed from the oven, the turkey should stand for at least 30 minutes before carving. This gives the cook time to bake extra stuffing and make gravy. Slight cooling also makes the bird easier to carve.

Gravy is made by deglazing the roasting pan with 2 to 3 cups of water, adding 2 to 3 tablespoons of flour (first mixed with cold water so that it won't lump), stirring until thickened, adjusting the flavor if necessary and straining over the chopped giblets.

Steamed Brussels Sprouts

If we have a large crop of Brussels sprouts, I often parboil and freeze them for winter use. If they have come from the freezer, I simply cook them less. Also, smaller sprouts need less final cooking. A taste-test will tell you.

No matter how much you hated Brussels sprouts as a child, allay your fears and try the homegrown variety. Never, never pick them before at least one hard frost. Eat them as fresh as you can. You'll notice a difference.

INGREDIENTS:

1 pound Brussels sprouts, cleaned and trimmed of stems and any
yellowed leaves
Water for a steamer
Salt
Splash of good white wine vinegar, white wine or lemon juice
2 tablespoons sweet butter

PROCEDURE:

1. Score the bottoms of the sprouts. Place them in the top of a steamer containing about 2 cups of water. Steam until the sprouts are tender, but not mushy, and bright green, about 20 to 25 minutes.

2. Remove the sprouts from the steamer. Put them in saucepan with the butter, lemon juice or wine and salt. Stir to mix the flavors and serve.

3. You may add any of a number of things to create a delicious and unusual dish. Crisp, crumbled smoked bacon, sautéed water chestnuts or crème fraiche are different ways to dress up an already tasty dish. Experiment.

Pastry Crust

The key to any pie is a crisp, flaky, fresh-tasting crust. It is easy to make, but you must remember that the harder you try, the tougher the result is likely to be. I use vegetable shortening because it seems to make a flakier crust. Sweet butter in the same amount may be substituted. It is tastier but makes a more solid, less crispy pastry. Try making pastry crust both ways (or with lard, the way our great grandmothers made it), and see which you prefer.

This recipe makes 2 10-inch crusts, a lower and an upper or two lowers.

INGREDIENTS:

2-1/4 cups unbleached flour
3/4 cup vegetable shortening
6 to 8 tablespoons ice water
Pinch of salt

PROCEDURE:

1. Put the flour and salt into a bowl.

2. Cut the shortening into the flour with a pastry cutter, pastry fork or 2 knives. Work quickly and stop while the mixture is still very lumpy.

3. Add the ice water and mix with your hands. You will know you've added enough when the dough begins to hold together.

4. Pat the dough down into the bowl. Cover and refrigerate it for about 1 hour to give the gluten time to act. The dough will be easier to handle.
5. Knead the dough just enough to make it hold together. Roll it out on a floured board to the size needed for the pie pan. Fit it into the pan. Trim the edges.

If you are making a custard sort of pie, like pumpkin, bake the lower crust at 500° for about 8 to 10 minutes before you add the filling. To keep the crust from shrinking on the sides, cover it tightly with aluminum foil. Remove the foil a couple of minutes before the crust is done. This will dry the outside and prevent it from absorbing the filling and becoming soggy.

New England Pumpkin Pie

INGREDIENTS:
1 pastry crust (see above)
1-1/2 cups fresh pumpkin puree (can be made ahead and frozen)
3 tablespoons melted butter
1/4 cup light brown sugar
1/4 cup maple syrup
1 teaspoon cinnamon
1/2 teaspoon freshly ground nutmeg
1/4 teaspoon ground cloves
3 eggs, separated
1/4 cup milk

PROCEDURE:
1. Preheat the oven to 375°.
2. Roll out the pastry. Line the pan and bake as described above.
3. Combine the pumpkin, butter, sugar, syrup and spices. Add the egg yolks 1 at a time and beat. Add the milk and beat. Adjust the flavors, if necessary.
4. Beat the egg whites until stiff and fold into the pumpkin mixture.
5. Pour the mixture into the pastry crust and bake for 45 minutes. When a knife inserted into the middle comes out clean, the pie is done.

This may be served with whipped cream with a little sugar added. The pie will fall a bit as it cools. The falling is normal. It is a light and tasty creation.

Apple Pie

INGREDIENTS:

1 pastry crust (see above)
6 to 8 tart cooking apples (such as Granny Smith, Winesap, Northern Spy
or Cortland)
1 cup dark brown sugar
1 tablespoon cinnamon
1 teaspoon freshly ground nutmeg
1/2 teaspoon allspice or cloves
4 tablespoons sweet butter

PROCEDURE:

1. Preheat the oven to 375˚.
2. Fit the lower crust into a 10-inch pie pan.
3. Peel, core and slice the apples.
4. Pile the apples into the crust so they are high in the middle and slope down at the edges.
5. Sprinkle the sugar and spices over the apples.
6. Cut the butter into 1/4-inch slices and place them on the apples.
7. Roll out the upper crust and fit it over the pie. Make a hole in the top to release steam.
8. Bake for about 45 minutes or until the juices are bubbling. Cool.

My husband likes apple pie with a slice of cheddar cheese on top. My children prefer vanilla ice cream. I prefer it plain. In any incarnation it is a favorite at our house.

DECEMBER

Now stir the fire, and close the shutters fast,
Let fall the curtains, wheel the sofa round,
And, while the bubbling and loud-hissing urn
Throws up a steamy column, and the cups,
That cheer but not inebriate, wait on each,
So let us welcome peaceful evening in.

—William Cowper
"The Winter Evening"

The Land

It is December, the time of darkening days and long nights; lumpy, frozen earth; bare-boned trees; ghostly bright moonlit hours and the beginning of the snow. Autumn tiptoes away, taking with it the remnants of things green and growing. Winter brings a stillness to the land.

After an absence of several weeks, we have returned to the country and to our garden, which still had life when we left. That is gone now. There is nothing but a fence around some earth, dead leaves blown about by the north wind, a few frozen cabbage stalks protruding from the emptiness and a sprinkling of frost and week-old snow painting everything white and silver.

Coming upon such barrenness and cold so abruptly makes the change to winter seem quite somber. We are not allowed a comfortable adjustment to the bleak and the silent. Suddenly, it seems, there is no cricket's hum, no conversation of crows or gargle of frogs, no crackling confusion of crisp leaves, no warble of water wasting down the nearby rill. Even the wintering birds who flock to our feeders direct their energies toward food rather than song, leaving the making of sound to the coyotes at night and the wind against the window panes.

Last night, as I lay enclosed in a deep winter sleep, a handsome fat moon rose in the small hours. I woke at about three to a room filled with colorless light, the moon casting long, spidery shadows of tree branches across the dusting of snow, which reflected a soft, cold glow back into the sky. The temperature outside was near zero, and the house was a safe womb against the chill and the eerie light.

I walked from room to room looking out the windows for signs of nightlife—a hunting raccoon or skunk or fox—and considered for the thousandth time the discomfort of such a night for those out in it, those without refuge. Whether they be today's homeless people or ancient savages huddling together for protection and warmth, a cold night outdoors is not what humans have been content to endure. To sleep in the open on a bed of frozen earth, lulled by the rustlings, scramblings and murmurings of unknown beasts, is an activity only enjoyed if the participant has other alternatives at other times. And even then, ardent outdoorspeople may feel more comfortable with a tent flap between themselves and the untamed.

Most of the members of our family are "ardent outdoorspersons," and over the years of camping trips (in warm weather) have found themselves from time to time at the boundaries of civilization. Camping out with a tent and a sleeping bag can never be mistaken for an ancient practice, but this nearness to the natural state can be edifying and—under certain circumstances—remindful of our separateness.

Once, our two younger sons, then teenagers, were hiking and camping together in the Smoky Mountains—bear territory. They knew that leaving food out at a campsite was a sure invitation for an ursine visit, so they hung their provisions high on the metal poles provided by the Forest Service. The smell of cooking food must have drifted into the forest, however, for sure enough as they lay in their tent, the growls and shuffles of a large bear could be heard as he picked through the camping equipment. He brushed against the tent. He rattled the campstove and threw down the empty skillet. He stayed and stayed, searching for food. Our sons, each not knowing the other was awake, remained silent in hope that they would be undiscovered and unmolested. The next morning, when the boys found that their heavy aluminum gas can had been neatly pierced in several places by powerful claws, they assessed the circumstances and opted to spend the next night at a motel, a wise recourse, but one only recently available to the human species in its multimillion-year history.

The first bipedal primates—those earliest of the human ancestors—though smaller than we are, were large by mammalian standards and ill-equipped to dig lairs big enough to protect themselves in the night. To sleep high in a tree, which they probably did, had its own obvious dangers and discomforts, and caves were not ubiquitous and were often inhabited by other, larger animals whose eviction was problematic at best. The search for a resting place safe from roaming carnivores could be a demanding business, and the night, when predators could lurk undetected, must have been long and menacing indeed.

I, a modern primate who pretends to fear nothing much, find darkness in the country too inhospitable, bleak and alien for comfort. Getting caught at dusk in the winter, which seems to turn instantaneously into darkness, can cause apprehension even in familiar territory, for the territory is no longer familiar. It harbors unseen mysteries and unheard hazards in its silent shadows.

I think of the streetlights of the city, the noise of traffic and the movement of crowds, for in the city we have disguised the night, purged it of its character, forbidden it to enter our dreams. We have transformed so much of nature for our convenience. It is only in the country, in the forest and perhaps in the night that our original minor role in the scheme of things may be recalled.

I try to imagine what human life was like in a primeval savannah or woodland eons ago, before the brain had worked out a method for creating shelter and keeping it safe. What were the first shelters and what brave and innovative soul devised them? The evidence is sparse. Mary Leakey, the anthropologist, has found an archaic circle of large stones that might have been used to support a crude twig yurt—but how and when and by whom?

Ancient hearths have also been found that indicate the human employment of an element almost as dangerous as the wild: fire, that gift of Prometheus that set us on the road to segregation from the rest of nature.

Lots of speculation has addressed the mystery of the first domestication of the earth's natural fires. From the facetious notion of holding a branch over the edge of a live volcano until it ignited to more serious views of saving and nurturing fires caused by lightning or lava, we've conjured up theories and visions of hairy cavedwellers gathered around a blazing hearth, grunting, cracking bones open to suck out the marrow and eating their enemies' brains.

There is a cave in northern China that contains a hearth five-hundred thousand years old. It appears to have been used steadily from its first settlement until the cave filled too high with the rubble of life to contain its inhabitants any longer. The process took thousands of years. Thousands of years of living and cooking and getting along together in one place, around the same fire. No wonder flames cast such a spell over most of us.

There is no place in our own country that can completely mirror the world as it was before the arrival of humans and their inventions. Even the western wilderness areas are bereft of the rich animal and plant life that preceded early human settlement. But still, there are places and moments when the elements of nature are strong enough to impart a kind of universal déjà vu in our brains, a quasimemory implanted millennia ago.

It happened to me in Tanzania, a part of Africa that was home to some of our earliest forebears. I was a tourist, hauled about in the safety of a Land Rover, a neophyte in a primeval wilderness. Growing up on the North American prairie had not prepared me for this other immeasureable land that delineated the power of nature both through its space and its age. It was land that bore the deep wrinkles of time and endurance.

For several days we were buffeted between the two—time and space—vast, untamed space in which we saw wildebeests by the hundreds, perhaps thousands. The most conforming of animals, but apparently the most prolific, they were always following, following, never renouncing the group, even if it meant drowning in a raging torrent.

We observed hyenas devouring the black-and-white-striped leftovers of a lion kill, while nearby the lions lazily digested their meal. They were within spitting distance of an impervious herd of grazing zebras, who were unwary of their enemies during their siesta and undaunted by the fate of their kin.

Giraffes gnawed at tender acacia treetops and elephants plundered lower vegetation. Gazelles loped in great herds. Thousands of flamingos sucked algae out of the shallows of saltwater ponds, while hippos lolled in a lethargy between meals of marinated greens. A lone mother rhinoceros stood resolutely by her newborn, while egrets hovered about her, waiting for the lumbering giant to stir up the grasses and dislodge a few edible insects from their hiding places. Ostriches and water buffaloes, jackals and herons and hundreds of other birds were participating, along with the occasional human, in the Darwinian game of life—giving and taking, living and dying and maintaining a balance that allows the system to continue. This was happening all around us without the interference of superhighways or incinerators. This was a land never dominated by its human component. The bipeds were just part of a sustainable whole, as they have been from the beginning.

Here we also saw a picture of the past that could be measured as we dipped down into a rift that exposed level after level of strata where our predecessors had made their lives. We picked up fossilized teeth of crocodiles and shard femurs of large cats. We found a jaw of an ancient ungulate and a few crudely manufactured stone handaxes as old as the gorge in which we stood. Looking over our shoulders from time to time, we thought about early humans and large cats and weapons, and later, in the night, we remembered.

We were staying at a small, rustic lodge on the southern Serengeti Plain, a bit of civilization in a wilderness far from the most minimal urbanity. We were walking from the dining room to our cabins. It was nighttime, and the wood fire–powered generator provided only rudimentary light, a fifteen-watt bulb in each room, for two or three hours each evening. There was no artificial exterior light of any sort.

As we trudged along, laughing and joking, a friend who was carrying a flashlight to help us find our path panned it across the savannah, and there, perhaps two hundred feet away, we could see eyes—large, red animal eyes—reflecting the flashlight's rays. Laughter turned to slow breathing. I think we all felt more than the usual amount of gratitude for the cinder-block walls that enclosed our narrow cots, and even more gratitude when we found lion and hyena tracks the next day at the place where we had seen those eyes. Night might not have been the same without that small light to deter the owners of the eyes, and shelter—shelter with controllable light and heat—was a deterrent our ancestors only painfully learned about.

Yet they survived. Prehumans lived a long time without sturdy shelters or the use of fire. As far as we can tell from the archaeological record, stone tools preceded fire-making or fire-control by up to a million years, and earlier progenitors lived without any detectable tools at all for a few million years before that. Yet they—and we—have survived to change the universe that gave birth to us and to tip its balance, perhaps irrevocably. One wonders if it all started with the need for refuge.

This weekend, which was chill with snow turning to rain and then ice, we spent much time in our cozy lodging before our own blazing fire, letting its flames tease our chilled fingers, its coals warm our backsides. We felt protected and warm, housed and enclosed. No need to strike out through the enveloping, unremitting darkness. No fear of being preyed upon.

Because we share the genes of our *Homo erectus* predecessors, the ones whose cave dwellings exhibit hearths used ceaselessly through the millennia, we must also instinctively share the reassurance of the hearth, the home. The flame that can harm can also enhance the dwelling, warm the body, cook the food and discourage hostile predators. It is a symbol of sanctuary, as food is a symbol of love.

The Garden

The garden is desolate in December, all frozen leaf mulch and bare earth. We hope for a good, solid snow cover to shield our plants and preserve our soil, but often in these last years we haven't been so lucky This year we have had a relatively dry New England December, fluctuating repeatedly from frigid to balmy, while in the prairie, I hear there is rain and flooding and in Jerusalem snow—a world turned upside down. Still, there is nothing we can do about the weather, so when crocuses poke their green shoots upward through the warm earth of an unseasonable winter's day, we can only hope they will be forced to retreat and save their blossoms for spring.

With the garden enjoying its hibernation and fall chores either finished or diminishing in magnitude, indoor plants are now the focus of horticultural fussing. Our windows are filled with the green, the floral, the ornamental and the edible. I love them all and have a hard time discarding any that still have a breath of life in them. Consequently, I have such relics as a thirty-year-old potted palm that is seven feet tall but has fronds only on its top eighteen inches. It is weak-spined, scraggly and certainly not a thing of great beauty, but it has survived the trials and travesties of city life: poor air, too little light, inadequate humidity and unconsidered watering programs. It was given to us when our first child was born as part of a dishgarden, and I never look upon it that I am not reminded of that magnificent moment. So on it grows, upward to the ceiling, defying all adversity and embracing life itself.

Keeping indoor plants alive amid the threatening fumes of steam pipes and gas jets or a population explosion of aphids or whiteflies (from whence do they find us?) is not so much a difficult task as an enduring one. It is here, inside in unnatural surroundings, that plants need the most attention and consideration. Poor things. We imprison them away from their natural surroundings; give them less light than they need; hobble their roots, disallowing them to reach out freely; expose them to dry and stagnant air and too often overwater them, underwater them or disregard the pests that provoke them. Yet they usually live on, providing oxygen in our hermetic homes and pleasure for our eyes and nostrils.

Some plants adapt to indoor conditions better than others, as represented by the lowly philodendron or the spider plant, but for every living plant there are basics that cannot be ignored. Most of us would shy away from setting our prize orchid on an operating radiator, but many of us overlook the effects of an overheated, arid atmosphere. Or we place a plant into a window corner that receives only an hour of sun, because it seems sunny and bright at the time.

Of the factors most essential to the survival of an indoor plant, the most important is light, closely followed by those of temperature and humidity. A south window will receive the most hours of direct sunlight; a north window will receive virtually none. One plant species differs from another in its sunlight requirements, so appropriate placement can mean the difference between growth and disaster.

Although some species, such as cactus, can withstand high temperature and lack of humidity, as a rule, cooler and more humid is better. Room or windowsill temperatures of between sixty and sixty-five degrees during the day and five degrees lower at night can accommodate many more plants than a house whose thermostat is set at seventy or higher. We keep the country house at forty-five degrees when we are away, and only sixty when we are present. These relatively low temperatures have never damaged any houseplants there. However, when painters were painting in the house last year, and apparently pushing the thermostats up high to accelerate the drying, the plants suffered.

In a centrally heated house or apartment, even moderate heat can generate a lot of dry air, so periodic misting is a good idea. Pebble-filled, watertight trays on which to set flowerpots will catch draining water, preventing it from languishing in the bottom of a pot and causing root rot. The water, safe among the pebbles, can then create condensation and some localized humidity. One may also water more thoroughly without creating a flood. It's a pretty effective system, but it's still a good idea to spritz.

Although we have indoor plants all over the place, our winter culinary gardens live in dining room windows, where the temperatures are cool and the sun is best. In neither the country nor the city do we have adequate natural light for raising fruiting vegetables, so the culinary collection is really one of herbs, not stick-to-the-ribs vegetables but those makers of tastes that can elevate the mundane to the sublime. These include bay trees, rosemary bushes, oregano, thyme of several sorts, winter savory, cilantro (which goes to seed and must be replanted often), parsley and a miniature basil that thinks it is spring.

The perennials of this group spend the summers outside and are moved indoors in early October several weeks before the heat is turned on. This allows them to acclimate to the darker and stuffier atmosphere before they must also deal with dry heat. They never do as well indoors—nothing does. But they are worth the effort. The whispering aroma of rosemary that rises as one brushes past the bush, or the heady sap of a just-picked bay leaf continually bring the breath of the garden into our winter lives.

My ways with houseplants have evolved over the years with no systematic plan, but they have been too successful to abandon. I follow the same organic-growing philosophy that rules my garden. I use natural fertilizers and organic sprays, but mostly I try to attend to each plant's individual needs. My aloe veras get hardscrabble soil and little water, for that is what they thrive on. Cyclamens live in the coolest windows. Finicky rosemary gets misted and fertilized. Bay trees, dauntless as they are, get occasional prunings—both roots and branches.

Useful volumes with lists of requirements for various types of houseplants abound, and these I recommend. However, as each house differs, so does each interior climate. It is frequent attention that brings vigor to a potted plant and horticultural success to its custodian.

My own winter potting corner is small and sparely appointed. I keep a collection of clay pots of all sizes, an old trash can full of potting soil (sometimes homemade, usually purchased), several trowels and a cultivator, pruning shears and garden scissors. I occasionally use plastic flowerpots. Being nonporous, they retain moisture better, but I still love the look of a used clay pot, stained with age, and earth and moss. I save the shards of broken ones to place over the hole in the bottom of whole pots. This allows drainage without earth leakage.

Once an herb is planted and on a windowsill, a watering can, a water-spritzer and an old kitchen fork or spoon for breaking up hardening soil are all I need. If aphids, spider mites or whiteflies appear, I spritz them with Safer's soap or a dilution of liquid dishwashing soap and water (about two tablespoons of soap to one quart of water). The pests are usually asphyxiated after one or two applications. If scale finds its way to us (it seems to love bay trees), I pick off each offender.

As dry winter weather gets more relentless, and if pots are small enough to transport, I also like to give all the plants an occasional shower and a holiday in a dank bathtub. If people can benefit from mud baths, surely plants may enjoy a cold shower.

Fertilizing houseplants requires some knowledge of the individual species and its needs: acid soil or alkaline soil, many nutrients or few, resting periods or none. Overfertilizing may be as discouraging to a plant as neglect. Most herbs do not require overabundant nourishment, but do flourish in a loose, friable soil that allows their roots to reach and absorb. While searching for a slow-acting and natural method of houseplant rejuvenation years ago, I read somewhere that coffee grounds and tea leaves are rich in the nitrogen-phosphorus-potassium triad. Here was a source for fertilizing that was being dumped in the garbage by most people, probably the same people who spend money on expensive bottled products. I began feeding tea and coffee mulch to my plants, watering with cold (never warm), diluted, leftover coffee or tea and sprinkling the grounds or leaves over the soil, evenly mixing them in. They slowly decompose, improving both the loam and the liquid that travels through the roots to feed our captive flora.

I have subsequently found that I am not the only one who puts kitchen residues in clay pots on a windowsill. A Brooklyn friend has told me that her mother, who retains some of the "old ways," not only fertilizes houseplants with coffee and tea but chops up citrus peels to feed the acid-loving plants. It is all really just another form of composting, only this time it is all done indoors. It is easy, little more trouble than throwing a teabag into the garbage (but do remove the leaves from the bag before you add them to the soil) and, best of all, it is free.

The Kitchen

The gardener-cook may consider the activities of December as the climax, the grand culmination of a year of bringing food from the soil to the table, observing its ingestion and beginning again. In December there is nothing fresh from the garden but plenty in the larder, and the prospect of holiday giving and entertaining whips us all into a frenzy of preparation.

The first weeks of December are devoted to cooking ahead, preparing for the arrival of family and friends during the holidays. Breads, cookies and cakes can be made well ahead of time, making me thankful for my freezer and aware that the keeping abilities of the old recipes for fruitcake, plum pudding and gingerbread must have saved the day for those cooks of yore. My great-grandmother's fruitcake was preserved not with modern chemicals or freezer storage, but with a cup or two of whiskey, administered every day or two, a few drops at a time. The older it got, the better it tasted.

Other useful December recipes are larder concoctions, ways of using the stockpile of stored food to make a last-minute dinner, mixing leftovers to create a new dish or making do with what is on hand because it's sleeting outside and the store is six miles away.

The following recipes begin with a few "make-ahead" foods that are valuable not only for holiday entertaining but for gift-giving as well. The rest are things we eat at Christmastime. Many of them precede the garden by years—even generations—and have formed the traditions of our family.

Governor Moody Cake

Governor Dan Moody held office in Texas between 1927 and 1931, but I have no idea why this cake bears his name. It has been the family fruitcake for as long as I can remember. It's heavy and moist, not as sweet as many fruitcakes, and full of calories. It is also quite large. I don't recommend it unless you have a group of people to help you eat it.

You will need a larger-than-average mixing bowl and an electric beater because the batter is too heavy to mix easily by hand. It must be cooked in a large tube pan (an angel food cake pan does quite nicely), for it needs the hole to cook evenly and rise properly. It can be made weeks ahead of time.

INGREDIENTS:

6 eggs
1 pound sweet butter
1 pound white raisins
1 pound chopped pecans
1 pound light brown sugar
4-1/2 cups cake flour
2 heaping teaspoons baking powder
1 tablespoon fresh nutmeg or mace
1-1/2 ounces lemon extract
Cognac, rum, whiskey or bourbon

PROCEDURE:

1. Preheat the oven to 275˚.
2. Cream the butter and sugar in a large mixing bowl.
3. Separate the eggs, reserving the whites in a clean, grease-free bowl. Add the egg yolks 1 at a time to the butter and sugar mixture, beating after each addition.
4. Sift together the flour, baking soda and nutmeg or mace. Coat the pecans and raisins with a little of the flour mixture to keep them from sinking to the bottom of the batter.
4. Add the flour mixture a little at a time to the butter and sugar mixture. Fold in the coated raisins and pecans.
5. Beat the egg whites until they are stiff and glossy but not dry. Fold them into the batter.
6. Add the lemon extract. (Don't leave it out. It is the ingredient that makes this such a distinctive cake.)
7. Turn the batter into a buttered and floured tube pan and bake at 275˚ for 2 hours or until a knife inserted into it comes out clean.
8. Turn the cake out onto a rack to cool. When it is quite cool, store it in a tin box or any tightly sealed, nonplastic container.
9. If the cake isn't to be eaten right away, put a piece of cheesecloth on top of it and periodically dribble cognac, rum, whiskey, bourbon (the southern choice) or whatever liquor you prefer, over it. This keeps the cake moist and fresh and improves its flavor. Don't dribble so much that it makes the cake soggy.

Sour Cream Coffee Cake

My family always told me that my sister's sour cream coffee cakes were better than mine, and I agreed. It wasn't until I begged her for her recipe for this book that I found out one of the reasons. My recipe calls for a half cup of butter, hers calls for one cup. It does make a difference.

This cake has always been my sister's contribution to Christmas breakfast. It is everyone's favorite Christmas food. The year that Jane moved back to Texas, she sent us this delectable wonder packed in a tin, covered with plastic wrap and surrounded by popcorn to keep it from crumbling on its bumpy journey. What a perfect replacement for Styrofoam bubbles. We fed the popcorn to the chickens (it was a bit stale) and felt good about one little portion of the ozone layer.

This cake freezes better than most breads and can be preserved until Christmas morning.

INGREDIENTS:

1 cup sweet butter
1-1/4 cups sugar
2 large eggs
1 cup sour cream
2 cups flour
1/2 teaspoon baking soda
1-1/2 teaspoons baking powder
1 teaspoon vanilla extract
3/4 cup chopped pecans combined with 1 teaspoon cinnamon and 2
*   tablespoons sugar*

PROCEDURE:

1. Cream the butter and sugar. Add the eggs and beat the mixture until fluffy. Blend in the sour cream.
2. Sift the flour. Measure and sift it again with the baking soda and powder. Fold it into creamed mixture. Add the vanilla extract.
3. Prepare a 9-inch tube pan by greasing it lightly but thoroughly with butter, then sprinkling with flour. Shake the flour about until it entirely covers the inside of the pan.
4. Spoon half of the batter into the tube pan. Sprinkle half of the nut mixture over the batter. Add the remaining batter. Top it with the rest of the nut mixture. Place it in a cold oven. Set the oven to 350° and bake it for 55 minutes or until a silver knife inserted in the center comes out clean.

Chicken Consommé

Since grocery store chickens are almost never sold with their feet attached anymore, few cooks have the opportunity to discover the wonders of chicken feet. In China they are highly prized and may be seen in shop windows stacked in artistic circles of protruding claws. In an older North America, they were not discarded, but were added to soups to heighten their flavors and, because of their gelatinous quality, cooked to make consommés and aspics. This I do with feet saved and frozen since slaughter time.

INGREDIENTS:

8 to 10 chicken feet (or whatever chicken feet you may have), with enough
raw chicken to make a rich broth (such as 4 feet, 2 backs and 2 necks)
2 small onions
1 carrot
1 or 2 slices celery root
Fresh or dried sage to taste
Fresh or dried thyme to taste
Salt
Pepper
Splash of dry sherry, cognac or rice wine
1 egg white for each cup of broth

PROCEDURE:

1. Scrub the chicken feet thoroughly, scald them and peel away the outer skin and place them in a saucepan large enough to hold water 2 to 3 inches over them. Add the onions, carrot, celery root, herbs, salt and pepper. Bring them to a boil and then reduce the heat to a simmer. Cook for about 2 hours, until the broth is reduced to about the level of the feet. Taste it and reduce further if the broth is not rich enough. Remove it from the heat.

2. Strain the broth through a fine sieve. The liquid will probably be murky.

3. Allow the strained liquid to cool, skimming off any grease that comes to the top.

4. Put the egg whites into a bowl. Using a wire whisk, stir a cup of the cooled stock into the whites. At the same time put the rest of the stock into a clean saucepan and heat it. When the stock is simmering, remove it from the heat and add, a little at a time, the stock and egg white mixture to the hot stock. Whisk it around.

5. Return the stock to the burner and again bring it to a simmer, whisking, until the liquid begins to bubble. Stop whisking. Turn the heat as low as

possible and let it barely cook for about 10 minutes. The bits in the stock will adhere to the egg whites. (That's why you shouldn't whisk any more. You want them to stick together without disturbance.)

6. Line the sieve with a piece of clean muslin or 3 or 4 layers of cheesecloth. Carefully ladle the finished stock through the seive into a bowl. Let the liquid drip through, but do not press it or try to help it in any way, or the "gunk" you've labored to remove will seep through too. Now add a splash of sherry, cognac or rice wine. Your consommé should be sparkling, clear and amber-colored.

7. This may be done several days ahead of use. Store in the refrigerator, where it will become gelatinous. To liquify simply reheat.

Chicken Liver Mousse

This recipe makes use of the livers of our butchered chickens. It is a festive and colorful dish that is not only delicious but decorative on a buffet table. It may be made several days ahead of time and left in its mold in the refrigerator.

INGREDIENTS:
> *2 cups clarified broth (see Chicken Consommé above)*
> *2 pounds chicken livers, washed*
> *2 small onions, chopped (about 1/2 cup)*
> *3 to 4 tablespoons butter*
> *Chopped fresh or dried sage to taste*
> *Salt*
> *Pepper*
> *2 to 3 tablespoons dry port and/or cognac*
> *1 to 1-1/2 cups heavy cream or ricotta cheese*
> *Raw vegetables for decorations (see below)*

PROCEDURE:
1. Melt the butter in a medium-sized skillet over medium-low heat. Add the chicken livers, sage and chopped onion. Gently stir for about 5 minutes. The onions should be translucent and the livers should be barely cooked through.

2. Pour the contents of the skillet into a food processor and process until you have a smooth pâté.

3. Add the salt, pepper and port and/or cognac. Process again.

4. Add the cream or ricotta cheese and process briefly to mix. Adjust the seasonings to taste. This mixture should be very smooth and thick enough to hold its shape. Don't overprocess it. If it doesn't mesh easily, take it out of the processor and mix with a spoon.

DECORATIONS:
   1 black truffle, thinly sliced
   1 carrot, thinly sliced
   1 celery root, thinly sliced
   Pimiento or broiled red pepper slices
   Scallion stalks
   Fresh parsley
   Cutters for making designs

PUTTING IT ALL TOGETHER:
   1. Line the bottom of a 1-quart mold with 1/2 inch of the clarified aspic. Place it in the refrigerator to set.
   2. Cut patterns from thin slices of the vegetables listed above. Sketch out the design you want on a sheet of paper with the vegetable colors in mind. You want a design that will cover the top of the mold, plus a few things on the sides.
   3. Remove the partially set aspic from the refrigerator and press the vegetables into it to make your design.
   4. Return it to the refrigerator to set thoroughly. When it is set, add another cup of aspic and gently and carefully swirl it around to attach to the sides of the mold. Return it to the refrigerator. Repeat this process several times until you have enough aspic sticking to the mold walls to hold the cut-out vegetables.
   5. Press the vegetables into the sides of the mold. Refrigerate to set.
   6. Carefully lower the liver mousse into the mold, not allowing it to touch the sides. Pour the rest of the aspic into the space between the mold wall and the liver mousse. Fill to barely cover the mousse. Refrigerate to set.
   7. Unmold the mousse by lowering it into a bowl of warm (not hot) water for a few seconds, and then carefully turning it onto a serving platter. If the mousse doesn't loosen, don't try to turn it back over. Press a hot, damp towel around the mold. Leave it until you hear the mousse drop.
   8. Garnish with fresh parsley.

Beet Salad

   Although beets are good keepers, our crop never seems to last beyond Christmas, no doubt because they are so delicious and so easy to prepare that we eat them frequently. Their last appearance is usually on a holiday table, festive and colorful, especially if they are Chiogga beets with their red and white stripes.

INGREDIENTS:
Medium-sized raw beets
Water to boil
Pinch of salt
Pickled red onions (see the July chapter)
Fresh fennel fronds, basil leaves or parsley
Horseradish sauce (see below)

PROCEDURE:
1. Scrub the beets. Do not peel or cut away the root end or the stalk end. Place them in a saucepan and cover with water. Add the salt. Bring them to a boil. Reduce them to a simmer and cook until a fork can be pushed into one easily. This may take 20 to 30 minutes depending upon the size of the beets. Smaller beets may be removed from the cooking water before larger ones. Do not overcook them. They should be tender but not mushy.
2. Place the cooked beets under cold running water and peel them. The skins will now slip off very easily. Trim the root and stalk ends.
3. Refrigerate the beets. Prepare the onions and the horseradish sauce. Refrigerate all until time to serve.
4. Slice the beets. Arrange the beets and onions on a platter, leaving a space in the middle for the horseradish sauce. Place the sauce in the center. Decorate with the fresh herbs. Serve.

Horseradish Sauce

Horseradish roots survive in the refrigerator all winter long, to be drawn into action when the need arises. They may be grated and covered with vinegar well ahead of time, but they are stronger in flavor if freshly chopped. That may or may not be an advantage.

This is one recipe for which a food processor is a treasured appliance. As I have mentioned, horseradish should never be harvested until after at least one hard frost, for only then will its intense flavor be established. However, I must add that the intensity of that flavor and aroma go well beyond that of commercially bottled horseradish, and the process of grating it by hand may bring not only tears but gasps as the sinuses fill with the heady nuances of what is to come to the tongue.

We serve this sauce not only with beets but with our traditional holiday rib roast and Yorkshire pudding (this time at room temperature). It also complements pot roast and fresh ham.

INGREDIENTS:
2 or 3 horseradish roots
Good white wine vinegar (not the herbal kind) or white wine
Yogurt or sour cream
Dijon mustard to taste
Salt to taste

PROCEDURE:
1. Peel the horseradish and chop it into 1- to 2-inch-long pieces. Process in a food processor until the horseradish is pulverized (or so long as you can stand it).
2. Remove the horseradish from the processor. Put it into a ceramic bowl, press down and mix in enough white wine vinegar or white wine to coat all of the horseradish. This mixture may be kept for weeks and used in other recipes as needed. (I think it can be kept for years without rotting. What hapless microbe would dare to enter?) However, the flavor is stronger and better the fresher it is.
3. Place the yogurt or sour cream in a bowl with a spoonful of mustard and a spoonful of salt. Stir. Mix in the horseradish a little at a time, stirring and tasting with each addition, until the desired flavor is achieved.

Baked Smoked Ham with Apricot Glaze

When the children were young, we gave an annual Christmas Eve tree-decorating and caroling party for our children's friends, who brought their parents along. Over the years, the food that was served became a mélange of sweet and savory, home-cooked and contributed by guests. It changed yearly, except for the ham. Like Li'l Abner's family ham, our traditional smoked ham could feed fifty or a hundred if you followed the rules and carved it paper-thin. It was delicious the next day or next week, providing snacks for houseguests and children. The chunks became curry. When all else was consumed, the bone became the basis for a hearty winter soup and then was given to the dog. I suppose the grease would have been saved for soap in my mother's day. All in all, a ham—smoked, cured or fresh—is a multipurpose food that goes a long way.

Cured ham arrives at the table only after a three-step process: curing and perhaps smoking, braising and finally glazing. For most cooks only the final step is a necessary task, for most hams purchased in the United States are precooked before they arrive at the meat counter. If a ham is bought at a country smokehouse, it is a good idea to ask if it has been cooked, and, if not, what procedure to use with it.

Since we have lived in the country, we have bought smoked hams from local smokehouses as well as smoked our own in a handy electric smoker that fits in the fireplace. By buying a hog from neighbors, we have acquired fresh ham, which looks and tastes like a huge loin of pork. It is another taste altogether. However we have treated a ham, it has been delicious, but that is because we have started with meat raised on real, unadulterated food and placed in our hands before it was canned, injected with water and additives or left to acquire the flavor of the plastic bag it was stored in.

I have tried to persuade our local butcher-curer to pickle a ham for us using salt but no nitrates, but to no avail. Saltpeter (potassium nitrate) gives ham its characteristic pink color and is partially responsible for its flavor. He feels it isn't ham without these two additives. Perhaps the nitrate isn't so bad for you once a year.

INGREDIENTS:

1 whole cured, smoked and precooked ham from a reliable smokehouse
    (between 12 and 15 pounds)
Whole cloves
White wine or apple cider
Apricot preserves

PROCEDURE:

1. Preheat the oven to 375˚. Wash and scrub the ham. Remove the skin and cut away any excess fat. Leave a thin layer of fat over the top.
2. Score the fatty top of the ham in a diamond pattern. Press a whole clove into the center of each diamond.
3. Place the ham in a large roasting pan. Pour in enough wine or cider to fill the pan about 1/2 inch deep.
4. Place the ham in the oven and roast it for 1-1/2 hours, basting it frequently with the pan juices. If the juices dry up, add more wine or cider.
5. Remove the ham from the oven and spread a layer of the apricot preserves over the top. Return it to the oven and roast it for 30 minutes more, continuing to baste it, or until a meat thermometer thrust into the middle registers 130˚.
6. Remove the ham to a platter. Deglaze the pan and skim the fat from the liquid. Reduce the pan juices and thicken with a little cornstarch. Strain and serve the juice with the ham along with horseradish sauce, mustards and chutneys.

Ham Bone Stock

INGREDIENTS:

Bone and bits of leftover ham
Extra liquid from deglazing the baking pan
Whole cloves
Whole allspice
Bay leaves
Sage leaves
2 or 3 onions
2 or 3 garlic cloves
Salt
Pepper
6 to 8 quarts water

PROCEDURE:

1. Put all the ingredients in a large stockpot and bring it to a slow simmer. Skim as necessary.
2. Reduce the liquid until the flavor is rich.
3. Allow the stock to cool. Strain it through a fine strainer. Refrigerate or freeze it until ready for use.

Bean Soup

INGREDIENTS:

1 pint dried beans, soaked for several hours or overnight
3 or 4 Egyptian onions or scallions, chopped
3 or 4 leeks, thinly chopped
2 or 3 tablespoons cooking oil or sweet butter
1 celery root, chopped
1 parsnip, chopped
1 cup carrots, chopped
2 to 3 quarts ham bone stock (see above)
2 bay leaves
Thyme or winter savory
Salt
Pepper

PROCEDURE:

1. Rinse the soaked beans and place them in a saucepan. Cover them with fresh water and a pinch of salt. Place the pan on a back burner to simmer.
2. Heat the butter or oil in a large soup pot. Add the onions and leeks and stir until they are soft and translucent. Remove them from the heat.
3. Carefully chop the root vegetables to a size similar to that of a cooked bean (unless you are using lentils or split peas, which will break down

into a mush). Add them to the soup pot. Add the ham stock and set the pot on very low heat. Add the salt, pepper and herbs. (Be careful. Your stock may be salty enough without much more.) Taste it and adjust the seasonings, if necessary.

4. When the beans have cooked for about 30 minutes and the soup has cooked for about 15, drain the beans and rinse them again. Add them to the soup. Continue to cook slowly until the vegetables and beans are as tender as you desire and the soup is thick and hearty. Adjust the flavors to taste. Serve hot.

MENUS

A Potluck Dinner in Winter

In January we arrive in the country on Friday night to a forty-degree house and a larder heaped with food. We light wood fires that burn all weekend and begin pulling things out of the freezer and preparing for the meals of the next two days. Often I start a batch of dried beans soaking before bedtime, and on Saturday morning use them in a kettle of chili or soup that simmers in the fireplace all day. I try to keep Saturday night's dinner simple, for time is limited and other activities beckon—hence, the custom of the potluck dinner.

Almost always in the country and almost never in the city do people, once invited to dine, say, "What can I bring?" In the winter our rural neighboors may arrive with holiday leftovers, pantry produce or freshly baked bread. Whatever the contribution, it always looks and tastes as it should—bracing and hearty—food to warm up the bones and fortify the body on a winter's night.

On one such evening, one couple brought a selection of cheeses, Greek olives and loaves of warm, homemade bread. Someone else brought a pot of lentil soup, and another, leftover fruitcake and a fine Christmas gift brandy. Yet another brought salad and more cheese. All this made grilling a loin of pork, preparing leeks and squash from our garden larder and using our now dwindling fresh eggs in a custard dessert an uncomplicated task.

Although this menu does not conform entirely to my January paean to fireplace cookery, the pork was cooked at the hearth on our sturdy "Tuscan Grill," the leeks were braised in a pot above the open fire and the soup could easily have been simmered over the flames. This is a meal to remember when a storm has knocked out the electricity or the propane tank has run dry.

> Hors d'oeuvres: Assorted Cheeses, Green and Purple Greek Olives and
> Homemade Bread (see April)
> Lentil Soup (see Bean Soup, December)
> Grilled Loin of Pork (see below)
> Braised Leeks (see November)
> Green Salad
> Floating Island (See March) and Governor Moody Cake (see
> December)
> Coffee and Brandy

Grilled Loin of Pork

INGREDIENTS:

> *1 loin of fresh pork*
> *2 cups dry white wine*
> *1 cup olive oil*
> *1 teaspoon peppercorns*
> *1 teaspoon salt*
> *Several teaspoons chopped herbs, fresh or dried (parsley, bay leaf, winter
> savory, rosemary or thyme)*
> *Chopped garlic (optional)*
> *2 cups ham or beef stock*
> *1 teaspoon cornstarch*
> *Splash of white wine (optional)*

PROCEDURE:

1. Prepare the loin by cutting a pocket between the bones and the meat. Place half of the herbs in the meat pocket.

2. Put the meat in a crockery bowl. Combine the wine, olive oil, peppercorns, salt, garlic and the remaining herbs and pour it over the meat. Allow it to marinate for at least 3 hours. Turn it frequently.

3. Build a fire under a grill. As the fire burns down, pull the logs to the front of the fireplace, leaving only hot coals at the back. Place the loin at the back of the grill. Cook it for about 30 minutes, turning every 5 to 10 minutes and spooning on a bit of the marinade. The meat must cook slowly, never being encased in flame, to be juicy and tender.

4. After 30 minutes, check the meat with a meat thermometer. When it registers 137°, it is done. Do not overcook it.

5. For the sauce, reduce the leftover ham stock (see December) or beef stock with the cornstarch. Add a splash of white wine, if you wish.

A Respectable February Dinner Party

In this month of raw weather, quiet speculation and indoor activity, an afternoon of puttering purposefully in the kitchen and then pulling out the good linen and china to set a table for a few friends is not an onerous task. The architect of such an evening wishes for the meal to be complemented by a lingering dinner conversation balancing, the cerebral and the sensual.

Last Christmas we were given an old magnum of an elegant Bordeaux. Now it has become a good excuse for a small party for wine lovers who can tell the difference between our gift and "the other stuff."

Here are recipes for a crown roast and its accompaniments, listed in the best order for preparation.

Black Bean Pasties (see February)
Crown Roast of Lamb with Red Wine Sauce (see below)
Wild Rice (see below)
Broccoli Romanesca (see below)
Sautéed Wild Mushrooms (see below)
Deep-fried Celeriac (see November and below)
Radicchio or Watercress Garnish
Tossed Salad with Cheeses and Fresh Bread (see April)
Poached Pears with Chocolate Sauce and Vanilla Ice Cream (see below)

Deep-fried Celeriac

Do the slicing preparation well in advance. Heat the oil and deep-fry the celeriac just before it will be needed to garnish the platter.

Wild Rice

INGREDIENTS:
> *2 cups wild rice*
> *8 cups water*
> *Salt*
> *2 to 3 teaspoons sweet butter*

PROCEDURE:
> 1. Wash the rice thoroughly, first by putting it in a bowl of cold water and draining away any foreign matter that floats to the top, then by rinsing it through a sieve or colander until any sand or dirt has been removed.
> 2. Plunge the rice into a pot of salted, boiling water. Simmer it uncovered for 45 minutes. Test it for doneness. The inner grain should be tender. When it is done, add the butter.
> 3. Keep it warm to use as the stuffing for the crown roast.

Crown Roast of Lamb

A crown roast of lamb may be carved into fourteen to sixteen rib chops, depending upon how it is butchered. This is enough for six to eight people, depending on the size of the roast. When we order a whole lamb from our provisioner in the country, we must decide whether to have the ribs cut into chops, left as two racks or tied into the crown roast. Crown roasts demand more than your average supper fare as accompaniments, but shouldn't be upstaged either. They should be carved at the table, or what is the point of creating a regal headdress to grace a platter? If no one volunteers for the job, however, two racks can be cooked, carved and creatively arranged with the vegetables in the kitchen.

INGREDIENTS:
> *1 crown roast of lamb*
> *1 garlic clove*
> *Salt*
> *Freshly ground pepper*
> *Optional: decorations for rib ends (paper frills are traditional, but carved vegetables such as radishes or olives may also be used; or, radicchio leaves or watercress can provide a pallet for the roast and its vegetables)*

PROCEDURE:

1. Have your butcher cut through the back bones of two racks of lamb, trim the fat and tie the meat into a coronet.
2. Preheat the oven to 400°. Rub down the roast with a garlic clove. Sprinkle it with the salt and pepper. Place aluminum foil over the exposed rib ends to prevent them from burning.
3. Place the roast in a pan and bake it for 10 minutes. Reduce the heat to 325° and continue to bake the roast for 15 to 20 minutes. When it is done, the meat should be pink and juicy. (The cooking time depends on the size of the ribs, so testing with a thermometer is a good idea. An internal temperature of 125° will give you a rosy-pink and juicy roast.)

Broccoli Romanesca

This broccoli, so beautiful and so hard to find in markets, was raised last summer in our garden, then parboiled and frozen in the fall.

INGREDIENTS:
2 or 3 large heads of Romanesca broccoli, divided into 2- to 3-inch florets
Salt
Lemon juice

PROCEDURE:

1. Steam the broccoli until it is just tender. Do not overcook it or allow it to lose its color. This should take no more than 5 minutes if the broccoli has been parboiled, about 12 to 15 minutes if it is fresh. Try to time it so that it will be done just in time to serve.
2. Remove the broccoli from the heat and from the pot. Salt it and sprinkle with a little lemon juice.

Sautéed Wild Mushrooms

INGREDIENTS:
1 pound fresh wild mushrooms, Porcini if possible (1 large or 2 to 3 small ones for each guest)
Sweet butter

PROCEDURE:

1. Clean any bits of grime from the mushrooms. Do not wash them. Remove the stalks and save them for the meat sauce.
2. Melt the butter in a large skillet. Sauté the mushrooms over medium heat until they are cooked but not too soft, under 10 minutes.

Red Wine Sauce

INGREDIENTS:

> *Pan juices from the roast*
> *3 large shallots, finely chopped*
> *Mushroom stalks*
> *Red wine*
> *1 teaspoon cornstarch*

PROCEDURE:

1. Place the roast on a platter. Keep it warm. Brown the shallots in the pan juices. Deglaze the pan with a little water. Reduce the sauce. Add the wine mixed with the cornstarch. Stir until the sauce clarifies. Remove from heat.
2. Strain the sauce. Serve it separately in a sauce boat.

Putting It All Together

This is a last-minute operation. The cook must forego the dinner conversation to become an artist and make this dish a jewel in his or her crown.

Center the roast on a large and attractive platter lined with radicchio leaves or watercress. Fill the center of the crown with the wild rice, piling it up to make a small dome. Arrange the broccoli, mushrooms and celeriac around the periphery. Decorate the ribs. Serve immediately to your astonished and grateful guests.

Poached Pears with Chocolate Sauce and Vanilla Ice Cream

INGREDIENTS:

> *1 pear per guest*
> *Sugar syrup (1 cup sugar boiled with 1 cup water for each pear)*
> *2-inch piece of vanilla bean or 1 teaspoon vanilla extract for every 4 pears*
> *Vanilla ice cream*
> *Chocolate sauce*
> *Fresh mint sprigs (optional)*

PROCEDURE:

1. Prepare the sugar syrup in a pot large enough to hold the pears. Peel the pears. Add the vanilla and pears to the syrup and simmer until the pears are just tender, but not mushy.
2. Drain the pears and let them cool. Refrigerate them until ready to use.
3. Just before serving time, remove the ice cream from the freezer to soften slightly. Warm the chocolate sauce.

4. To serve, fill the bottom of a serving dish with ice cream. Place the pears on the ice cream, standing upright. Dribble warm chocolate sauce over each pear and garnish with a sprig of mint, if desired serve extra chocolate sauce on the side.

A Family Birthday in March

March and April are months filled with family birthdays and memories: the births themselves; the early parties where hotdogs, cake and ice cream constituted the menu of choice; a meal that spilled onto the floor and wound up in the stomach of our perpetually hungry Labrador retriever; meals peripheral to the more exciting games and songs, opening of presents and blowing out those pivotal four (or five or six) candles with one to grow on.

Though I no longer bake cakes designed to look like trains, Easter bunnies or moonscapes complete with astronauts, I can't think of March without envisioning a birthday dinner.

> Oysters and Clams on the Half Shell
> Beef in Phyllo Pastry (see below)
> Pan-roasted Herbed Potatoes (see below)
> Green Salad with Dilled Green Beans (see July)
> Chocolate Soufflé or Angel Food Cake (see March)

Beef in Phyllo Pastry

When I first made Beef Wellington for the family using Julia Child's recipe, it was such a sensation that thereafter it was always requested for birthday dinners. I feel that her version, like her versions of everything else, is unbeatable. I wouldn't even try to improve on it. Here, however, is perhaps a peasant rendering. It is fashioned after a lamb dish we had in Greece many years ago. If you have access to a Middle Eastern or Greek market, phyllo pastry is easy to find. It is also easy to use and takes a good deal less time than brioche or puff pastry.

INGREDIENTS:
1 filet of beef, trimmed and tail removed
2 to 3 tablespoons sweet butter
1 pound mushrooms, finely chopped
5 or 6 shallots, finely chopped
Splash of white wine

> *2 to 3 tablespoons heavy cream*
> *Salt*
> *Pepper*
> *1 pound chicken liver mousse (see December) (optional)*
> *1 package phyllo pastry*
> *Melted sweet butter*
> *1 egg white, beaten*

PROCEDURE:

1. Preheat the oven to 400°. Trim the filet of fat, connective tissues, head and tail so that you have a neat, compact piece weighing about 5 pounds.
2. Sear the filet in a skillet with butter or by broiling. Set it aside to cool.
3. Sauté the shallots in butter. Squeeze all the liquid you can from the chopped mushrooms by putting them in a dish towel and wringing it until liquid stops dripping out. Add the mushrooms to the shallots. Add the wine, salt, pepper and heavy cream. Cook until the mixture is no longer soupy.
4. Open the package of phyllo pastry. You must work quickly with this because it dries out and stiffens rapidly after it has been unwrapped. Keep what you are not using in its plastic wrapper or covered with a barely damp towel. Open out 1 sheet of phyllo and brush it with melted butter. Put another sheet on top of that. Brush that with butter, and continue until you have stacked 12 to 14 sheets (they are very thin). Check to see if the first sheet is large enough to go around the roast with an ample overlay. If it looks like a tight squeeze, don't lay the sheets directly on top of each other, but overlap them to create a larger surface area. If you must do this, you may want to use more sheets of pastry.
5. Place the roast in the center of the layered phyllo. Carefully cover it with the mushrooms and/or liver mousse. Fold the pastry around the roast until it completely covers the meat and dressing. Seal it closed with the egg white. Place it in the oven and bake it for about 40 minutes or until a meat thermometer registers about 130° when inserted. This will give you rare, pink meat and a crispy brown crust.

Pan-roasted Herbed Potatoes

INGREDIENTS:

> *Small whole potatoes*
> *Salt*
> *Pepper*
> *Minced herbs*

PROCEDURE:
1. Scrub potatoes and cut away any bad spots.
2. Place around roast to cook.
3. Sprinkle with salt and pepper and herbs before serving

April and the First Spring Greens

When the New England climate reluctantly allows the earliest traces of green to enliven the landscape, many of us who scrutinize each infant leaf find this a time to celebrate the end of one cycle, and the beginning of another, with the first fruits (actually leaves) of spring, combined with the last of a previous growing season.

There are no flavors like those humble green tastes of April, many of which are wild. Here is a wild and tame dinner.

Leek and Potato Soup with Fresh Sorrel (see April)
Broiled Veal Chops with Dried Fennel (see January)
Polenta (see February) or Spoon Bread (see April)
Wild Greens Salad (see below)
Homemade Bread and Cheeses (see April)
Blackberry Cobbler (see July; made from last summer's frozen berries)

Wild Greens Salad

INGREDIENTS:
Newly sprouted wild violet leaves
New dandelion leaves
Fiddlehead fern shoots, parboiled, depollened and cooled
Chopped chervil
Vinaigrette
Johnny-jump-ups or pansies (homegrown and unsprayed)

PROCEDURE:
1. Wash the greens and toss them with the fiddleheads and the vinaigrette.
2. Garnish with the Johnny-jump-ups or pansies.

A Sunday Brunch in May

It is difficult to organize a gathering around the hope of freshly caught fish. However, if there are enthusiastic anglers about the house who love to get up early, and if fish are biting somewhere in the vicinity, the following brunch is a late-morning possibility. If they come back empty-handed, a fine omelet of fresh eggs may be substituted. Hens are reliable.

Fruit Juices and Fresh Fruit
Raw or Steamed Asparagus with Homemade Mayonnaise (see March)
Fresh Pan-fried Trout (see May)
Buttermilk Biscuits with Honey and Sweet Butter (see November)
Coffee

June and the Flavors of the Far East

Those fast-growing, cool weather–loving greens that were planted in early spring are at their best now, whether they are from one's own garden or from a local greengrocer or farmer's market. We eat a variety of new and delicate lettuces daily, increasingly taking them for granted, forgetting how different they taste at other times of year.

The sprouting Chinese greens are held in higher esteem. Largely unavailable in our country markets, their uncommonness sets them apart, but it is their actuality we most celebrate. The cabbages, Bok chois and Taisai greens have a delicacy and tenderness this season not found at other times of the year, and in collaboration with the first crisp, sweet snow peas and pungent cilantro, these exotic foods form the foundation of many a Chinese dinner.

Here is an example. The strawberries and rhubarb remind us that we are in New England.

Soup Taipei (see June)
Spareribs Oriental (see below)
Green Chinese Vegetables (see June)
Snow Peas with Mushrooms (see June)
Soft-Shell Crabs with Cilantro (see below)
Rice
Strawberry-Rhubarb Pie (see June)

Soft-Shell Crabs with Cilantro

Coriander/cilantro is a staple in my garden. Since it matures and goes to seed quickly, I plant it two or three times a season to make sure I have a ready supply at all times. I use both seeds and leaves for a variety of recipes.

INGREDIENTS:

8 soft-shell crabs, freshly killed and cleaned (1 per person)
Flour
Salt
Pepper
About 1/4 cup sesame oil
2 or 3 garlic cloves, chopped
Equal amount of gingerroot, chopped
About 1/3 cup light soy sauce
About 1/3 cup good red wine vinegar
Handful of fresh cilantro leaves, chopped

PROCEDURE:

1. Dredge the freshly washed crabs with flour, salt and pepper. Heat the sesame oil in a large wok or skillet. Stir-fry the crabs, turning them frequently and adding a bit more oil, if necessary, to cover the cooking surface. (However, the oil should not exceed what will be absorbed by the crabs and the flour.)

2. While the crabs are cooking, which shouldn't take more than 5 to 10 minutes, combine the garlic, gingerroot, soy sauce and vinegar in a small bowl.

3. When the crabs are crisp and lightly browned, remove them to a serving plate and keep them warm. Pour the sauce mixture into the wok and stir until it is thickened. Add a little water if the sauce becomes too thick. Strain the thickened sauce to remove any lumps and pour it over the crabs. Sprinkle with cilantro and serve.

Spareribs Oriental

INGREDIENTS:

1 rack lean spareribs
1/4 cup low-salt miso (soybean paste)
1/4 cup hoisin sauce
1/4 cup sesame oil
Scant 1/4 cup light soy sauce
4 to 5 tablespoons sugar
1 tablespoon five-spice powder (equal amounts of ground peppercorns, fennel seeds, cinnamon bark, star anise and cloves)

PROCEDURE:

1. Preheat the oven to 400°.
2. Blend all the ingredients except the ribs. Adjust the seasonings to taste.
3. Place the rack of ribs on a metal baking rack in a large baking dish.

Add 1 inch of water to the bottom of the pan. Brush the top of the ribs with half of the sauce mixture.

4. Bake the ribs for 20 minutes. Then turn, brush the other side with sauce and bake for 20 minutes more. Check for doneness. If they are not brown, reduce the heat to 350° and continue to cook for 10 or 15 minutes more. If they cook too fast and begin to char the sauce, reduce the heat sooner.

5. Remove the ribs to a cutting board and cut them into individual pieces. Serve hot.

A Picnic in July

In our family of environmentalists and pragmatists, there are three prerequisites for picnic provisions: easy transportability, convenient edibility and minimal "litterability." Our children convinced us long ago that a wilderness site must always be left as it was found. Even the evidence of a fire must be obscured and nothing left behind to disturb the next visitor's sense of nature unbound. The father who knows best insists on simplicity, no unnecessary baggage, nothing fussy. Everyone relishes the possibility of munching away unencumbered by utensils, maybe at the top of a waterfall.

The following picnic menu requires no knives, and if you eliminate the potato salad, no plates or forks, yet the flavors from this picnic basket are not meager.

Fried Chicken Anita Perez (see July)
Pan Bagnas (see July)
New Potato Salad (see below)
Dill Pickles (see July)
Raw Sugar Snap Peas with Aioli (see Mayonnaise, March)
Fresh Raspberries, Cherries and/or Blueberries with Sour Cream or Yogurt Sweetened with Brown Sugar

New Potato Salad

INGREDIENTS:

2 pounds new potatoes, washed and scrubbed, but unpeeled
1/2 cup fresh dill, chopped
1/2 cup chopped pickled onions (see the July chapter)
1/4 to 1/2 cup olive oil
Pepper
Salt

2 to 3 tablespoons good balsamic vinegar
2 tablespoons mustard

PROCEDURE:
1. Boil the potatoes until soft. Allow them to cool.
2. Cut the potatoes into bite-sized pieces. Toss them with the other ingredients. Adjust the seasonings to taste.

A Dog-Day Supper in August

In the old days, country folks had "summer kitchens," which were sometimes in the basement, but always away from other living areas. Such kitchens were used predominantly during those long hours required for canning garden produce, and they were always meant to keep the cooking heat out of the way.

Our twentieth-century answer to the summer-kitchen heat problem is the charcoal grill. Father cooks hamburgers on the patio. Diners stand around drinking tall iced beverages and enjoying the aroma of carbon.

In the following menu, only the squash blossoms need indoor cooking. Everything else may be prepared so that the heat can spread to the four winds.

Appetizer: Squash Blossoms (see July)
Charcoal-Grilled Steak
Salsa (see September)
Corn on the Cob Roasted in Hot Coals (see January)
Grilled Peppers and Eggplant (see below)
Tomatoes with Fresh Basil and Vinaigrette (balsamic vinegar and olive oil)
Homemade Fruit Ice Cream (see June)

Grilled Peppers and Eggplant

INGREDIENTS:
Sweet peppers, cut in half and seeded
Eggplant, sliced
Olive oil
Salt
Pepper
Chopped garlic
Fresh oregano

PROCEDURE:
1. Marinate the sliced vegetables in the other ingredients for at least 1 hour.
2. Place the vegetables between the 2 sections of a mesh vegetable grill and clamp shut. Place it on the charcoal grill. Cook, turning frequently, until the vegetables are tender but not overdone.

A Vegetarian Dinner in September

September for the gardener can be a whirlwind of picking, cooking and preserving for winter. Vegetables that have been sluggish all summer now tantalize, not only by producing in abundance but by demanding timely attentions and tangible considerations.

A day of canning tomatoes, pickling cucumbers and parboiling broccoli for the freezer is not conducive to spirited thoughts of dinner, yet there are usually people about with stomachs demanding attentions of their own. What could be easier after a day of canning than a make-your-own pizza dinner? Well, sending out for pizza is easier, but maybe not quite as good.

> Antipasto: Roasted Peppers, "Sun-dried" Tomatoes (see September),
> Cheeses, Celery, Radishes, Dilled Green Beans (see July), Cooked
> Beans with Aioli (see Mayonnaise, March) and Anchovies.
> Garden Pizza (see August)
> Green Salad
> Raspberry Granite Garnished with Mint (see July)

A Cider-Making Party in October

When we have a good apple crop, we make cider with the windfalls —pear cider too. Our cider press must be a hundred years old, but its heavy iron knobs and teeth still perform as they should, grinding up apples or pears in one section, then pressing the sweet juices out into a four-gallon pot. The group effort on this project includes friends, who gather fruit, work the press and drink the cider, and chickens and geese who consume the fruit residues. Dinner afterwards begins and ends with the flavor of apples. Cider is also good with a splash of dark rum.

> Apple Cider
> Lamb and Squash Curry (see October) with Green Tomato Chutney (see
> September)
> Yogurt Spiced with Ground Coriander Seeds, Salt and Pepper

Kimchi (see October)
Basmati Rice
Chapatti (see below)
Applesauce Bread (see October)

Chappatti
This Indian bread is easy to make and delicious for all its simplicity.

INGREDIENTS:
2 cups whole wheat flour
Salt to taste
3/4 cup hot water

PROCEDURE:
1. Sift the flour and salt together. Add the water.
2. Knead the dough until it holds together and isn't sticky. Add more flour or water as you need. Set it aside for at least 1 hour.
3. Divide the dough into 10 balls.
4. Rollout each ball into a very thin, flat, round piece.
5. Heat a skillet (without butter or oil) and quickly cook each piece of bread on each side until it begins to brown. Then put the bread under a broiler for a few seconds. It should puff up like a very thin pita bread. Keep it warm until served.

November and Thanksgiving
Our nationally prescribed Thanksgiving date, though a harvest festival, is celebrated too long after the New England harvest to correlate with the feast celebrated by the Pilgrims and their aboriginal saviors. This first Thanksgiving was celebrated after reaping the first harvest in 1621, and many Thanksgivings followed it. But it wasn't until 1863 that President Lincoln proclaimed the fourth Thursday in November as a national holiday, more to symbolize the hope for a united nation than to honor the gleaners in the fields. Nevertheless, the day follows a worldwide pattern that has celebrated the gustable garden since—I'll wager—its invention.

Thanksgiving is my favorite holiday. Because I love to cook and to have friends and family gathered around, it combines these best things in a relaxed, uncomplicated way.

For the last few years, Thanksgiving dinner has not been in the country but in our Brooklyn home. Our children arrive eager to see old high-school classmates, and a group of old and dear friends are always with us, representing several generations.

Folks begin to arrive in the early afternoon, usually with wonderful surprises to sustain us until the bird is ready and the dinner begins.

Mozzarella Cheese with "Sun-dried" Tomatoes (see September)
Roasted Sweet Peppers (see September) and Anchovies
Oyster Bisque (see November)
Turkey with Corn Bread and Biscuit Stuffing (see November)
Cranberry Sauce
Crudités
Steamed Brussels Sprouts (see November)
Marinated Carrots (see November)
Baked Squash (see October)
New England Pumpkin Pie (see November)
Apple Pie (see November)

December and a Holiday Buffet

I think holiday menus, of all menus, are more bound up in family tradition than any others. We remember with such mythic attachment those tastes, colors and textures of our tractable years. I, for one, remember a certain cherry jello salad, set in a ring mold and filled with canned Royal Anne cherries, canned pears and canned pineapple slices. I loved it. I was even allowed to help make it. I made it for my children, but only once. New York sophisticates at an early age, they hooted at my creation, expressing dismay at my temporary (they hoped) lapse of taste. But I still remember with pleasure that jello mold, bright and shimmering red on the table, a metaphor for sweet Christmas.

Today our holiday menus are more varied than those of the jello-mold days. We live in a time of experimentation and in a place where the world's foods merge. Our markets and seed catalogs offer an expanding range of possibilities. Our friends and extended family bring a profusion of foods and food notions into our lives. We explore them all.

At our annual Christmas buffet dinner and caroling party, the informality of the evening corresponds with the multifarious dishes prepared. There is something for everyone.

Baked Smoked Ham with Apricot Glaze and Horseradish Sauce (see December)

Chicken Liver Mousse (see December)

Homemade Breads (see April)

Curry of Winter Vegetables (see Bean and Squash Stew, February)

Mushrooms Marinated in Vinaigrette (balsamic vinegar, olive oil and herbs)

Beet Salad (see December)

Brie Baked in Pastry Dough (see below)

Middle Eastern Olives (green, purple and black)

Raspberry Linzertorte Cookies (see below)

Governor Moody Cake (see December)

Brie Baked in Pastry Dough

INGREDIENTS:
1 round of Brie
1 pastry crust (see November)

PROCEDURE:
1. Roll out half of pastry crust, place whole cheese on crust.
2. Roll out second half of crust, place over cheese and cut and crimp edges.
3. Place in 350° oven for 15 to 20 minutes, until crust is light brown.

Raspberry Linzertorte Cookies

This recipe makes cookies shaped like miniature wreaths. They look pretty, taste good and freeze beautifully.

INGREDIENTS:
3/4 pound sweet butter, softened
1 cup confectioner's sugar
1 egg
2 cups unbleached flour, sifted
1 cup cornstarch
2 cups finely ground pecans
Raspberry preserves

PROCEDURE:
1. Cream the butter and sugar. Add the egg and mix until all is smooth and fluffy.
2. Sift together the flour and cornstarch. Add this to the butter and sugar mixture. Mix well. Add the pecans and mix well again.
3. Form the dough into a ball and chill it for several hours.

4. Preheat the oven to 350°.

5. Roll the dough out thinly. Using a large (3-inch) cookie cutter or upside-down glass, cut out cookies. Using a smaller, round cookie cutter, cut a hole out of the middle of half of the large cookie circles.

6. Bake the cookies on an ungreased pan until they are barely browned, about 10 minutes. Remove them from the oven and let them cool.

7. Spread the raspberry preserves on each whole cookie. Press a cookie with the cutout in the middle on top, making a sandwich with a red center.

INDEX OF RECIPES